D1012047

A NEW MAN

San Diego Christian College
Library
Santee, CA

Praise for *A New Man...*

It has been a pleasure knowing Rev. Hoise Birks over five decades. His life and his book are transparent testimonies of Paul's words to the Romans: "The just shall live by faith." Hoise, in each of his stages of life, has refused to walk by sight. He has dared to trust his Lord and his Lord has never let him down.
Dale Rhoton
Founding member, Operation Mobilization

Hoise had a fantastic ministry in places we may deem difficult. This book will increase your faith and widen your horizons.
Rev. Dr. Virgil Lee Amos
General Director, Ambassadors Fellowship

...Reading the account of his travels let me know how God had touched Hoise, heart and soul, to risk everything and enter countries hostile to the Gospel....Our prayer is that it will encourage other men and women of color to obey Jesus' command to "go into all the world and preach the Gospel."
Dr. Leroy Yates, Sr.
Pastor Emeritus, Westlawn Gospel Chapel, Chicago, IL
Psychotherapist, Specialist in Christian Counseling

266.92
B619Hn

A NEW MAN

MISSIONARY JOURNEYS OF AN AFRICAN AMERICAN

Rev. Dr. Hoise Birks

HB Publishing Company
Stockbridge, GA

Copyright © 2012 by Rev. Hoise Birks

All rights reserved.

Published in the United States by HB Publishing Company
P.O. Box 2171, Stockbridge, GA 30281

Library of Congress Cataloguing-in-Publication Data
Birks, Hoise 1933-
A New Man: Missionary Journeys of an African American/ Rev. Hoise Birks
p. cm.
Photographs and Timeline of Key Dates included.
Ministry. 2. Missionary Work. 3. Inspirational Literature.   I. Title.
Library of Congress Control Number: 2012917092

ISBN 978-1-467-54665-2

Unless otherwise noted, Scripture quotations are from the King James Version (KJV) of the Bible.

Scripture quotations taken from the New American Standard Bible', Copyright © 1960, 1962, 1963, 1968, 1971, 1972, 1973, 1975, 1977, 1995 by The Lockman Foundation. Used by permission (www.Lockman.org).

Scripture taken from the New King James Version®. Copyright © 1982 by Thomas Nelson, Inc. Used by permission. All rights reserved.

THE HOLY BIBLE, NEW INTERNATIONAL VERSION®, NIV® Copyright © 1973, 1978, 1984, 2011 by Biblica, Inc.™ Used by permission. All rights reserved worldwide.

No part of this publication may be reproduced, stored in a retrieval system, or transmitted in any form or by any means—electronic, mechanical, photocopy, recording, or otherwise—without permission of the publisher of the book.

Printed in the United States of America

Cover Design & Photo Insert by: Clive Williamson, On Target Communications
Typesetting by: projectluz.com
Editing by: Mary C. Lewis, MCL Editing, Etc.

Includes Photographs.

Copies of A New Man may be ordered at: info@HoiseBirks.com

10 9 8 7 6 5 4 3 2 1

First Edition

Printed and bound in India by
Authentic Media, Secunderabad 500 067, India
E-mail: printing@ombooks.org

DEDICATION

To my Lord and Savior Jesus Christ,
and to my miracle wife, Cynthia.

CONTENTS

Part Three: Extending Horizons and Heading Home, 1965 - 1969

FOREWORD

Hoise Birks came into my life like a wind out of heaven. From our first encounter, I could see the hunger for reality and God in his life.

I receive many manuscripts and can only read some of them or parts of them, but here is one I went through from cover to cover, sometimes breaking into weeping.

We have been friends for 55 years. Hoise is my first African American friend I am ashamed to say, though I had many beginning stage friendships in Maryville before I went to Moody Bible Institute where I met Hoise. My own racism was very subtle due in part to being from an almost totally white town in New Jersey. As a kid, even Italians seemed a bit different.

I think this book is a must read for omers [participants in Operation Mobilization], ex-omers, and our prayer partners. You will learn things about our movement that I only learned reading it.

If we could get copies of this into the hands of African Americans, and even other ethnic groups, I believe the Lord will use it.

One of the most powerful and popular books of our day is *Radical* by David Platt. The message of this modern book was more or less not only the message of our movement in the 1960s, but our lifestyle and hour-by-hour way of living. We were to soon learn how complicated and difficult it was to live that way and maintain that Revolution of Love that Hoise is speaking about in this book. Hoise had already left Operation Mobilization before the really big Grace Awakening hit our movement.

Hoise is very kind to me in this book, but I have been crying for several minutes realizing how in some ways I failed my dear brother and how often I lacked a pastor's heart and sensitivity.

Only years later visiting the Martin Luther King, Jr. memorial in Memphis did I see more strongly how I had failed the black people in my own nation and how blind I really was. I wept that day and went into the streets of Memphis speaking to any black person who would listen and trying to apologize and ask forgiveness.

Hoise was a pioneer in missions ahead of his day, but not many would listen due to the complexity of our churches and society.

Maybe this book will somehow do what we failed to do and help see an army of African Americans and other Americans thrust out into the needed mission fields where there are still hundreds of millions who have never once heard or read the Gospel. As you read this I wonder if you might step into the shoes of Hoise Birks for the next generation.

Dr. George Verwer, 2012

PREFACE

This autobiography is for God's glory. Over the past twenty to thirty years, my wife Cynthia has encouraged me to record the life experiences that the Lord has allowed me to have for His glory. As she and I scroll back over my life, after I accepted Christ as my personal Savior in Fairbanks, Alaska, there is much to give God praise for. At the same time, our hearts' desire is that this autobiographical glimpse of part of my life might be used to encourage and challenge other people—young people, older people—to give of themselves and their time and efforts to make Jesus Christ known to individuals that know Him not as their personal Savior.

In the course of being married for thirty-six years, Cynthia and I have talked many times about the experiences the Lord allowed me to have. Her enthusiasm and encouragement about these experiences, along with that of many friends has helped me to share my written testimony with others. Whenever I've had the opportunity to give a testimony or speak in a church, many have said, "Oh, my goodness. This should be in a book!"

I must admit that at first I did not sense the urgency, but I'm 78 years of age now, and the more I think about it, I am convinced that it would be wise to record what God has allowed me to do and accomplish by His grace. At 78 years of age, it's really not over yet. My heart's desire is to continue to serve Him until He takes my last breath.

My ministry, since I accepted the Lord, has been strongly oriented toward foreign missions, and of course, that takes in the whole world. But before I get into talking about foreign missions, I want to give a background of my life—where I was born and reared, where I went to school, and where, after joining the Air Force, I accepted Jesus Christ as my personal Savior.

Hoise Birks, 2012

ACKNOWLEDGMENTS

This book came about, to a great extent, as a result of a conversation with my cousin W. N. Raven, Ph.D. His suggestion that I speak my experiences onto a tape and send the tapes to be transcribed and typed by Cris Wanzer at Manuscripts to Go in Geyserville, California was right on target. Those tapes eventually became this book. Thank you, Doc "Cuz" Raven. Thank you, Cris for your skillful deciphering of my taped conversations as you typed the transcript/manuscript and offered encouraging words along the way.

I must acknowledge those who have had a tremendous influence on my life and development, because this book is about what God has done in my life and God always uses people. I am thankful for the way God used the life and example of George Verwer, the founder and former international director of Operation Mobilization in my life, beginning at Moody Bible Institute, continuing overseas and throughout the following fifty-four years up to the present day. Another person God greatly used was Bakht Singh, the godly leader of indigenous work in India who kept me by his side for the four years I was with him there. It is hard to estimate the effect on me of his life of prayer, faith, and childlike trust in God. I thank God for my longtime Lebanese friend Fouzi Ayoub. God bound our hearts together in a truly close-knit bond of fellowship, from the time we first met at Swansea Bible College in Wales in 1962 through our secret undercover work in Iraq in 1964 through our visits to each other's homes in the 1970s, 1980s, and 1990s. I will never forget the grief and heartbreak I felt the morning of March 24, 2000 when I learned that Fouzi had been called home to glory as a result of an automobile accident during a short-term mission trip in Mali, West Africa. I learned much about humility from Fouzi and I look forward to seeing my good friend in heaven.

I am thankful for Westlawn Gospel Chapel in Chicago, Illinois for the influence the believers had on my life while I was at Moody Bible Institute and overseas, and on the life of my wife when she went there as a new Christian and was nurtured and built up in the faith. We both appreciate their faithfulness to the Word of God and their determination to remain a lighthouse in the Lawndale area on Chicago's West Side for over fifty-seven years. A special thank you goes to Dr. Leroy Yates and his wife Beverly of Westlawn who have mentored and counseled us as a couple over the years. We are thankful, too, for the faithfulness of Harvey and Doris Rollerson of Westlawn. Thank you, Brother Harvey for teaching my wife all of those Sunday school lessons which helped her to grow in grace. Thank you to Dr. Melvin Banks and his wife Olive, founders of Urban Ministries, Inc., also of Westlawn. Dr. Banks recommended my excellent editor Mary C. Lewis. Ms. Lewis, of MCL Editing, Etc. does excellent, professional work and is a pleasure to work with.

I am thankful to the pastors and believers at Galilee Gospel Chapel in Queens, New York for their support and encouragement of the short-term missions' trips I have taken while in fellowship with them. Thanks to the book's gifted graphic designer, Clive Williamson, also of Galilee Gospel Chapel, who has been a friend for many years and who is quick to attribute his creative gifts to the Creator God. A special thanks to Dr. Robert White; when you were pastor at the Clarendon Road Christian and Missionary Alliance Church in Brooklyn, New York you were a steadfast anchor to our family with your wise counsel and guidance.

I am thankful to the many OMers who were team members and who taught me much and helped to shape my life as we travelled to over twenty-eight countries in nearly eight years. Thank you for your grace and patience as the Spirit of God worked on me. Thanks also to the many who supported me with monetary gifts and prayers while I was away for eight years. Your willingness to do this while only receiving my prayer letters and not being able to see my face for such a long stretch helped make the life experiences in this autobiography possible. I thank each of you.

Finally, I want to express sincere thanks to my family. I am thankful for my parents, Maudell and Elder Birks; while not perfect, they brought me into the world, worked hard, and stayed together in marriage for fifty-seven years. I am thankful for my children Daniel and Lisa and for what I have learned from each of them. Words cannot express how much I appreciate my miracle wife Cynthia. She has encouraged me each step of the way. She has helped in many ways, with the preliminary editing and proofreading of the manuscript and with keeping the entire project on schedule. In this and other matters, her assistance has been invaluable.

It is always difficult to acknowledge each and every person involved in a project, so if I have missed anyone, please know that it was not intentional. I am humbled by all of you who have reached out to help me. Thank you for allowing God to use you.

Hoise Birks

KEY DATES

1933	*Hoise Birks is born in Cincinnati, Ohio.*
1957	*Birks becomes born again while stationed with the Air Force in Alaska.*
1957	*He enrolls at Moody Bible Institute in Chicago, Illinois.*
1958-60	*Missionary trips are taken to Mexico.*
1960-61	*Evangelism experiences occur in Chicago.*
1962	*Birks joins Operation Mobilization (OM) in Europe.*
1962	*OM begins summer crusades in Europe.*
1965	*A four-year missionary effort in India begins.*
1969	*Hoise Birks returns to the U.S.*

PROLOGUE

Childhood

I was born on July 4, 1933 in Cincinnati, Ohio. I often comment that I was a born revolutionist, and many of my friends, knowing how Christ revolutionized my life, laugh about that. My family lived in the Tremont Building at 651 W. 5th Street. On the first floor was a small storefront which my mom and dad rented after we moved into the building. They operated a delicatessen store where we made sandwiches and sold ice cream, soda pop, candy, sour and dill pickles, bread, milk—all the items a delicatessen store would carry.

To the right of the store was Jackson Elementary School, and to our left was St. Luke Baptist Church, a small church that our family attended. The Tremont had four floors of apartments, with two families on each floor. We lived on the third floor. The Tremont Building was quite prestigious at that time, an attractive, well-maintained brick building amidst other storefronts and shabby looking homes in the neighborhood. The tenants were proud to live in such a building.

The Family Store in the Community

Needless to say, since we owned a store, we had many friends. We also had some enemies who were jealous of our circumstances and who spread rumors about our family. Some said that the children in our family, including myself, were unwashed and ill-mannered. This really irritated my mother. But there also were friendly people living in the building. Mr. Enell, for example, worked at a local clothing store, and always spoke of us very highly. Another family in the building, on the first floor was an elderly lady and her husband, Mr. Jess and Ms. Willie. She was confined to a wheelchair and was a very loving woman. When we were little kids, she used to talk to us about what we would be doing during the day, especially during the summer when we were outside. I never forgot Ms. Willie. She had kind words to say, and even though she heard some bad reports about our activities in the community, it never changed her attitude toward us. She always stands out in my memory when I think of my young childhood.

At this time in our family, it was my mom and dad, my older sister, Mary Helen Birks, myself, and my brother Edward Birks. Later my parents had three more children, James, Arthur and Patricia. We were an influence in the community and in school. During World War II, I was around 10 years old and the school was selling defense bonds. Of course, we had a little more money than most people in our community; Dad used to give us extra money to buy up to fifty dollars' worth of defense bonds every week. The school was impressed with that, and of course, we were happy to have the bonds for later use. For as long as I can remember, our friends got discounts at the store, and sometimes the schoolteachers sent us to get them Pepsi-Colas to have with their lunch. We were active and well-known in the community and the school.

My Father's Influence

My father owned a car, a Model T Ford, and that was really something at that time. People really looked up to us for owning that car. I remember that shiny little black car well. But before he had the car or the store he had a business collecting waste paper.

He was a self-made businessman originally from Macon, Georgia who arrived in Cincinnati as a young man. He got to Cincinnati by being a hobo. During the 1920s and 1930s hoboing was common. A person traveled around by hopping on a freight train, illegally, because no ticket had been purchased, riding in open cars until he got to his destination, and jumping off. After being in Cincinnati for a while my father met my mother, who was about 15. Apparently he made a good impression on her family. My mother and my dad united in marriage when she was 16.

My father started out with his paper business by carrying a burlap sack collecting waste paper to resell. Shortly afterward he got a wheelbarrow-type cart. If you can picture my father using a little pushcart to collect cardboard boxes, breaking them down manually and tying them up and selling them at a waste depot (nowadays we would call it a recycling center) for a few pennies a pound, then you have the picture of what my father did. After about a year, my father fulfilled a long-held vision and bought a used truck, which allowed him to go around to office buildings and collect larger quantities of used paper and boxes. In those days, and especially later, during World War II, paper was very lucrative because it was used to produce certain military items.

My dad was coming home with between $50 and $60 a day. Not only were we were able to rent the space for the store with the money my father was making, we were able to rent an apartment in the Tremont Building and buy the Model T Ford. He was a hardworking man who got up at four o'clock in the morning and got out into the elements six days a week. He would finish up about two or three in the afternoon; come home, take a bath, eat, talk to his wife and be with her in the store, and spend some time with his children. We, of course, were very happy to see Dad, a very industrious person and a faithful man to his family.

Early Interest

Like my older sister Helen, I graduated from Jackson Elementary School and went to Stowe Junior High School, a twenty-minute walk from where we lived. At Stowe, I developed an interest in jazz; I learned to play the tenor saxophone and played in the school bands. Even though I did not practice as I should have and wasn't performing like Dad expected, with the help of a private teacher, and with playing in the school band and marching band, I learned to play well. To this day, I feel very fortunate to have experienced this great source of education.

Right from Wrong

Another thing I noticed at an early age was that my mom was not really honest in her dealings with people who came in the store. I remember one man who came in and said, "Mrs. Birks, I have a job and I did not have any breakfast. I was wondering if I could buy some cornflakes from you, and borrow a bowl from you and some milk, and eat it here so I'll have my strength when I go to the job."

My mother said, "Oh yes, of course," but she charged him double for the milk and sugar, and $4 to use the bowl and spoon.

Even at my young age, I thought that was terrible. I knew it was dishonest and taking advantage of the man, and I let her know about it. Of course, she gave me a backhand and almost knocked me under the table, so I never tried that again. I could sense a difference between right and wrong, even though I wasn't able to put my finger on the reason.

A Young Believer

That brings to mind the church we attended. St. Luke Baptist Church was directly to our left. My mom and dad got us out of bed every single Sunday to go to church. About 75 percent of the time Mom and Dad were with us, but the other 25 percent of the time, they were not with us. At church, we heard about Jesus Christ for the first time. We used the little Sunday school cards from Standard Publishers, and we learned about this Person, Jesus Christ, who came into the world to die for the sins of all.

At that time, the Gospel didn't make much sense to us. Of course, as I grew older, it began to influence my heart more and more as I witnessed what was going on in my own family and in the store. I could sense that the message of the Gospel was contrary to some of the things that I was doing in my own life. My desire was to live according to the standard put forth in the Bible and according to the message that I was hearing about Jesus Christ, God in the flesh, who came to die on the Cross for me and for all who are lost. It was difficult to understand, though. Why would He come to die for me? I pushed it to the back of my mind, didn't think about it too much, and went about my activities as a young teenager, doing the things that most teenagers do, and contemplating even more contrary things as I grew older. But I began to develop early in my life a sense of the truth of the message of the Bible. I tried to convince myself that not only is it the way to go, but I thought about sharing this with other people and trying to get them to come to the church. Looking back, I can see that God had a plan for my life even as I was growing up, and before I came to know Him personally.

One summer when I was a teenager, I was walking the streets and a very elderly lady stopped me and said, "Son, can I talk to you?"

And I said, "Yes, ma'am."

She said, "Did you go to church Sunday?"

"Yes, ma'am," I said. And I had gone to church that Sunday.

She said, "That's good. I'm happy to hear that, because God is going to use you. God wants to use you."

I thought, *she doesn't know what she's talking about, she doesn't know what's in my heart. I want to be a musician.* But even though I bit my tongue, I realized that she spoke with great conviction. I believe it was an important moment for me, because I am convinced that God was working in my life and had a plan for my life all along.

Challenges to Right and Wrong

Often when we came home from church, the atmosphere wasn't church-like. My mom frequently criticized the pastor, and gossiped about so many different subjects, including the people in the church. This was confusing to me. We went to church to learn about the way that people should live, how to love one another, how to treat one another, and how to pray for one another. But the actions in our home were so contrary.

A lot of conflict was taking place in my home—and I have thought about this for a long time before talking about it, because it seems like I am revealing some unmentionable things—and it shook me up a lot. In the midst of what God was doing in our family, that is, giving my father strength to work and bring in such money, and having a popular, prosperous store, my mom and dad argued a great deal about how the money would be handled. She disagreed with him in so many ways, and made it clear that she was going to control the money whether he liked it or not. I thought it was very unloving of my mother to have that attitude.

One day my mom and dad began to argue and she began to hit him. He was trying to keep her from beating him up, and finally things got so heated that she brandished a gun they owned and threatened to shoot him. Fortunately, she only hit him on the head with it. But still, I was terrified. Up until this day I'm thankful that at least she didn't shoot him. We had the gun because people had come in the store several times to rob it. This happened about once a month for about three months in a row. I am glad that the gun was never used to shoot anyone, including Dad.

I believe that the Lord protected my father from harm; now that I'm a Christian, I am convinced that it was the Lord's doing because we would have been devastated. There were times during junior high school when I felt so insecure in response to all the arguments and fights between my parents that I thought I had better start saving some money for my future. This was a regular part of my life and still happens in many homes.

Some of my friends came from broken homes and I envisioned my family also becoming broken, so I thought that I had better begin to prepare for taking care of myself. I opened a savings account at a bank in Cincinnati. I used to buy malt tablets, for 15 cents, which I ate to kill hunger pangs, and I put the rest of the lunch money Mom gave me in the bank. The agent at the bank thought I was a very smart young man and he told me he felt for sure I would be a millionaire by the time I was an adult. But it was a desperate move in my young life to try to secure my future, because in many ways my home life was potentially unstable.

Potential Glimpsed

I graduated from Stowe Junior High two years after my sister Mary Helen. While I was at Stowe, the principal, Mr. Phillip, gave students money for every B or A grade they made in their subjects. My first year, I did so well I earned $20. Mr. Phillip was a black man who was convinced of the importance of education, and he did everything he could to encourage young black men and women to get an education.

After I followed my sister to Woodward High School, I met a young man who had gone to Woodward; he said that with my size and build, the coaches would want me to play football. I made it clear to him I wasn't interested in banging heads playing football, I wanted to get an education; I wanted to play in the band, and I still had a dream of becoming a jazz musician. But sure enough, the coaches pointed out that because of my size and great physical shape, I should play high school football and then I could get a college scholarship. They were persuasive, and after a couple of weeks I succumbed to their influence.

After trying out on the freshman team I did well, and at the end of the first season I had made the all-city team. It was quite an honor. When I came back my second year to Woodward High School I was much more motivated to do well in football, which I did for the rest of high school. When football was not in season, I played in the band and I felt very good about what I accomplished in music and athletics.

Football and College

My football record enabled me to receive several scholarship offers to leading colleges. One of these colleges was the University of Kentucky. At that time, Paul Bryant was the head coach there and he sent me the invitation to attend. Lots of people told me that it was a very prestigious opportunity; I would have been the first black person to play at the University of Kentucky, which would have been a great honor. But to this day I'm thankful for my coaches at Woodward. They said that frankly, the Civil War was practically still going on in the South, and were I to play football at Kentucky I would probably risk physical injury or even death.

I was also offered a scholarship to Miami University in Oxford, Ohio which was only thirty-five miles from Cincinnati. Also, I had a friend who was playing on the team who encouraged me to come to Miami. In the end, I enrolled there. I envisioned going home every weekend, which was a foolish plan because I should have been planning to stay on campus to study.

The freshman team was doing well, but I was not maintaining good grades. A counselor graciously and respectfully pointed out I'd lose my scholarship and have to leave the school if I didn't maintain a certain grade point average. Unfortunately, I felt that I could play football and study at the same time, and that doing both was no big deal. But it wasn't true. Keeping up with my classes and rigorous football practices left me too fatigued to improve on my homework and exams. Discouraged and confused, I flunked out of Miami University in my first year.

PART ONE:

Navigating a New Path

1957 - 1961

CHAPTER ONE

An Unpredicted Preparation

Joining the Air Force

Not long after my time at Miami University came to an abrupt halt and I went back to Cincinnati, the draft board called. The board informed me that I would have to make a decision about going into the Army. I went to the draft board's local office and explained that I had just left school but was planning to go back. They said, "Well, we'll sit on your papers and give you a chance to get back in school so you won't have to go into the service, but stay in touch with us."

So, I worked for a while with the Cincinnati Highway Maintenance Department and made a good salary for a single person. After about six months, I got a letter from the draft board telling me that I needed to make a decision. Rather than going into the Army, I thought it would be wise to try to go into the United States Air Force, which would afford me courses of study in technology that I could use in civilian life once I was discharged. As I recall it I took the test and failed it the first time. The commanding officer said, "I think you can do better than this. Take it over, and see what you can do." Sure enough, I got a score of 95, and they took me into the United States Air Force.

Actually, by this time I was ready to leave Cincinnati. I was depressed about having flunked out of college; it seemed as though my life was going nowhere, and the same was true for my friends. As a matter of fact, one of my close friends, an extremely intelligent mentor who tutored me in high school algebra and knew a lot about world events and how to make a lot of money had become a surprising disappointment. I had admired and looked up to him. One evening, as we were relaxing and discussing things, he suggested that I smoke a "little pot" with him. I was surprised. I never knew that he was involved in the drug scene. Initially I said no to his offer, but for the next few weeks he continued to press me to smoke marijuana. I was very uncomfortable with this pressure and felt that based on our friendship I would soon give in and begin to do drugs. It occurred to me that he was using our friendship to eventually turn me on to drugs. I was relieved to escape into the Air Force.

I told my father I had enlisted in the Air Force, which meant that I was discontinuing my plans for college and would be leaving home soon. I was looking forward to it; I was really very confused and frustrated. I had applied for several jobs, and other than the highway maintenance position a college degree was required. So I was reluctantly entering the Air Force and leaving my family. On the day of my departure, my mom was sad, of course, and my brothers and sisters were sad, as was I. But my father came with me to the recruiting office. That really touched me, because it showed my dad loved me. He had spent a lot of time with me when I was small, talking with me and playing with me, and I was very appreciative of those times with my daddy.

At the time of departure, the Gideons, a group which distributes Bibles, passed out New Testaments to everyone who was in my group. For the first time in my life, I began to read the Bible every single night before going to bed. While I was at Woodard High School, there was an event where students were asked to take part. Someone suggested that perhaps I would be interested in reading a portion of the Bible, which I'd never read before. We had a Bible in our home, but my father only took it off the shelf twice a year. He blew the dust off, and read a portion at Christmas and Easter, and put the Bible back on the shelf. The Bible was not read any other time in my home. I remember I chose to read the Beatitudes at the school event, and I was impressed by the contents. As I went into the service, I had the strong desire to read a portion of the New Testament every single night. No matter what time I went to bed, I read a portion of the New Testament.

Discovering a Field

I underwent basic training at Samson Air Force Base in New York and after completion I took a series of aptitude and placement tests in every field. By God's grace, I scored high on the electronics and mechanics tests, but I desired to be an Air Force policeman. I admired the men wearing the blue suit and white gloves with the big .45 holstered at their side. After looking at my records, the Air Force counselor pointed out that since I did very well in mathematics and mechanics I might want to consider something other than being a policeman. Also, the counselor said, "You would not make a good policeman. You don't have the attitude. You can't hurt anybody, and you can't shoot anybody."

I laughed about that and questioned whether he was right, but I respected his judgment. I said I wanted an interview to become a jet pilot, and he arranged that. But during that interview my weight became an issue; they said I was too big to fit into an airplane cockpit. The news depressed and discouraged me, but I was allowed to train as a jet engine specialist. My counselor convinced me that since the future airplanes would be jets, I would be able to get a good job at an airline as a jet engine mechanic making a good salary when I was discharged from the Air Force. That was appealing to me.

Next I was sent to Chanute Air Force Base in Illinois for technical training as a jet engine mechanic. I was very excited and looking forward to my studies of different types of aircraft, including supersonic jet bombers, with different types of engines and different types of systems. I studied very hard and did well. I was always asking questions, and it paid off. I graduated with the fourth highest grade in my class of thirty.

Stationed in Alaska

After graduating from the technical phase of my Air Force experience, we were encouraged to apply for three parts of the world that we would like to serve in. My first choice was Hawaii, my second choice was South America, and my third choice was the Caribbean—all places with warm climates. I had never traveled outside the U.S. before, but I had read about those three places and was looking forward to another phase of a grand education.

When my request was reviewed, I was informed that I was going to be sent to Fairbanks, Alaska. I was astounded. I thought, *Wow, Alaska? I didn't apply for Alaska.* Most of what I knew about Alaska was that Eskimos lived there in little ice houses called igloos. I didn't know anything about the military there, and of course, I didn't want to live in an igloo or be in a cold climate. I was determined to get out of this assignment. I received permission to speak to the commanding officer. Airmen were encouraged to speak freely with this officer so I told him that it seemed that someone had made a mistake in my assignment.

He asked me, "What part of the world did you express that you would like to be assigned to?"

I told him Hawaii, South America, or the Caribbean.

"Well, airman," he said, "I'm busy right now, would you be kind enough to come tomorrow? We can talk about this further." He was a very gracious commanding officer, and I felt he was really considering my case.

But when I came the following day, he got a telephone call while I was there and again he apologized and asked me to come the following day. I came back three times and experienced interruptions each time. Finally, the officer said, "Airman Birks, you will go to Alaska."

I almost wept on the spot, but I maintained enough presence of mind to salute, do an about face, and go out the door. I did, however, weep bitterly once outside. I could not reconcile myself to going to Alaska, and I continued to envision myself living with Eskimos in ice houses.

After a thirty-day furlough, I reported to California to be transported to Alaska. From the Air Force base in California, I went by ship to Anchorage, Alaska, and then by train to

Fairbanks. The year was 1954. To my surprise, it was springtime, there was no snow around, and the days were beautiful and sunny. Also to my surprise, I was assigned to a dormitory of 500 men. I discovered that Air Force military personnel stayed in dormitories of 500 men, really a community. One thing that reduced some of my anxiety about being assigned to Alaska was the fact that I met quite a few very friendly airmen while there.

Experiencing Nature for the First Time

In addition to taking extension courses at the University of Alaska in subjects such as psychology and government, I also took advantage of leisure activities available at the base. From April to October, the days were extremely long and it rarely got dark. It would get dim, not dark, and thanks to recreational equipment made available to airmen there were opportunities for all kinds of outdoor activities. There were lakes that the government had stocked with fish, and there were bicycles to ride. I used to take a bicycle on the weekend and ride all the way to Ileson Air Force base, twenty-five miles away. I truly enjoyed the ride and the scenery. Wild bears, caribou, and deer were among the animals I saw in Alaska.

I discovered that Alaska was incredibly, hypnotically beautiful. Coming from a dirty industrial city like Cincinnati, with its smokestacks, trains, cars, and grime, I had never experienced starry nights, the Aurora Borealis or Northern Lights, the snow-capped Mt. McKinley, to say nothing of the natural flora and fauna of a place like Alaska. The state's beauty calmed my heart and reduced the anxiety, doubts, and frustration I had felt ever since I had flunked out of college. The ghetto where I was born and lived in Cincinnati was not a beautiful place. There was a lot of crime and people were killing each other every day. As a young person, I had big questions about the meaning of life, and at times wondered if life was even worth living. I certainly was not content and had no peace.

In Alaska, I could sense order in the universe and the beauty and order of the creation restored my belief in the Creator. One of the things I really experienced during my initial time in Alaska was a high level of peace in my mind. The contrast between the tempo of Fairbanks and the tempo of Cincinnati caused me to breathe deeply, exhale deeply, and relax. This feeling of peace and beauty and the sense that there was order in the creation was something I couldn't sense in Cincinnati. For the first time in my life, I perceived nature's order: I noticed that when it rained, the grass grew, and when the grass grew, the caribou ate the grass, and we ate the caribou.

My doubts began to fade as I realized that there must be an intelligent Being behind this order, and if there is intelligence and order, there is reason and purpose. I began wondering what my purpose in life might be. Later I would learn that an intelligent Being is indeed behind the creation: He is God. Psalm 24:1 says:

> The earth is the LORD's, and the fulness thereof; the world, and they that dwell therein.

Accepting Jesus as Personal Savior

Soon after I became acclimated to my assignment in Alaska, I took the initiative to find out about the base chaplain and church where airmen could go. I was happy to find out about the chapel choir and I took the opportunity to sing in the choir. And once I made attendance at the Air Force base chapel a regular event I had the opportunity to teach Sunday school. Heaven knows, I didn't know anything about teaching Sunday school but they allowed me to do that, and I was coming up with some crazy stuff that they should've told me was incorrect. I knew very little about the Bible, and I should not have been allowed to teach Sunday school. I think they were interested in having military personnel take part, but it was very destructive to me, and to others too, because what I was teaching was nowhere in the Bible. I was not a Christian at that time.

However, an important friendship emerged. I met someone who attended a church in the town of Fairbanks. His name was Ron, and he encouraged me to come and visit the Native Baptist Church that he had been attending. The people were very loving. There were missionaries from America, and since it was a native church there were many converted Eskimos in the congregation. They were very educated, warm, and friendly, so naturally my visits captured my heart. They taught the Bible in a clear way and the doctrine was solid and sound. I had never heard teaching from the Bible like that. I began attending every Sunday, and I added the midweek prayer and Bible study meetings to my scheduled activities. I stopped going to the chapel on the Air Force base.

As a result of attending this church, I accepted Jesus Christ as my personal Savior. The experience revolutionized my life. In addition to the love, fellowship, encouragement, and warmth that drew my heart to the church in Fairbanks, I was there during a series of meetings by a visiting pastor. For the first time in my life, I was exposed to the Bible as the true Word of God. This visiting pastor preached a series of sermons from the book of Daniel in the Old Testament. He was a very competent pastor, a very godly man who knew the Bible and secular history as well. In his sermons this pastor showed that many of the prophecies regarding secular history mentioned in the book of Daniel had come to pass, such as those about the

Greek and Roman Empires, and the prophecy concerning the first appearance of Jesus Christ. Hundreds of years before Jesus Christ was to appear on the face of the earth, the Bible had prophesized how He would come, where He would come, and where and how He would die. This pastor mentioned that the book of Daniel not only spoke of the first appearance of Jesus Christ, but it also spoke of how Jesus Christ is going to return the second time.

As you can imagine, this actually blew my mind. I attended the meetings every evening. The speaker gave convincing information that the Bible was the divinely inspired Word of God. The speaker made reference to I Peter 2:20-21:

> [20]Knowing this first, that no prophecy of the scripture is of any private interpretation.
>
> [21]For the prophecy came not in old time by the will of man: but holy men of God spake as they were moved by the Holy Ghost.

For the first time in my life I was exposed to another portion in the Bible, Hebrews 1:1-3:

> [1]God, who at sundry times and in divers manners spake in time past unto the fathers by the prophets,
>
> [2]Hath in these last days spoken unto us by his Son, whom he hath appointed heir of all things, by whom also he made the worlds;
>
> [3]Who being the brightness of his glory, and the express image of his person, and upholding all things by the word of his power, when he had by himself purged our sins, sat down on the right hand of the Majesty on high;

Before I was confronted with the truth of the Bible, I had been like many young people: I questioned whether the Word was true, whether the Bible's authorship was authentic, whether it was full of myths and whether it was reliable. Based on my personal background, I was also concerned that many who claimed they were Christians did not act like Christians. Even in the church in Alaska where I was going, some people were acting and talking like they were not Christians. Others were not showing an interest in Bible study; I did not see congregants who brought their Bibles; in those days they just sat and listened to the message. So at these special meetings, the visiting pastor's statements were really blowing my mind. The minister was insisting that the Bible was God's Word and could absolutely be trusted as divine truth. He said that God had brought the Bible into being to glorify Himself, and that from beginning to end, the Bible speaks about the person of Jesus Christ who was sent to help man pull off what man could not pull off by himself.

A Witness and a Conviction

At the same time of my attendance at the special meetings in Fairbanks, several airmen on the base were trying to witness to me. They were genuine Christians who loved the Lord, but I was not very nice to them at first. They tried to give me a leaflet or a pamphlet about the Person of Jesus Christ, and I rejected them in a hostile way. My mind was filled with thoughts like, *"You racist pigs, telling me about Jesus Christ when you have suppressed my people and those of us who are African Americans, and you talk about Jesus Christ..."*

I rejected them and I rejected what they were saying. After a period of time, I became convicted about the way I was treating them. I found it difficult to sleep at night because of this attitude, but I didn't know that it was God Himself convicting me and giving me discomfort. I just felt so uncomfortable. Each time I was on the Air Force base and saw these guys coming, I crossed to the other side of the street. I glared at them with an extremely angry face to drive them away, and of course they picked up on my hostility. After a while, they stopped trying to approach me. I was satisfied to a certain extent. But I was becoming miserable inside myself. I felt guilty because these men hadn't done anything to me; they were warm, friendly people, and I felt bad about being mean toward them.

Well, after the week of special meetings at the Native Baptist Church, an invitation was given to those who wanted to receive Christ. I kept thinking about the speaker's emphasis on the first part of the book of Daniel, which prophesied that Jesus Christ would come the first time and that He had come, and the later part of Daniel, which prophesied that Jesus was coming again. Now, I had no doubt that Jesus had come the first time, just as the Bible said He would. I could not negate that. The speaker reminded everyone that they should be ready when He comes the second time. I knew that I was not ready. I knew that I was not right with God.

The speaker had explained that the word "sin" simply means coming short of God's standards. I certainly came short of what God required. I felt guilty about my lying, cheating, hostility, and stealing. I thought, *What's the use of living?* I was miserable and actually thought about committing suicide. My parents had taught me that the most important thing in the world was money. If you had money, life was worth living. Without money, life would be miserable. We were privileged above many in our community and still there was no peace in my family or my heart. So I knew that money would not bring me peace.

"Why Not Tonight?"

When the invitation was given at the end of the special series, encouraging those to come and give their lives to Jesus Christ, I broke out in a cold sweat. I was clinging to the back of a church pew. I was torn. I did and I didn't want to step forward. I wanted to go because I didn't have the peace that only Christ could give, but I didn't want to go forward and embarrass myself. Later I learned a Bible verse in which Jesus explains that peace is in Him. In John 16:33, Jesus says:

> These things I have spoken unto you, that in me ye might have peace. In the world ye shall have tribulation: but be of good cheer; I have overcome the world.

I know now that God was drawing me to Himself during those special meetings at that Baptist church in Alaska. I also found out that the Christians on base to whom I had been hostile had been praying for me to come to Christ. During the final night when the invitation was given, we sang the hymn "Why Not Tonight?" Can you imagine a more appropriate hymn than "Why Not Tonight?" In my mind I was trying to give all kinds of reasons why I should not go forth and accept Christ as my personal Savior. I told myself I wasn't dressed properly. I told myself that I'd come back and do it later. Also, I was not quite sure that this time would be any different from a previous time when I thought I had come to Christ.

A while back in Cincinnati, I had gone forward as a kid at our family's church to be baptized. I had programmed it so I would go in the evening when my friends would not be there; I did not want to be embarrassed in front of them, and baptism was more or less a family rite. My parents expected that sooner or later, every family member had to go forward to be baptized. When the day came for my baptism, I went down in the water a dry sinner, and came up a wet sinner. There was no change in my life. I lived as I had lived before, without God, and having no control over my life. The same was true for my family members and many other friends that I knew who called themselves Christians.

Finally, as the invitation was being given at the church in Fairbanks, I overcame all my doubts and objections and wholeheartedly gave my life to Christ. I reasoned in my heart: *Lord, I believe that Your Word, the Bible, is true from beginning to end. I believe that Jesus Christ came to save me and to reconcile me to Yourself. By faith on the authority of Your Word and Your Word only, tonight I accept You as my personal Savior and make You Lord of my life. I give You everything I have, and everything I ever hope to have, to make You known, by life or by death.*

I shared the decision I had made with the church. I had been in dialogue with two very lovely people there. They had really wooed my heart, and I was at ease with them. One was John Smith and one was John Powell. I still maintain contact with John Powell, who later became a psychologist and was a chaplain at the University of Michigan.

The night I received Christ, there was no bouncing off the wall, and there were no visions of any kind. I did, however, experience a sense of peace that I had never experienced before. I had a sense of contentment and a joyous conviction that my search for meaning and purpose in life was over. Somehow, I just knew that I had made the greatest decision in my life, that I had really found what was missing to give me fulfillment.

CHAPTER TWO

Born Again in Alaska and Churched in Washington

From Fairbanks to Spokane

I accepted Christ as my personal Savior on August 5, 1957 in Fairbanks, Alaska. I was so excited and happy. I called my family and told them the good news. When I told my mom, she said, "Well, we've always been Christians, so what are you talking about?"

I said, "Mom, you wait and see."

When I told my brothers, they said, "Yeah, yeah, man, we know, don't try to pull any games on us. We're blood, man, we know you. We are just waiting for you to come home."

So many wonderful things happened to me in Alaska. I went from not wanting to go there to extending my stay there for an additional year. I was able to save a lot of money, to say nothing of chalking up nine credits at the University of Alaska.

Most importantly, this was where I came to know Christ as my personal Savior. I was thankful that God had used Alaska's natural beauty, along with the loving Christians I met while there, to prepare my heart to accept His Word and allow me to have the most miraculous experience in my life.

Still, the time came to accept my next Air Force assignment. When I left the base in Fairbanks, I was assigned to Geiger Field, a large military installation near Spokane, Washington. I was fortunate to immediately make contact with a wonderful church, the First Baptist Church in Spokane. Dr. Walter Bridge was the pastor at that time, and I really liked the preaching and teaching of the Bible from a spiritual, humble, and scholarly posture. Like the pastor in Alaska, Dr. Bridge brought together science, biblical and secular history, and many bits of information to support the fact that the Bible is God's divine Word.

The Navigators

In addition to the First Baptist Church, I came in contact with the Navigators while I was in Spokane. The Navigators are a para-church ministry which is strong on Bible memorization and witnessing for Christ. In Spokane, they had a servicemen's center that featured games such as pool and ping pong and refreshments such as coffee, tea, cake, and pie prepared by local Christians. But their main interest is witnessing to military personnel, sharing the Bible with them, and hopefully and prayerfully seeking an opportunity to lead them to a saving knowledge of Jesus Christ.

At that center I really learned to witness to people personally by using the Bible. Ron York, a very astute, godly Christian leader who was then the director of the Navigators in Spokane, taught me a lot about witnessing to servicemen, as well as to people on the street, and how to pass out Gospel tracts and leaflets like those I had received from the Christian men on the Air Force base in Fairbanks. I learned so much, and I discovered later that the Navigators are the Christians who often follow up on converts from the Billy Graham crusades.

In my humble opinion, there's no group like the Navigators. They not only know the Word of God, they teach individuals, one on one, about the Bible and how to share with other people. In my experience, they do not jam it down a person's throat; they just logically and respectfully share the Scriptures with individuals. I have seen much fruit from their work. By God's grace, after approximately fifteen years I renewed contact with Ron York, who is living in Idaho now. He continues to be a real source of encouragement in the Lord.

I had grown quite a bit spiritually in the Scriptures before leaving Alaska, and between the Navigators and Dr. Bridge's ministry, I grew much in the Lord.

Deciding on the Pastoral Path

I had about a year left in the service when I first went to Spokane. With my discharge coming up, the big question was: What was I to do with my life? I had a desire to go to school, to learn more about the Bible, and to serve the Lord; in my mind, this meant becoming a preacher. The Baptist preacher was the model in my head; I thought that I wanted to be a preacher and was thinking about the best way to prepare myself. A well-known Bible scholar, Dr. Sidlow Baxter, was coming to First Baptist Church from England. I made sure that I had vacation time available so that I could attend the meetings that featured him. I asked the Lord to lead me through his series of messages as to where I might go to school. This seemed a logical, sensible request to put before God. I had been talking to Dr. Bridge and he said that the Lord will make it clear to me, but I felt that I needed specific guidance.

Dr. Baxter arrived, and he gave a series of messages from the New Testament. After his week of meetings, I told him my testimony, about how I had accepted Christ as my personal Savior, and my desire to go to a school where I could learn more about the Bible. I asked for his advice.

Dr. Baxter said, "Well, you know, I don't know much about the schooling system here in America, but I do know that there's one school that is true to the Word of God. If you go to some of these other schools, even though they may be Christian, they may not hold to the fact that the Bible is God's Word, so they come up with anything and everything."

Then he said, "The only place that I can think of that I would encourage you to prayerfully consider going to is the Moody Bible Institute."

I said, "Where's that?"

"Chicago," he said.

During my military service, I had watched science films by Moody where a professor named Dr. Moon explored the mysteries of science to show how the natural creation supported the truth of the Bible and what it says about the Creator. So I was familiar with the name Moody, but I didn't know where the institution was located. I decided to follow up on Dr. Baxter's suggestion. Once discharged from the Air Force, I stopped off in Chicago on my way back to Cincinnati, and I visited Moody Bible Institute so that I could apply to attend the school.

Enrolling at Moody Bible Institute

While in Chicago, I stayed at the YMCA nearest Moody and had an unusual experience. I ran into a young man with whom I had attended Woodward High School. We also played on the same football team. I remembered that he was a strong, professing Christian: He carried his Bible with him at school, he read his Bible, and before football games, we asked him to pray. Everyone was sure he was going to be a minister. Since I had become a Christian, I was delighted to see him at the YMCA in Chicago. I began by telling him how his life had made an impression on me when I was at Woodward.

He interrupted me and said, "I'm no longer interested in that foolishness."

I was so shocked to hear him say that, especially in the tone in which he said it, that I spoke no more of spiritual things. We continued to talk for awhile, but I had a hard time recovering from my shock.

The following day I visited Moody's admissions department and expressed my desire to become a student. They gave me all the proper papers and they said, "We really have a waiting list. It might be a year or two before you are accepted."

Of course, that was very discouraging. I looked at the person who was talking to me and wondered why he didn't tell me that in the first place. I felt like he'd been leading me on, but I didn't say that, of course.

After I got back to the YMCA I met another young man in the cafeteria, and we began to talk. I began to direct the conversation in order to discover where he was with God in terms of Jesus Christ. He said that he wasn't a Christian, but he'd thought about it.

I asked him if he wanted to become a Christian, and he said, "Yes."

"Would you mind if I share with you from the Bible how you can become a Christian?" I asked.

"No, not at all," he said.

With God's help and by God's grace, I shared verses with him that helped him accept Christ as his personal Savior. These were verses such as I John 5:11-12:

> [11]And this is the record, that God hath given to us eternal life, and this life is in his Son.
>
> [12]He that hath the Son hath life; and he that hath not the Son of God hath not life.

Another salvation verse is Romans 10:9:

> That if thou shalt confess with thy mouth the Lord Jesus, and shalt believe in thine heart that God hath raised him from the dead, thou shalt be saved.

The young man said, "I've always wanted someone to show me the way and how to do it, and I feel today God has really heard my prayers."

That was a time of rejoicing. I was happy that the Lord led me to Chicago, not only to apply to attend Moody Bible Institute, but also to meet my old friend who had lost his faith, so that I could pray for him, as well as to meet and make friends with a young man who was ready to begin his faith.

I made my way home to Cincinnati, Ohio.

A Brief Stay in Cincinnati

My mom and dad were happy to see me, of course. I related many stories to them about my military experience and was happy to be home. Every day's focus began with the Bible. I got up at six o'clock in the morning and studied my Bible for about an hour.

Unfortunately, this became a point of tension between my mom and me. "Why are you reading that damn Bible so much?" she asked once she discovered how I was spending my mornings.

I was shocked at her attitude! Before I went into the Air Force, she was concerned about me staying out late at night; my siblings and I were only allowed to stay up late on the weekends. She would tell me to be home no later than two o'clock Sunday morning, but sometimes I came home at three, even four in the morning. Whenever I did that, my mom was waiting up for me: "Where have you been?" she'd ask. "I told you not to come home later than two, I've been worried about you, something could have happened to you out there and now here you are coming in at four o'clock. And whether you like it or not, you're getting up at seven to go to church."

"Yes, Mom," was my response. But now, after I accepted the Lord as my personal Savior, her concern didn't involve me running the streets. Even though I regularly was home by nine in the evenings, she told me that I was going crazy reading the Bible so much.

Mom's criticism continued for days on end. I felt so bad about her disruptions in the morning that I decided to go down in the basement to read the Bible. I was relatively young in the faith and I didn't want to lose my faith in Christ. I wanted to cling to Him, and one of the main ways for clinging to Christ in my new life was clinging to the Bible.

But then my mom began coming down to the basement, disturbing me. "You're still reading that damn Bible. You need to get you a job." Well, Mom knew that I looking for a job. I had applied to attend Moody but wasn't sure how long I'd have to wait to get in the Bible school, and I was really scared at that moment because my mom was using all of her motherly powers to break my faith in Christ. Here again I experienced the Bible, the Word of God coming to my rescue, to encourage me.

Romans 8:35-39 says:

> [35]Who shall separate us from the love of Christ? shall tribulation, or distress, or persecution, or famine, or nakedness, or peril, or sword?
>
> [36]As it is written, For thy sake we are killed all the day long; we are accounted as sheep for the slaughter.
>
> [37]Nay, in all these things we are more than conquerors through him that loved us.
>
> [38]For I am persuaded, that neither death, nor life, nor angels, nor principalities, nor powers, nor things present, nor things to come,
>
> [39]Nor height, nor depth, nor any other creature, shall be able to separate us from the love of God, which is in Christ Jesus our Lord.

After reading that portion of Scripture, I decided that it would be wise for me to move from home. I had tried to live at my parents' house but my mother was all over me with her unwarranted criticism. My dad left for work about four in the morning so he was not home when my mom was criticizing me for reading the Bible. Even though he was passive in some areas, I feel sure that he would have stood up for me in this situation. I respected my mom, and I was going to respect her, but I felt that I wasn't strong enough to take all the abuse and not let it affect my walk with Christ. Not only that, I knew from experience that much of my mom's philosophy did not work in our home, and actually did not work for anyone. I did not want to go back to the presence and influence of those beliefs, so I moved to a YMCA residence in Cincinnati.

I continued to read the Bible there each morning and as often as I wanted. I went out and witnessed to people on the street about Christ, and I had the opportunity to speak at some of the rescue missions in Cincinnati and in nearby Kentucky. I was keen to serve the Lord. While in Cincinnati I was in fellowship with a dear brother named Tom Wells. He headed one of Cincinnati's rescue missions where I helped out, and we had wonderful conversations and fellowship which encouraged me and kept me strong in the Lord. To this day Tom Wells is doing very well in the Lord. He's a pastor at one of Ohio's leading churches.

Shortly afterward, to my surprise, I got a letter from Moody Bible Institute. After being home for only a few months, they informed me that my application had been accepted. I didn't have to wait a year or two; I could feel free to come to Moody the first opportunity I had. I was jumping and shouting hallelujah. I could see how the Lord had led me in the midst of what was happening at home, to make the decision to move out, stay close to Him, and serve Him while I waited on Him to direct me. Of course, I packed my bags right away and I was off to Moody Bible Institute.

Early Influences at Moody

At Moody Bible Institute, I was well received and encouraged in my studies. Because the school did not have adequate housing facilities for every student, and it was growing at that time, freshmen had to stay at the residential quarters of Lawson YMCA, which was less than two blocks from Moody. Along with approximately thirty other freshmen, I stayed at Lawson. One of the students who enrolled the same semester I did was

George Verwer, who was later to become the founder of the mission organization with which I became involved.

At the time George seemed to be a very unusual student, and some students referred to him as a whacko. In our classes together, he always raised seemingly untimely and idiotic questions. But the questions turned out not to be idiotic or untimely, but were very pertinent to our class discussions. His shoes and clothing were a little frayed, and his hair was long. While I was staying at the YMCA, I continued to take time in the evenings to go out on my own and pass out tracts and Gospel leaflets. Sometimes, instead of going back to Moody for supper, I used that time to distribute tracts in the surrounding community. Even though almost all of the day students at the time were white, Moody Bible Institute was in an African American community so I related well to residents. Often I saw George Verwer in the same neighborhood, passing out Gospel tracts, too.

George Verwer, Dale Rhoton, and Send the Light

I came to know about George Verwer's life while we were at Moody Bible Institute. At the age of 14, George had received a copy of the gospel of John from Mrs. Dorothea Clapp, an elderly lady who had prayed for eighteen years for the students in her local school, Ramsey High School, and on the first page he wrote a pledge to read it each day. At that time, George had a reputation at the school for causing problems and drawing attention to himself. Mrs. Clapp prayed not only that students at the high school would come to know Jesus Christ in a personal way, but that they would be witnesses for Him in many parts of the world. She didn't know that one of the students her prayers would impact would be George Verwer specifically or that God would change him from a troublemaker to a young man greatly used of Himself.

Three years after he made his pledge, George Verwer accepted Christ at Madison Square Garden in New York City, at a rally in 1955 that was organized by Jack Wyrtzen, the founder of an organization called Word of Life. Billy Graham was the speaker. I learned that George went to the meetings with an attractive blonde young woman on his arm. He was interested in the Christian message because of the prayers of Mrs. Clapp and the gospel of John that he had been reading, but he says that he was not sure about the kind of meeting or the evangelist. But there in Madison Square Garden under the ministry of Dr. Billy Graham, he accepted Christ as his personal Savior. His life was literally turned upside down.

George was a senior in high school when he became born again and he immediately began winning his friends to Christ. He arranged Gospel meetings and the Lord used him to lead many to a saving knowledge of Himself. When he graduated from high school, he went to Maryville College, a Christian college in Maryville, Tennessee; also there was a friend of his, Dale Rhoton. One year later, George transferred to Moody Bible Institute and Dale transferred to Wheaton College, a Christian college in nearby Wheaton, Illinois. Later, Dale and George helped to found the mission organization Send the Light, Inc., which later became Operation Mobilization.

Prayerfully Considering Missionaries

At Moody, we were blessed to experience two main conferences during the school year. One of the conferences was during Founders Week, honoring the history of Moody Bible Institute. Missionaries came from all over the world to present missions and challenge students to prayerfully consider joining their mission upon the completion of school.

The other main yearly conference was held at Moody Church and was called the Keswick Conference. (Moody Church had no legal affiliation with Moody Bible Institute; it was simply named after the famous evangelist who founded the school.) Many famous speakers and evangelists from all over the world came to speak at this church. For the first year and a half that I was at the Bible school, free time from studies on most Sundays enabled me to attend Moody Church, a twenty-minute walk from the institute. The church provided such a nourishing ministry in which you could learn the Word of God and the Spirit of God clarified the truth to my heart.

The Keswick Conference was named after a place in England where conventions emphasizing a deeper Christian life were held. The speakers at the Keswick Conference often ministered the Word of God powerfully, and made a deep impression on the students. Many made lifelong commitments to serve God during the conferences. The speakers challenged students to walk in Christ-likeness, and live a broken, humble, and prayer-drenched life that allowed the Spirit of God to work in a mighty way through them.

Both conferences were accompanied with much prayer. I had experienced this power while in Alaska. After I accepted Christ as my personal Savior, I discovered that the men who had been witnessing to me had asked the church to pray for me. Every congregant of Native Baptist Church was praying for me. They had what they called cottage prayer meetings in their homes, and they had evenings of prayer in which they prayed earnestly that I would be saved. With such earnest prayer going up, I did not have a chance on earth other than accepting Christ into my life.

At Moody, students were privileged to take part in student prayer bands. Once a week, an hour was given to prayer groups which were organized to pray for specific countries, for specific missionaries, and for specific mission groups. At the time I was a student, prayer was greatly emphasized at Moody Bible Institute, because it was believed that it enabled God to empower His servants in the great task of reaching the world with the Gospel and it enriched the lives of believers. When students saw how the Lord answered prayer, and how they were empowered to accomplish feats in their own lives, they were encouraged to pray even more. This is one of many qualities that distinguish Moody Bible Institute from many other places of higher learning.

During the conferences, developing an effective prayer life was something the missionaries greatly encouraged the students to do, apart from their studies and apart from any other type of learning or preparation they would make for going to the mission field. I believe that God used the fruit from these annual conferences to affect the whole world. My life was certainly changed and challenged, as was that of George Verwer. Later, as we did missions work we could trace our motivation back to many of the speakers at those conferences.

As I began to settle into my studies at Moody, I discovered that the program was structured so students would really have to study. We didn't have much time for any activities other than study. Moody Bible Institute is referred to by some as the West Point of Christian schools in terms of Bible learning and I felt very privileged to be there. Of course, I was eager to learn as much about the Word of God as I possibly could, and it was indeed an experience in my life that I will never forget.

During the second part of my first year, available space in Moody's dormitory enabled me to move on campus, and I felt more a part of the school and closer to the functioning of everything. At this time in the late fifties, I was one of five African American day students at Moody out of a student body of about 1,000. There were about ten other black students from countries in Africa and the West Indies. Interestingly, of about 1,000 evening students at Moody, about 90 percent of them were African American. At 820 N. LaSalle Blvd. on Chicago's Near North Side, Moody is about fifteen minutes from downtown Chicago and is close to a densely populated African American section which, until the first decade of the twenty-first century included a housing project known as Cabrini-Green.

CHAPTER THREE

Illinois: Training for Ministry

Westlawn Gospel Chapel, Chicago

Midweek, Moody Bible Institute had a release program, in which students were assigned to churches in different communities. At these churches we taught the Bible to young people. Many of the pastors were steeped in oral tradition but didn't always teach the Bible accurately. Congregants were not being nourished properly with the Word of God, and of course, such men and women often were not really walking with the Lord themselves, so they came up short in terms of their spiritual lives.

Through Moody's release program, I came in contact with several African American churches in Chicago. One was Westlawn Gospel Chapel, a Bible-centered African American church on Chicago's West Side in a section called Lawndale.

This church was actively involved in teaching the Word of God and witnessing for Christ in the neighborhood and in the prisons. Unlike many churches that talked about such activities but never got around to it, I was really impressed with this church because they had a prison ministry where they visited inmates in Chicago's correctional facilities and witnessed to them. Some of the inmates accepted the Lord and joined the church. Working with the churches' inmate visitation ministry was a vast source of experience for us students.

One of the first brothers I met in this church was Dr. Leroy Yates, a microbiologist. It was unusual for an African American pastor to have secular work and carry out a ministry. The same was true for the two other pastor/elders in this church, Dr. Melvin Banks and Pastor Harvey Rollerson. All of them were professional people. Dr. Banks was founder and CEO of Urban Ministries, Inc., an African American Christian education publishing company; Harvey Rollerson was a school principal.

Ministry with Dr. Samuel Stephens

Dr. Yates of Westlawn Gospel Chapel introduced me to another very godly man, Dr. Samuel Stephens. He was a mature brother in the Lord who knew the Bible extremely well. Dr. Stephens was the first African American registered pharmacist in Illinois. I was impressed by his humble, influential life. Once when President Nixon came to Chicago, Dr. Stephens had the opportunity to speak to him about the needs of housing, jobs, and education in the African American community. His pharmacy was on Chicago's South Side, at 505 W. 51st Street. On the weekends, Saturdays mainly, I visited him in his pharmacy and drugstore. He had seven telephone lines so that doctors could have a direct way to reach him to order medications for patients. His brother, also a pharmacist, worked with him and a third pharmacist; it was a busy shop, serving the community.

Dr. Stephens had been used of God to help initiate three Christian fellowships, including Westlawn. He used his finances and influence to support these three assemblies so that the Word of God might be taught and preached. During the midweek, he developed his own Christian businessmen's association which met at a branch of the YMCA on Wednesdays around noon. He encouraged African American businessmen to come and hear the Word of God, and he pointed out to them that what they had experienced in terms of getting an education and their success in business was due to God's grace. Of course, his ultimate purpose was to encourage Christians to give thanks to the Lord for His goodness, and to seek ways for them to use their resources to help others to come to the same knowledge of Jesus Christ.

On several occasions he encouraged me to speak to the businessmen. They were happy to hear that I had accepted Jesus Christ as my personal Savior in Alaska while in the military, and they encouraged me in the ministry in many ways, verbally at times, as well as monetarily, which helped me with school expenses. One day Dr. Stephens asked if I would visit a family living near his pharmacy whose son had deep emotional problems, which I did. The family was happy about the results of my visit and greatly encouraged me to continue spending time with their son, which I did for the rest of the semester.

Dr. Stephens was influential in many ministries, encouraging individuals to serve the Lord, preach the Word, and help our people. He contributed money to many mission groups, including those associated with Moody Bible Institute. Moody had a group of stewards who went around the world soliciting funds for the school. Once a steward that came to Dr. Stephens' pharmacy expressed to Dr. Stephens that his wife was ill and needed some medication, which came to something like three or four hundred dollars. Dr. Stephens gave it to this man as a gift in the name of Jesus Christ.

This godly man was an influence in my life in so many ways. He challenged me and encouraged me to take part in many of the ministries which he had initiated or had a part. One day, seeing how I was exercised to use literature like Gospel tracts, leaflets, New Testaments, and Christian books to witness for the Lord, he encouraged me to set up a book table on a sidewalk along 63rd Street near his drugstore. His rationale was that many young people would pass by and it would be a wonderful way to reach them with the Gospel by giving them literature. He pointed out that even though I would not be able to spend much time with them, at least I could put some of God's Word in their hands.

Naturally, my heart was greatly inspired. After notifying the precinct's patrolmen so there would be no problem about my presence, I was able to do the book table a few days a week. One sign of encouragement occurred sometime after I had the book table set up. A plainclothes policeman came by and said that he was happy to see me there with the books. He mentioned that if I had any problems, he would be nearby keeping an eye on me.

That was the nature of Dr. Stephens' influence as well as his burden, getting God's Word out and encouraging those of us in the ministry in every possible way to be effective in preaching and distributing the Word of God.

Ministry with Inmates

Along with Dr. Yates at Westlawn, Dr. Stephens also challenged me about visiting the inmates at Cook County Jail. Later, since I had a heart for ministering to inmates, I was able to arrange through Moody Bible Institute to use the midweek practical ministry to visit the jail. Sometimes I also arranged to go along on Sunday mornings with a church group as they conducted services at Cook County Jail. At the jail I met Chaplain John Irvin, who also was the director of chaplain's services with the Light Bearer's Association, a chaplain's organization. Brother Irvin was a very loving, humble man who spent many hours at the jail. He was extremely happy that the Lord had burdened me to visit the individuals there. Later he created office space for me, so that inmates who wanted permission to visit the chaplain's office could meet me for private counseling.

I learned a lot from talking to the different inmates and hearing about their experiences. They were incarcerated for various reasons, but they all had a need to know the living God. Over a period of time, some responded to the Gospel and accepted Jesus Christ as their personal Savior. At times Chaplain Irwin would ask me to fill in for him at the Cook County Jail when he was away for a week or two.

After several months, I was surprised and encouraged when Chaplain Irvin gave me a small monetary gift to encourage my heart and cover minor expenses. After about a year, Chaplain Irwin burdened me to visit the Cook County House of Corrections next door, a similar, newer facility that housed mainly teenagers. One of the encouraging factors about the ministry at the House of Corrections is that I was also given office space for private counseling sessions. By God's grace, I was able to maintain that ministry as long as I was at Moody

Bible Institute. With the Lord's help and encouragement from Chaplain Irwin, Dr. Yates, and from Dr. Stephens, I learned a lot about prison ministry through my experiences at Cook County Jail and the House of Corrections.

Influencing Others

On some Sundays at Westlawn Gospel I was encouraged to preach the message for the day and teach a Bible class. This was another phase in my life, after accepting the Lord as my Savior in Alaska in which I grew tremendously in the Lord. To this day I am thankful for the influence and spiritual mentoring of men like the pharmacist Dr. Stephens, and others such as Chaplain John Irwin; Dr. Leroy Yates, Sr.; Dr. Melvin Banks; and Brother Harvey Rollerson. I was a new Christian and they impacted me greatly.

One day I had the book display set up on 63rd Street and a young man named Arthur Jackson came by. He was a young African American who told me he was an activist and interested in what was happening in Africa. He asked, "What do you think of Lumumba?"

At that time Patrice Lumumba was the leader of the Congo. I had been reading about him in the newspaper. I could see that this young man thought deeply about things and so I responded by asking him, "What do you think about Jesus Christ?"

He was a bit stunned by the question. I told him that while Lumumba had a lot on the ball, his qualities paled in comparison to those of Jesus. The Lord led me to share with Arthur Jackson that there was a man more awesome, attractive, powerful, and challenging than Lumumba, and this man is Jesus Christ.

Arthur looked at me strangely when I told him that, but he continued to listen. My word to him was simply that Jesus

Christ came to earth to die for him because He loved him. Arthur said he had gone to church all of his life and he was still attending church, but he told me that he had never heard the Gospel the way the Lord allowed me to explain it to him that day on 63rd Street. It wasn't too long after we began talking that I asked Arthur Jackson if he would prayerfully consider accepting Christ as his personal Savior based on what the Bible said.

He looked at me for a few seconds with a deeply sincere, thoughtful expression on his face, and said, "Yes, I would like to accept Jesus Christ as my personal Savior."

My heart was filled with joy as I shared with him several verses from the Bible, including John 3:16; Romans 3:23; Romans 6:23 and other verses pertaining to salvation. Afterward I folded up my table and gathered my books, and he and I walked back to Dr. Stephens' drugstore. He shared with Dr. Stephens what he had just experienced. Of course, Dr. Stephens was ecstatic. He reflected on the fact that what the Lord had led him to help me with was coming to pass: Arthur Jackson was a living testimony of a person who had come by the book table and accepted Christ as his personal Savior.

I kept in touch with Arthur Jackson who later went into the military. He married a beautiful Christian girl, and he and his wife were sent to serve, of all places, in Alaska. After his discharge, he returned to Chicago and became very active in his own church like never before. Shortly afterward, I contacted his pastor about the possibility of prayerfully ordaining him for the ministry, which he thought was a wonderful idea. In due time, Brother Jackson was ordained as a preacher of the Gospel of our Lord and Savior Jesus Christ. He and his wife have two children. God used him tremendously. It is not likely that

Arthur Jackson would have ever used his resources for God's glory if God had not changed his heart. Arthur Jackson and his wife are in my life to this present day and remain a great source of encouragement; they are trophies of God's saving grace.

A Fortuitous Meeting and a Different Future

While at Moody Bible Institute, Pastor Alan Redpath, the pastor of Moody Church, invited me to have lunch with him. Naturally, I was excited that such a spiritual man, the pastor of a church with such a reputation would ask me to join him for lunch. I accepted the invitation, and after lunch he began to share with me that he had heard about my ministry at Moody, that he had a burden for assisting a smaller church in an African American community which was associated with Moody Church. He was wondering if I might agree to become the pastor of that church. He assured me that I would be well compensated.

As I thought about the offer, I weighed several factors. On the one hand, it was an honor to be offered such a position by such a revered pastor, and there was certainly a need for solid Bible teaching and evangelism in the African American community. My recent experiences with the book table and inmates seemed to confirm my capabilities. On the other hand, I thought about my studies. I came to Moody to study, and I felt strongly that I was in a preparatory stage. I knew I should stay at Moody and continue my studies.

Reluctantly, I turned down his offer. The Lord gave me the grace to tell him that it would not be wise for me to accept such a position; I would not be able to commit to the time necessary to pastor the people and do my studies at the same time. He assured me that he understood; he had been praying about it and he felt my response was the answer from the Lord. Dr.

Redpath said that he would continue to pray for God's leading in my life.

The Network Expands: Troubled Souls and Other Evangelists

While at Moody Bible Institute, I had another very encouraging experience when a group from Wheaton College, one of America's leading Christian colleges, asked me to speak with a man who was a gangster. They knew that I had worked with men in prison, I had grown up in a neighborhood with more than its share of criminal activity, and I probably could relate somewhat to this man. He was about 45 years old and had just been released from prison. Because of his association with gangsters he had given information to the authorities about their activities, and he made it clear that he felt he did not have long to live. The Christians who were witnessing to him wanted him to be sure that he knew Christ personally. This knowledge would give him comfort and confidence: even if he was killed, he would have eternal life. The group from Wheaton sought me out at Moody, and I agreed to witness to him about Jesus Christ.

One Sunday we met at the Claiborne Gospel Hall on Chicago's Near North Side. I shared my testimony and explained the Gospel to him. He said that he had already accepted Christ, but he acknowledged that my witness was very encouraging. Although my time with him was brief, the incident was an example of an experience which reinforced me in terms of my ministry. The Lord was allowing me to learn and to be effective for His glory, and it was an experience I shall never forget.

Also during my time at Moody Bible Institute, as I visited various churches, I met a group of Christians who were really concerned about missions and praying for individuals like me.

I met one such couple at a prayer meeting. He was a minister and traveling evangelist and his wife was a very godly woman. They had a daughter, whom I will call Deborah, who was a schoolteacher. She loved the Lord and she taught the Bible and played the piano and organ at her church in New York. This couple was eager for me to meet their daughter. Sister Ayers Smith, another friend of mine from Westlawn Gospel Chapel, was an African American who was involved in children's evangelism; she also mentioned Deborah. Sister Smith said that it would be wonderful if somehow Deborah and I met and shared each other's ministries and supported each other in prayer. I was in my early 20s and had not had a relationship with any young lady since I had accepted Christ as my personal Savior, and I was hearing that Deborah was a believer and dedicated to the Lord. It occurred to me that she might be the Lord's choice for my life.

Around this time I met Deborah during a time when she was visiting Chicago. Her parents invited me to their home and introduced us. Deborah showed an interest in me, and a desire to get to know me better when time allowed, which encouraged my heart. From 1957 through 1960, my time at Moody Bible Institute was one of activity, learning, and new experiences.

Taking Evangelism Seriously: Verwer's Challenge

At an annual Keswick meeting at Moody Church, Dr. Oswald J. Smith, the pastor of the famous People's Church in Toronto, Canada, spoke. He said that he was convinced that if enough of God's people were committed to evangelism, the world could be evangelized, especially with the printed page, in a short period of time. At the end of his message he invited anyone to come forward who was burdened to give their lives to the task in obedience to our Lord's last command in Matthew

28:19-20, to go throughout the world to preach the Gospel. I was seated near the middle of the church and saw a person streak past, down the aisle. When he got to the front, I saw that it was George Verwer, my classmate, who had run all the way to the altar.

The next day, after getting back to Moody Bible Institute, George asked the administration if he could speak to the entire student body at our weekday devotional period. George's challenge was this: prayerfully consider going with him to Mexico during our Christmas vacation on a mission of evangelism.

As George pointed out, Mexico was very close to the United States, less than 2,000 miles from Moody Bible Institute. He told us that very few Mexicans had any part of the Bible in their homes as they were practically unreached by the Gospel. Thousands of people were going into eternity without knowledge of the Savior. George told us that the least we could do was to go to Mexico for about ten days during our Christmas recess to distribute Christian literature and do our part to reach the nation for Jesus Christ.

But, Should I Go?

Several students responded to George's invitation. The Lord spoke to my heart, but I rationalized that George and others probably wouldn't want me to go; I was an African American and the group was white. I wrestled with this reasoning for several days. *Well, maybe I want you to go too, the Lord was saying.*

Finally, I went to Brother George Verwer and said, "George, what would be the possibility of me coming along with the group to Mexico during the Christmas recess for a time of evangelism?"

Oh, he was so excited! He was jumping and shouting, "Yes, brother! Please come! We really want you to come! It won't be a problem at all! We would really love for you to come." Of course, I was encouraged, but his enthusiasm was a surprising contrast with my assumption that I would not feel welcomed.

He provided some details that helped me get up to speed. They planned to have orientation meetings so that participants would know what to say, what to bring, and how to prepare. He also emphasized the importance of prayer before going on a crusade like that. It was important to know God's will, pray that God would prepare our hearts, and pray for our needs and the needs of the people we were trying to reach. They were planning on having a prayer meeting on Friday. Such an undertaking should certainly be bathed in prayer, he explained, and the Lord would make it clear to everybody who should be involved. So he was putting out the word that all the students at Moody and students from other Bible schools that had heard about the trip should gather Friday evening about nine o'clock for prayer.

I made sure I did all my homework and caught up with my work for the weekend before going to the prayer meeting. Of those in attendance, there were about fifty students who came for the session to hear about the trip to Mexico. George Verwer expressed that the most important thing was prayer, not only about whether or not one should go to Mexico, but also in view of the nature of the Christian's spiritual warfare. We were graciously reminded, "For we wrestle not against flesh and blood, but against principalities, against powers, against the rulers of the darkness of this world, against spiritual wickedness in high places" (Ephesians 6:12).

Spiritual Warfare Isn't Easy

It was very wise on George's part to remind us that our task ahead would not be easy. The devil himself would be upset. If anyone thought about doing anything effectively for Jesus Christ in Mexico, then we could be assured that the devil would try to hinder it and attack in many different ways. On the other hand, our hearts were greatly encouraged by Jeremiah 33:3:

> Call unto me, and I will answer thee, and show thee great and mighty things, which thou knowest not.

I was greatly impressed with the prayer meeting. Before then, I had never attended a prayer meeting whose focus was taking on a whole nation for the cause of Jesus Christ. We were encouraged to claim verses like John 14:14:

> …Ask any thing in my name, I will do it.

It is a simple matter of taking God at His word. Over time George often reminded us that since we were engaged in a spiritual battle, in order to win, we had to use spiritual weapons such as prayer. He encouraged us to exercise our faith and just believe God for things like how we would get to Mexico and where we would stay once we got there. At Moody we were learning to expect great things from God and to attempt great things for God. Of course, there were those among family members and others who said it made no sense for any Christian group to try to attempt these things while still in school. But at Moody we were being taught the Bible and we were being challenged day by day to trust the word of God and to trust God to do what He promises in His Word. We were not just lowly students; the Lord's commission is for each of us to go throughout the world and preach the Gospel.

At George's encouragement, we met every Friday evening for prayer for the trip to Mexico.

The challenges were great. For example, we were challenged to pray for one million copies of Gospel tracts. As far as we knew, most Christian groups did not print more than 2,000 tracts for distribution at any given time. We had heard about the desperate need in Mexico, and I realized that on many an afternoon while carrying out my book table ministry on the South Side, I passed out 2,000 tracts. In a country like Mexico where people have a great need for something spiritual to read, distributing a million tracts in a week did not seem impossible to us at the time.

Another major challenge was transportation. We needed a truck for transporting us, our belongings, and the literature. Another dream was to open a Christian bookstore through which the Gospel could flow. People could buy Bibles, receive free Christian literature, ask questions, and be presented with the Gospel of Jesus Christ. The location of the bookstore, and a local congregation that would run the store were all items for prayer. We were also challenged to ask God to scrutinize our hearts for wrong motives and for known or unknown sin. We prayed that God would help us to allow the Holy Spirit to search our hearts for anything that might hinder our prayers.

Even though our goals were ambitious, God was gracious. He rewarded our faith. Here we were, barely able to pay our tuition, and yet God did these amazing things because they were burdens, first on His heart, and then on ours.

CHAPTER FOUR

Southbound: Evangelizing in Mexico

Background on First Missionary Trip to Mexico

Since George himself had been saved through the ministry of the printed page, that is, the gospel of John that he read each day when he was in high school, he was exercised to use literature to reach others even though circumstances prevented him from spending significant time with them. On many different occasions, as George Verwer did personal outreach with his friends back home in New Jersey, he began to use books and Gospel literature more and more. That was why I saw him out on street corners in Chicago when I was doing similar evangelism while at Moody.

He realized that selling Christian books could be so effective that in 1958, along with his friend Dale Rhoton, he established the Send the Light ministry. At that time his mother did most of the paperwork and book inventory, but it was the beginning of a ministry for which God had burdened him.

Brother Verwer's vision for Mexico was inspired by a trip he'd taken in 1957 with two friends, Dale Rhoton and Walter Borchard. They took Gospel literature to Mexico and according to George, within seven days almost all the literature was gone. He said that they saw people fight to get a copy of the gospel of John and ran across fields to pick up a Gospel tract. They met hundreds of people who had never even seen a portion of God's Word. After their first summer in Mexico, George knew that God wanted him on the mission field as soon as possible.

Prayerful Preparation: Confessing and Sharing Testimonies

Many of us attending that first prayer meeting were impressed and convinced that Brother Verwer's heart was really on fire for the Lord, that he was deeply concerned about reaching the lost with the Gospel. The room was filled with the Spirit of the Lord. You could sense that the presence of the Lord was there and everyone was at ease, excited, and joyful about the challenge. There was a willingness to say yes to the Lord, and a willingness to open our hearts and confess sin.

In my case, I still felt some guilt about some of my sinful activity while in the Air Force before I accepted Christ. I remembered how I used to do loan sharking amongst the military personnel. I made loans to individuals for money they needed, charging them 25 cents on a dollar. To my amazement, quite a few of the young men came forward; each weekend I was loaning out hundreds of dollars for a 25-cent return on each dollar. Now that I look back, only God's grace kept me from getting caught and court-marshaled. I wasn't aware at the time that I was doing something wrong. I was just out of high school, and I felt that I was performing a service and making a profit. It didn't occur to me that I was doing something contrary to Air Force policy.

So then and there at that prayer meeting, I squared it with the Lord and confessed that the loan sharking was very wrong. I believe the Spirit of the Lord brought it to my mind: the Lord was indicating the need for a confession, even though the loan sharking took place long before the prayer meeting.

I also struggled with the bitterness I had toward whites, which was a result of the way I was treated as an African American. Some white students at Moody were not at all friendly toward me and I could sense their hostility and prejudiced attitudes. This was a special problem to me because these students were supposed to be Christians. Another thing that bothered me was some of the school's policies. It did not seem fair to me, and perhaps you could say there was racism involved, that in a school of 1,000 students, only about ten were black. On the other hand, with the student population at evening classes being the opposite composition—almost 90 percent were black—it could make one wonder why that was the case.

I really had to put my bad attitudes and bitterness before the Lord; I knew that He was not pleased with my spurts of resentment. At times it made me angry with various students in the school. It made me angry with the school's policies. At times I thought about leaving the school, and I was crying out to God to help me remain at an institution where I was learning the Word of God. The Word of God had changed my life in such a dynamic way and I was desperate to grow in the knowledge of God's Word and to know more about His purpose for my life.

At that prayer meeting, I confessed my bitterness and resentment. The peace that surged in my heart was clarification that God had forgiven me.

This first prayer meeting about Mexico was expected to take one or two hours. But when we finished our prayers and our confessions of sin—some of which had never been shared before—it was six o'clock Saturday morning! The prayer meeting had lasted all night and time had gone so fast. It was so refreshing, and there was such joy in our hearts that even at six in the morning, it was difficult to end the meeting and depart. We gave each other loving hugs and we could sense that God was binding our hearts together. We felt united and ready, in the name of Jesus, to make an assault on the devil's territory in Mexico.

Other Needs: Transportation and Funding

Transportation was one of our challenges. A brother among us, George Hanert had an uncle with a fleet of trucks, and one of his trucks had been put on cinderblocks because it was nearly unusable. After George Hanert shared our situation with his uncle, he said, "Well, you can have the truck, but I doubt if it will even get outside of Chicago. Take it and just see." We prayed about it and had the truck checked out. It was ideal for carrying a large amount of literature and students in the back. We decided that the female students would travel separately in an old dusty car, which we would pack with literature.

George Verwer had the wisdom to challenge the group in two important aspects: we were to maintain very strict rules in terms of social contact between males and females, and we had to raise our own financial support. I had a few war bonds which I had purchased while I was in the Air Force, and they'd grown to maturity with interest. Normally I wouldn't have released those war bonds; I had plans to use them for myself. But when the thought came to my mind that the Lord had saved me in Alaska, had delivered me from myself, had commissioned me, and had burdened me to tell others about Jesus Christ, I made the decision to cash in the war bonds to pay for the expense of my first missionary trip to Mexico to reach lost souls for Jesus Christ.

Other students had similar testimonies. They had hi-fi (a precursor to stereo) sets for which they'd paid large sums of money, but they couldn't really use them at Moody Bible Institute because students' rooms only were allowed to have certain items, so these were sold to pay for the trip. We were not allowed to initiate campaigns raising money for going to Mexico, but we were challenged personally to burden our churches to stand behind us and to pray for us. If they were exercised to share and give donations, we encouraged them to do so.

We continued to have Friday night prayer meetings and planning sessions and we continued to seek God's answers through prayer. The group continued to grow; most of our nights of prayer were on campus, but some were at a Gospel mission near the school.

Departure for Mexico

Christmas recess of 1958 arrived and the day came for departure. In addition to the tons of literature and our sleeping bags, we had some canned food to minimize the cost of our stay in Mexico and to reduce the chance of eating food that might be contaminated or that would give us an upset stomach. It was a comfortable ride, really, in the back of the truck. While the young men planned to sleep back there, arrangements were made beforehand for the young ladies to stop along the way and stay in the homes of believers so that they would not have to sleep in the car the entire trip. We had cut windows in the side of the truck in order to allow more sunlight to come in, as well as to do distribution through the windows once we got to Mexico and went through various towns.

We left Chicago and headed for Mexico City, stopping for the night at Little Rock, Arkansas at the home of some Christian believers. They knew about our trip and had invited us to visit them so that they could encourage us and provide refreshment and overnight accommodations. The ten guys in the truck stayed in their garage. Dr. Cook was with us, a professor of Spanish at Moody; he strung his hammock up in the garage and was soon asleep. I had my sleeping bag as did several others and we camped out in the garage. It was exciting. I felt like a real Christian soldier for Jesus Christ, roughing it on the way to Mexico. The next morning, our hosts also gave us a light breakfast and coffee and we were on our way to Mexico City.

We were aiming for Mexico City as the center of operations and tried to save as much time as possible traveling. We took turns: one person drove, and the others slept or took part in strategy discussions as well as prayer. We prayed for Mexico, for its people, for other parts of the world, for safety as we drove down to Mexico and for safety once we arrived. We also were rejoicing all along the way, realizing that God was allowing us to proceed with no hindrances, no accidents, and no mechanical problems. It was a time of rejoicing and giving thanks.

Being Likeminded: The Ministry in Mexico Begins

Brother George Verwer had contacted several churches in Mexico ahead of time and had shared our burden with them. He also encouraged the churches to supplement their ministry by participating in our distributions of Christian literature in their community. In response, many of the local pastors wrote back and said they didn't have the time to carry out the ministry, do distribution, and follow up on people after the initial contacts were made. We assured them that we would be willing to do distribution under their supervision if they allowed us to.

Once we got to Mexico and began our efforts, in many cases we were exercised to help local pastors and local churches in a practical way. We assisted with some domestic responsibilities such as sweeping the floor and arranging chairs, so members of the church could be freed up to go out and distribute Gospel tracts. In this way, the Word and the ministry became known to Mexicans by Mexicans as well as through our evangelism.

Many of these churches allowed us to spread out our sleeping bags in their sanctuaries. During the orientation and the prayer meetings, Brother Verwer reminded us that since we were soldiers of Jesus Christ, we should be willing to forsake all and endure hardship for the sake of the Gospel. He said that we should be willing to eat anything put before us by the Lord's people, to be submissive to them, and to esteem them and their ministries above our own ministries.

There was great joy in our hearts as we went forward. The Holy Spirit brought various portions of His Word to our minds to help us grow. One portion that came to my mind as we moved among the Christians in Mexico was Philippians 2:2-4:

> 2Fulfil ye my joy, that ye be likeminded, having the same love, being of one accord, of one mind.

> 3Let nothing be done through strife or vainglory; but in lowliness of mind let each esteem other better than themselves.

⁴Look not every man on his own things, but every man also on the things of others.

Coming from a prosperous country like America, and working in a poor country like Mexico, I worked hard not to have a haughty attitude and to not allow the devil to fool me into thinking that I was superior. I knew that whatever Satan tried to tell me was superior, whether it was my money, my status, or my intelligence, it would be a lie. According to the Word of God, all that we are, all that we have, and all that we ever hope to have, we owe it all to the love of God. Philippians 2:2-4, especially the part about esteeming another brother better than myself, was becoming real as I ministered in Mexico. I had read it before, but I had never practiced it like this.

We made a short stop in Saltillo and after about two days of more driving, we arrived in Mexico City. We went to the home of some local believers who allowed us to park the truck near their property. Some of us alternated sleeping in the truck at night so we could protect our belongings. The believers made toilet and bath facilities available to us, a tremendous encouragement.

Each morning we were up early and out for distribution. Since we were truly neophytes we were grateful for the help we got from Wycliffe Bible Translators. We learned a lot about their ministry, including the discipline and training that they insist on from their missionary candidates, and we felt good in terms of how the Lord was burdening us and challenging us to live as soldiers. We gave our time, strength, and resources in order to get the Gospel out to the lost.

One of our main tracts, put together by Brother George Verwer was titled "Who has the truth, the Protestants, or the Catholics?" This was a very clear presentation to provoke people to do some critical thinking about the faiths of Protestantism and Catholicism. Verwer's content didn't bash anyone; the material challenged individuals to consider the truth in light of the context of the Bible. We also passed out a card with about eleven different individuals' pictures on it from several different countries. The card showed that believers are from many different ethnic groups and a variety of countries; one thing we have in common is the fact that we all have Jesus Christ as our personal Savior.

First Experience with Correspondence Course Tracts

Another piece of literature we had produced beforehand which was a strategic element of our distribution was an invitation to send for a correspondence course. We gave individuals a tract, and on the back was an invitation to write in for a free Bible correspondence course. In time we found that thousands of individuals sent in to study the Bible by way of correspondence. This was a tremendous encouragement to us. Many testified to the life-changing effects of the free correspondence courses; after studying God's Word in an organized fashion, they made a decision to accept Jesus as their Savior. As we went along in our ministry, we were amazed at the number of people who wanted to know more about the Word of God, and when we saw that individuals were writing in because someone gave them a tract, it increased our vision for literature.

There was also a three-way benefit. Local churches got addresses and names of individuals requesting correspondence courses, and the churches followed up to invite the people taking the courses for a time of fellowship and growth at the local church. As a result of the campaign in Mexico, the local churches were greatly strengthened and encouraged, just as we students were during our time there.

CHAPTER FIVE

Spreading the Word: Saltillo and Sunshine Gospel Mission

Christians' Encouragement in Mexico

It would have been impossible for us to get established in any way on our first trip to Mexico, if not for the local Christians who encouraged us, who gave us a place to wash, a place to park the vehicles, and who looked after us continually. The believers provided much encouragement. Other than Dr. Cook, most of us didn't know much Spanish. We knew a few phrases, such as "thank you," "good morning," and "good evening". We learned more of the language by being among Mexicans and talking to them. As we gave out Christian literature in Spanish, it also gave us an opportunity to converse; of course, this is the best way to learn a language. The local people were always willing to help us practice our phrases, and to correct our pronunciation or syntax, and though humbling, it was a good position to be in since we were learning Spanish free. In addition, this was yet another circumstance that showed us how we were certainly not better than our Mexican brothers and sisters.

Eager Responses to God's Word

By going out early in the morning we were there when the masses were moving about and going to work. With hundreds of thousands of people rushing to and fro in the morning, a few thousand pieces of literature did not last long. Most people were eager to get something to read that was free, especially teenagers and college-age students, and we were happy to be able to give them a portion of God's Word. About noon, we returned to where we were staying, had lunch and since this was the hottest time of day in Mexico, we took a two-hour siesta (nap), until four o'clock. As the sun went down and the day got cooler, we drank tea or a soft drink, and then we were out again, into the streets distributing Christian literature to thousands of people making their way home after a hard day's work. This short-term mission trip to Mexico was indeed a productive, joyous experience.

A Special Bookstore Opens in Saltillo

In addition to distributing Christian literature, we wanted to establish a Christian bookstore. Most mission manuals encourage missionaries to live in an area maybe five or ten years and study the situation before opening a Christian bookstore. We believed, however, in view of the massive population explosion in Mexico during the late fifties, that there was a special urgency in getting the Gospel out and waiting for five or ten years was not an option. So by faith, we believed that God would honor our vision of starting a bookstore.

A bookstore offered a number of benefits. Not only could thousands of pieces of literature be distributed, including Bibles, but individuals could come in and ask questions about the Bible and about any question relating to Christianity. Those working or volunteering at the store could be trained so they could answer questions, and perhaps visitors would be led to a saving knowledge of Jesus Christ. We cried out, "Lord, help us to open a bookstore in the city of Saltillo." We prayed that the Lord would raise up committed people from local churches to take on the responsibility of the bookstore. Local churches in Mexico were happy to have us there for fellowship, sharing, and laboring along with them because they could see that the desire in our hearts was to simply spread the Gospel of Jesus Christ and not start our own empire. The Lord wonderfully answered our prayers and helped us to establish the mission team's first Christian bookstore in Saltillo, Mexico.

My time in Mexico was one of extreme soul searching and intense activity. After doing distribution each morning and late afternoon, we had a meeting in a church practically every evening. Since we were a mixed group of Americans, the local people were curious about an African American traveling with white students. They had heard a lot about racism in the U.S. and they were interested to see us working together. At times the devil would try to convince me that I was in the wrong place. Why was I traveling with these white people? They could do their own thing. I could do my own thing. But what I had experienced at Moody Bible Institute was God was speaking to my heart. He reminded me that I had been bought by His blood, my life had been changed by Him, and He had united my heart with a group of young people who had the same desire to make Him known to others who knew Him not.

God's Task: "Even unto the End of the World"

I knew that God has a definite task for those who accept Him as their personal Savior. He desires to work through them to accomplish His task of reaching the world for His glory, and I was firmly convinced that God is willing to use any believer to fulfill His global purpose. At Moody, we were being challenged go to the ends of the earth for Jesus Christ, even as we are lovingly exhorted by Jesus in Matthew 28:18-20:

> [18]And Jesus came and spake unto them, saying, All power is given unto me in heaven and in earth.
>
> [19]Go ye therefore, and teach all nations, baptizing them in the name of the Father, and of the Son, and of the Holy Ghost:
>
> [20]Teaching them to observe all things whatsoever I have commanded you: and lo, I am with you alway, even unto the end of the world. Amen.

So that was it. I had this opportunity with these students to go forth for Jesus Christ, not thinking of myself, and not worrying about what other people would think about me. Before I went on the mission, I had come across many pastors who tried to discourage me by telling me that it made no sense to go all the way to Mexico when there was so much to do here in our own community. Plus, they said, you speak English and they speak Spanish so there would be a language barrier. Many things were said to try to discourage me from following the Lord's leading and going to Mexico. But no matter what our differences were, all of us on the trip realized that we were His, that He called us to accomplish a task, and it was not about ourselves, it was about Him.

So there we were in Mexico, in the Spirit and the power of the Lord, and in His love. While there, God increased love amongst us in a way that I'd never experienced. That was the icing on the cake concerning the Christianity I was experiencing. You can imagine I had some reservations as to how the mission would work out, and how team members would respond to me. In reality, I experienced the love of Christ through the lives of believers in a way I had never experienced it before.

After our evening meetings, when the team came back together, there were times of praise and thanksgiving. Team members had a chance to share testimonies about how God had worked during the day as they passed out Christian literature and spoke to people on the street. Having been exposed only to Catholicism, the local people had many questions about the literature we distributed, and about the person of Jesus Christ. After having their questions answered, several people accepted Christ as their personal Savior right on the street and came to the church meeting that night. Each day was a new experience for us, and we became quite emotional as we prepared to return to the United States from Mexico. We were amazed at how our hearts had been bound with the local Christians in Mexico in such a short time. Such a grip of Christian love is difficult to put into words.

Return Trips to Mexico

After returning to Moody Bible Institute, only a day or two passed before we were back into our routine schedule of disciplined study habits and regimentation. We did have an opportunity to give a testimony to prayer groups at the institute concerning our trip. Many students were happy to hear how the Lord had answered prayer on our behalf and they told us that they had been praying for us while we were gone. Several students made a commitment to continue to pray for what was accomplished in Mexico. Personally, I thought of the Christmas recess trip as a once in a lifetime experience. It was far from it.

During the spring semester, the thought arose among the students, *"Why not go back to Mexico this coming summer?"* It was a challenge. We would have to pray for twice as much in terms of the resources needed for being in Mexico during July and August, and for possibly two to three times more literature than we prayed to have for distribution during the Christmas recess. So again we reminded ourselves how wonderful it would be to go back to Mexico. We saw the response when we went at Christmas recess. We ran out of literature in a few days, the local people were wonderfully responsive, and there was an overwhelming need for the Gospel. As we met with each other at the school and talked about it, we felt in our hearts: *"Yes, let's do it again. Let's ask the Lord to help us believe Him for what's needed to return to Mexico during the summer."* We did not want to stay in America and spend our time doing things we considered less important than getting the Gospel out in Mexico.

As we met each other day after day in class, in student devotional time, and in prayer meetings, it seems that all of our hearts and minds were going in the same direction and with the same desire; with the Lord's help, we would go back to Mexico during the summer of 1959 to give more time to reaching that country for Jesus Christ. Along with our prayers for specific needs, and for our effectiveness during the summer mission, we prayed that we would be able to open another bookstore.

At times we thought maybe this would be too much, but then we reminded ourselves that God is willing to do far above anything that we can even ask or think of. By the Christmas 1959 outreach, a bookstore opened in Guadalajara, the second largest city in Mexico.

Over and over as we meditated on the Word of God, our hearts were encouraged to attempt great things for Him, and to look to Him for the faith to accomplish them. I think of a verse found in Isaiah 65:24:

> ...before they call, I will answer; and while they are yet speaking, I will hear.

During my time with the team, one of my greatest experiences was living the truth of God's Word when I simply put my faith and trust in Him. I was experiencing a closer relationship with Jesus Christ. My mornings of devotions deepened as I reflected on answered prayer. God was doing a work in my own life by teaching me to love, not only my fellow brethren, but each individual that I had an opportunity to talk to about Jesus Christ. Not everyone was happy to hear our message. Some became irate, cursed us out, took a tract and tore it up and threw it in our faces. Those could have been discouraging moments, and at times they were for a while, but then we reflected upon the fact that we sent Jesus Christ to the cross, so these little challenges and incidents only served to make us more dependent on the Spirit of God.

So we began to beat the drum louder and louder in preparation for going back to Mexico. Several new students were interested this time, while others felt that they had to work during the summer months and get funds for fall tuition and other needs so they could not return to Mexico.

Since I had been discharged from the Air Force and was getting veteran's assistance and money from the GI Bill which was helping to pay my way through school, I could use that for my summer expenses as well. Thus, I felt at peace about going back to Mexico. Again the team's truck was packed with tons of literature and our belongings, and the guys on the trip were in the back of the truck. The girls on the team rode in a car filled with literature and provisions. It was exciting to share our faith and pass out literature. These trips to Mexico were the highlights of my time at Moody.

Neckties Lead to a Prison Stay

In the summer of 1960, I had a frightening experience that tested my faith. I was arrested and put in prison. During one interim period in Chicago, we met some Christians who had a clothing store. They gave us clothing to give to people in Mexico. One of the donations was a box of brand new neckties. We thought it would be a good idea to give them to individuals who accepted our Christian literature and donated 5 or 10 cents for a Gospel tract.

We stopped in the city of Matamoros on our way to Vera Cruz during our trip to the country in the summer of 1960. As we were passing out tracts, and I was passing out ties along with the literature, I was apprehended by an undercover policeman. I tried to explain, but he didn't believe my story about giving out free ties. He couldn't understand that a person would give neckties to people for taking pieces of Christian literature. Since he was not a Christian, it was reasonable that he neither understood, nor believed us. No doubt he was convinced that I was an unlicensed vendor. As a result, I was arrested and taken to prison.

That particular day I was the only one on the team with a few neckties left. Therefore, it appeared that I was the only one distributing the ties. My colleagues tried to reason with the police officials that I was innocent and I was not selling the ties, but they didn't want to hear anything. They took me to a prison in the city of Reynosa and signed me in. At first I thought I would be there for some time with that false accusation because in Mexico, unlike the U.S., you are guilty until you are proven innocent. I was taken to a one-room cell that held two African American prisoners from the United States. It was very tight living quarters. They let me keep my sleeping bag, so I actually slept on the floor for the first day I was there.

Then the devil began to attack me. He said, "See, I told you that you should not have come to Mexico with this group of students. Look at what's happening to you. God says He loves you and you are doing what He wants you to do, and yet He's allowing you to go to prison?!"

God's Word Comforts

The devil was trying to arouse me, but again God's Word came to my mind with such comfort, and I thought of a portion of Scripture, I Peter 4:12 (*Amplified Bible*):

> Beloved, do not be amazed and bewildered at the fiery ordeal which is taking place to test your quality, as though something strange (unusual and alien to you and your position) were befalling you.

God used this portion of Scripture to bring such comfort to my heart. Meanwhile, my Christian brothers were working on my behalf outside the prison. They were visiting the prison's officials and letting them know that they had made a mistake by putting Hoise Birks into prison: He's not a criminal, my mission brothers and others insisted, and imprisoning him is a terrible thing.

Meantime, the two Africans Americans in my cell questioned me. They assured me that since we were all black people, I could be open with them. They did not believe my story, either; they tried to get me to tell them the real reason I was in Mexico. I took the opportunity to take them all the way back to Alaska with me, to the time when I accepted Jesus Christ as my personal Savior. I told them that when I was saved, I declared that I would be willing to go to the ends of the earth and share Christ by life or death. I gave them the whole story.

My cellmates scratched their heads for a while, trying to figure out if I was really being truthful, or if I was trying to pull the wool over their eyes. They offered me cigarettes and were surprised that I did not smoke. Then they questioned me about my girlfriend, and I told them that I did not have a girlfriend at the time and that I was in Bible school in Chicago. After two days, I think they were convinced that my testimony was genuine. Other prisoners were sticking their heads in the door trying to find out what I was about, and the officials were coming in and out to see if they could find out anything about me that was contrary to what I was saying.

Service in Prison

I was incarcerated in a prison in Reynosa, a small town several miles from Matamoros. The first Sunday I was in the prison, the guards allowed the inmates to attend a Christian service conducted by Christians who came into the prison. Of course, I attended. I knew one or two of the ones they were singing in Spanish and I sang heartily, praising the Lord.

After the meeting the Christians giving the service came to me, asked me what my story was, and offered to help me.

I let them know that they could contact other Christians and asked that they all pray for me. I told them that my colleagues and friends with whom I had come to Mexico were working on my behalf. They were happy to hear that, and they assured me that they would do everything they could to help me until I was released.

One morning my cellmates informed me that in a day or so there would be an "inner court" held by the prison's officials. The officials would look over the information they had on prisoners and decide who should stay and who should be released. I was told that when that day came, they would have all the recently incarcerated prisoners line up along the wall surrounding the prison. When the day for inner court was announced, I joined a line of about thirty prisoners, to hear the results of the investigation. When my name was called, with great joy I heard that I was being released. Psalm 147:6-7 came to mind:

> [6]The LORD lifteth up the meek: he casteth the wicked down to the ground.
>
> [7]Sing unto the LORD with thanksgiving; sing praise upon the harp unto our God:

Once I rejoined them, the team members rejoiced with me and we all praised God for answering prayer.

The devil tried to attack me again by saying that I had caused problems for the team, with them spending less time distributing the Gospel and having meetings because they had to run back and forth between Matamoros and Reynosa, looking after me and trying to get me released. I felt a little bad about that for a while, but the Lord encouraged my heart when they assured me of their love and expressed how the Lord had burdened them to pray for me. They put their arms around me and hugged me. So, it was all in the mix in terms of what God was doing. God was binding our hearts together in love in the body of Christ, and I had never experienced this before.

After I was released, we gathered where we were staying, and after giving thanks and praise to God, I rededicated my life to the Lord. After the experience of imprisonment, I realized that He surely would never leave me or forsake me.

After I was released from prison, I went with the team for the rest of the summer to the city of Vera Cruz on the eastern coast of Mexico. Vera Cruz is a beautiful city, and the people were so loving and hospitable that it encouraged our hearts in many ways in terms of distributing Christian literature throughout the city. Another advantage was that since Vera Cruz was on the ocean, there was a lot of seafood, which made our stay less expensive. We ate fresh fish every day.

We were also burdened to pray for a bookstore to be opened in Vera Cruz, and the Lord wonderfully answered our prayer. The summer of 1960 included a fruitful trip to Mexico and another Christian bookstore, all to God's glory. Before we knew it, the summer was over and we headed back to Chicago for school.

Back in Chicago: Studies at Moody

A few days later we were on our way back to Chicago. Once again we settled into school. At the end of that semester, the winter of 1960, school officials informed me that since my grades had been borderline in the preceding semesters my grade point average was not high enough to merit my graduation from the school. I could not return to the school unless I improved my grade average. I had two choices. I could attend Moody Bible Institute in the evening, take courses in theology and Greek, and bring my grade point average up. Or, I could attend another secular school and earn an average of B or A, and then I could come back to Moody Bible Institute.

Well, I was really hurt and discouraged. I felt I had given myself to my studies properly at Moody Bible Institute. I never questioned the grades that I received. I talked it over with George Verwer, the leader of the student mission group.

He said, "Well, Hoise, I think it would be wonderful if you just do what they suggested, and see how the Lord will lead."

As I considered his suggestion, I remembered a previous, similar experience. Once before, after I had been informed that my grade point average was too low, I took two papers on which I had received very low grades and I shared them with other students in the same class to see the difference in our answers. I found that there was no difference in our answers. I decided to talk to the two professors and just try to get a full understanding of why I received very low grades. The professors explained that, as a pastoral student, I should have written in a more pastoral way than the crude outline form I had used. Of course, I understood, to a certain extent. But what confused me was that the information was there, and was not honored.

This time, I talked it over with other students, and they echoed George's suggestion, encouraging me to take evening classes and see how the Lord would lead from there. I decided to follow this advice and enrolled in evening courses at Moody, joining a population that was 98 percent African Americans, the opposite of what I had known at the day school. Many in the night school were Christians who worked fulltime during the day and studied the Bible during the evening at Moody Bible Institute. The evening classes were not as intense as the day classes.

A New Direction Emerging

While I was going to school in the evenings I worked at a cold storage plant where turkeys and other meats were stored in a large building. I really appreciated the job and the money I made.

At the end of the semester, I received C's in the evening courses and these grades were not high enough to qualify me for reentry into Moody's day school. I was deeply discouraged, thinking that I wouldn't have a chance to fellowship with my fellow team members and pursue the burden and vision that was on all our hearts. This included not only going to Mexico, but eventually, many of us prayed, to other parts of the world.

During the time that the ministry from Moody went back and forth to Mexico, the teams spread out and went to different cities. Even though I was no longer going with them, I stayed in contact with my former teammates and continued to pray for them. They continued to experience success on each missionary trip. In the course of this ministry in Mexico, more than seven Christian bookstores were opened, in Saltillo, Monterrey, Mexico City, Vera Cruz, and Guadalajara. Team members were not allowed to solicit funds by sending out prayer letters or other correspondence. We were challenged to share with individuals who knew us and supported our ministries about the work, and if they were exercised about giving a love gift to us toward the work, they could feel free to do so. That's how many of the bookstores came into existence, and local Christians in each of those cities staffed the bookstores themselves.

We were so encouraged and amazed at what God had done in such a short length of time in Mexico through a small group of seemingly insignificant students who were trusting Him and taking His word by faith, that we began to pray for other countries where Christianity wasn't readily accepted. We thought of Spain, which at that time was closed to the Gospel. Franco was in power, and evangelical Christian activity was restricted. We thought of Muslim countries like Turkey, where Christianity was not allowed, and where Christian lives would be threatened if they passed out even one tract.

At this point in my life, now that I was no longer at Moody, I wondered if I would ever have another chance to have a active part in reaching other countries for the Lord as I had done with a group in Mexico. Not only that, many of the Christians I knew in churches in Chicago were saying discouraging things like "There's so much here to do, why are you going to Mexico? Why would you want to go to Spain? Why are you even thinking about going to Turkey?" But as I continued to seek the Lord, He encouraged me to continue to pray regarding His leading for my future, my relationship with the team, and His direct will in my life at that point.

I stayed in close communication with George Verwer. He had graduated six months before I left Moody. Occasionally we met and talked, and we corresponded with each other in between. He was praying for my ministry, and I was praying for his as well.

Sunshine Gospel Mission: All Things Become New

When I left Moody Bible Institute, I did not have much money. Some Christian friends had a ministry at Sunshine Gospel Mission on North Clark Street in Chicago and I began staying there and helping out. This was a mission for men who were having hard times, often living on the street without food or shelter. The mission served meals three times a day and provided overnight shelter. As a rescue mission, the most important part of the program was eventually to have the men listen to the glorious Gospel of Jesus Christ and share the love of God with them.

One of my friends at this mission was Ralph Buss, a dear brother in the Lord, who was on staff there and had an effective ministry with teenagers undergoing difficulties. He counseled them, nurturing them into spiritual maturity, and teaching them how to share their faith with others. Ralph also did construction work; he was a very beautiful person, and he touched my life deeply. I moved into Sunshine Gospel after I left Moody as I prayed and prepared for what God had in store for me next. I really believed that at some point He wanted me to go to Europe with the group that had started at Moody.

I helped out with the ministry at the mission, and during the summer months Sunshine Gospel's leadership encouraged me to assist with the Christian Youth Camp. Most of the teenagers who came to the camp were African Americans and I was greatly encouraged to use my gifts, as an African American, to share with these young people, especially since most of the staff at the mission was white. I was impressed by Ralph and others who were engaged in secular work, and yet spent a lot of time and energy on weekends, after work, and sometimes before work, pouring themselves into these young people. With the love of God, they truly reached out to these youth who were confused and getting into all kinds of trouble. After many of them heard the Word of God and felt the love that came from these beautiful Christians, these teenagers decided that they too wanted to accept Jesus Christ as their personal Savior. What happened next is described in II Corinthians 5:17 (*New King James Version*).

> Therefore, if anyone is in Christ, he is a new creation; old things have passed away; behold, all things have become new.

That's what took place in many of these young lives. Everything became new. They way they talked, the places they went, the friendships they developed, the activities in which they participated; everything changed, as is true in any life that is submitted to Christ.

While I was staying at this mission, I continued to work at the deep-freeze storage corporation. My responsibility, along with that of my fellow workers was to load and unload the trucks that came and to put the frozen food into freezers. Since I was not married at the time, the federal government through its income tax was a big recipient of my paycheck. But I was really blessed and thankful to have a job that paid good money, and to have a place to stay where I did not have to pay a penny. I was experiencing God's provision and God's faithfulness every day. It brings to mind the hymn "Great Is Thy Faithfulness." This hymn is based on Lamentations 3:22-23:

> [22]It is of the LORD's mercies that we are not consumed, because his compassions faileth not.
>
> [23]They are new every morning: great is thy faithfulness.

The Mission Moves to Europe

Even though I was discouraged about having to leave Moody, I knew without a shadow of a doubt that God had led me there and that He had put me in contact with George Verwer and other students of like faith. After George graduated from Moody in 1960 he married Drena Knecht. George met Drena in the autumn of 1958 when he went to get a Moody science film and she was the secretary in the office. At the time Drena was attending night school at Moody. After they were married, they went immediately to Mexico and continued the mission. A few months later, they went to Spain. By the autumn of 1960,

George and Drena were living in Madrid with their newborn son Benjamin. When George returned to the United States in the summer of 1961 to share with churches about the Spanish ministry and to challenge other young people to take part in fulfilling the Great Commission, he contacted me in Chicago.

We had a good time of fellowship at a local restaurant. Then he challenged me to prayerfully consider returning to Europe with him when he came back through Chicago. George pointed out that anyone can work in a cold storage building, or do secular work of any kind for that matter. Very few Christians had the vision to take the Gospel to the ends of the earth.

PART TWO:

Overseas for the Lord

1962 - 1965

CHAPTER SIX

"Gospel Bombs" in Spain

Joining Send the Light

Even though I had money to pay my way to Europe, I had questions and doubts. How long would I be in Europe? Since each team member had to raise his or her own support, where would I get the money to support myself in the ministry? What would it be like to minister overseas and be so far from home? As I pondered these questions in my heart, the Spirit of the Lord brought portions of His Word to my mind to comfort my heart and encourage me to move forward in faith. I think of another Scripture, John 15:7-8:

> [7]If ye abide in me, and my words abide in you, ye shall ask what ye will, and it shall be done unto you.
>
> [8]Herein is my Father glorified, that ye bear much fruit; so shall ye be my disciples.

When I thought of the challenge, my mind went back to Alaska. I thought of how God saved me when I was not able to find joy or purpose in life and at times, I was contemplating suicide. I thought of the joy and comfort my relationship with God brought me along with His precious Word. I knew that it was a tragedy that so many were perishing without the hope of ever knowing Jesus Christ as their personal Savior. I thought of the many godly believers that God had used to help me come to Christ and grow as a Christian.

I let the cold storage company that I worked for know that I would be resigning at the end of the month with the anticipation of going to Europe to do missionary work. My co-workers were happy that a young man like me would be giving my life to serve the Lord. Many of them commented on how wonderful it would be if other young people would have the same burden and passion.

The Lord also allowed me to initiate the paperwork and receive my passport. Shortly afterwards, Brother Verwer mentioned that he was leaving the West Coast and coming back eastward, and he wanted to know if I was going to Europe with him. I was happy to tell him know that not only did I have my passport, I had made all my plans for departure to coincide with his arrival in Chicago. We decided to meet and drive back to New Jersey and then prepare to go to Europe.

I was excited to be going by faith to Europe to reach individuals with the Gospel. Of course I had to leave behind my friends and relatives in Cincinnati, Ohio. My mother told me that someone else could go to Europe. She said, "We need you here at home. We need help, and you'll be so far away. Besides, what if something happens to you?"

I assured her that the Lord cares for His own and I would be fine.

George Verwer and I were booked on the ocean liner *Queen Elizabeth*. George brought many boxes of powdered milk for the teams in Europe, because many of them didn't have fresh milk as they traveled and the powdered milk was a donation. George was also a collector of used postal stamps and in Europe there was a big market for used stamps. He had thousands of stamps dating back many years, and selling them in Europe would bring a good amount of money for the ministry.

This was the second time in my life traveling on an ocean liner. The first time was when I was in the Air Force and I sailed from Oakland, California to Fairbanks, Alaska. That was a military ship, however, and nothing like the luxurious *Queen Elizabeth*. During our five-day voyage, we spent a lot of time studying and having fellowship in the cabin. We shared our life's ambitions with each other and spent hours in prayer for team members, for ourselves, for our family members, and for a lost world.

About the third day I got seasick. It wasn't severe and some sleeping tablets that the steward gave me took care of it. I was out for hours as we made our way across the Atlantic Ocean.

First Stop: Cherbourg, France

We departed the ship in Cherbourg, on the west coast of France. They didn't really dock the ship. The ocean liner stopped off the coast and a large barge came out to the ship. I was surprised because I thought they were going to dock at a normal berth and then we would come off the ship like we got on. Instead, a big barge came and met the ship and took individuals and their luggage getting off at Cherbourg and not planning to go to the ship's destination, England. Since our final destination was Spain, it made more sense for us to get off at Cherbourg.

The first team that had gone to Europe went to Spain. George and his wife and baby lived in Madrid, working underground, really, because under the rule of Franco, Christian evangelism was not allowed. Individuals who were distributing Christian literature and having Christian meetings could be arrested and penalized by the government of Spain. So, George and I, our baggage, some books, the boxes of powdered milk, as well as the postal stamps were unloaded, and we took the barge to the city of Cherbourg.

At Cherbourg customs officials detained us because of the contents of our luggage. The officials were suspicious of the many boxes of powdered milk, and let us know they suspected the boxes contained cocaine. George explained that the boxes of powdered milk were for teams of young people in Spain who were living by faith and who had given their lives to serve the Lord. Also, the customs officials were concerned about all those postal stamps. In France, postal stamps are a big industry, especially very old stamps. They told us that those stamps should have been registered, and George said it would be very gracious of them if they would forgive us this time and allow us to go. By this time, all the other passengers were gone from the terminal and the officials were still asking questions.

Finally, we were released from customs and allowed to take the powdered milk and stamps with us. We knew that it was because people had been praying for us. George had made plans for us to rent a truck in Cherbourg and drive all the way to Madrid, Spain. There also was a driver in France who helped us with part of the driving. This particular model of truck had two bucket seats up front, so I was in the back of the truck as they drove south through France toward Madrid.

Next Stop: Spain – A Closed Country to the Gospel

By God's grace, after about ten hours of traveling from Cherbourg, we arrived in Madrid and rendezvoused with the team there. Everyone was joyful at our arrival, and we had a time of prayer and thanksgiving for the safe trip the Lord had given to us. George shared with them about his trip in America, and they were happy about the addition of their dear brother Hoise Birks to the team.

As I mentioned, Spain was a closed country to Christian missionary activity of any sort—laws in Spain made evangelizing illegal. Weeks and months before George Verwer ever went to Spain he made contact with the local Christians and shared with them the burden that was on his heart to reach the people of Spain. To the Christians already working in Spain, the strategy that George Verwer shared was bold and risky. His burden was to reach the thousands of villages in Spain with the Gospel, and at the same time make an impact on large cities like Barcelona and Madrid. The vision included opening bookstores, too, and putting Gospel posters all over the city. Some respected the burden and vision, and did not believe that George was a sect or cult leader, but they had never heard of such a large burden and vision. It was like a dream and as they looked at George Verwer, they outwardly saw no indications of a person with hundreds of thousands of dollars to pull this off, or of the hundreds of thousands of people needed, perhaps, to do it. They knew that humanly speaking, it could not be done.

While many of the local Christians were excited that a group wanted to reach their fellow citizens with the Gospel, some of the missionaries working in the country at the time expressed fear that the Spanish government would be displeased with all of this frenetic activity and put all missionaries out of the country. Some missionaries had been put out on one or two occasions. For many years, most missionaries in Spain had worked at an extremely slow and cautious pace.

One missionary was irate. He stood up in a meeting and said that this young, inexperienced man (George) was going to ruin the work that he and others had been laboring to do for forty years in Spain with this vision of his. The man said that even though the ministry had been slow in terms of individuals accepting Christ as their personal Savior, they did not need anyone to come in and ruin things.

There was a lot of tension in the room after this angry missionary made his speech. So, what was the response? Was George Verwer going to respond with similar anger? Were the local churches going to say that these missionaries have been with us for many years, we know their work and we're going to stick with them, so pack your bags and go back to America, because what you're talking about at this point—it's difficult to see that it will ever become a reality?

"Gospel Bombs" and Correspondence Courses

After the smoke cleared away, some missionaries went their way and fortunately, the local churches encouraged George to stay and to pray that God would show him and the local church how such evangelistic activities could take place. This was not going to be simple. First of all, it was impossible to go out in the street passing out Christian literature. That was against the law so we couldn't do as we had done in Mexico and the U.S. We did pray about the possibility of taking one of the trucks which had been driven from England, and cutting windows in the truck's side panels, similar to what we had done as we drove to Mexico.

We decided to use this method and we loaded the truck with Gospel literature which had been prepared by the team in Madrid. There were about five Americans with the team in Madrid, and about five or six Spaniards who were operating from an apartment we had rented. During the day the team would stuff envelopes with several items, including a small gospel of John and a tract with information about a correspondence course where individuals could get further information if they wanted to know more about Jesus Christ and the Bible. We sealed the envelopes and put thousands of them into boxes in the back of the truck at nighttime beginning about midnight.

Our team drove through Madrid and many small surrounding towns at night, throwing the envelopes—which we called "Gospel bombs"—over the fences into yards. If there was an obvious mailbox that we could get to without difficulty and without calling attention to what we were doing, we put the envelope in the mailbox. Mostly though, we just drove around throwing Gospel literature over walls and into yards and praying that God would cause the people who received them to respond to the love of Christ and to the truth of His Word.

Even though God had clearly told us to go into the whole world and preach the Gospel, some, like the missionaries who had been in Spain for years, questioned our tactics; they clearly thought our tactics were too aggressive. Some asked if it was right to disobey the law in order to distribute Christian literature. When we were back at Moody Bible Institute, the Lord had laid on our hearts not only Spain and Mexico, but other closed countries such as Iraq, Afghanistan, Turkey, China, Russia, and Soviet bloc nations. We were convinced that since the Bible was so clear about our commission to win the world to Christ, we should obey God rather than man.

We had the Lord's mandate to go unto all the world and preach the Gospel; His commandment was supreme above every law. By life or by death we had decided in our hearts that we would obey God rather than man.

As a result of receiving those Gospel packets, many people wrote in to request the correspondence course in order to study the Word of God. This was not our only method. Another tactic that the Lord brought to our minds was to buy telephone books of all the towns and cities in Spain. Using addresses from the telephone books, the team typed a note introducing the Christian literature and encouraging the recipient to write in for the correspondence course. We put these notes into envelopes and mailed them. This was a big expense in terms of postage, since we sent them all over Spain. But the response was huge. Amazingly, thousands of people wrote in to study the Bible. This was encouraging to our hearts. As George pointed out to Spain's Christian leaders, it was one way to reach people and get an overwhelming response, which indicated a tremendous interest in knowing about the Gospel. Spaniards had seen many images of Jesus on the cross but in most cases, it never was explained to them why He died on the Cross.

We knew of a town that didn't have a telephone book, and we were concerned about how we could reach those people. But in that town the telephone operator got a copy of the correspondence course and apparently she told so many people about it that a lot of people wrote in from that little town. More than 25,000 people from across the country wrote in to study the Bible. We were filled with joy that so many wanted to know more about the Savior who had revolutionized our lives and brought us such joy, peace, and purpose.

Lord, Can We Open a Bookstore?

After a period of time, in addition to distributing literature from the truck and sending out mailings, we began to pray that we could open a Christian bookstore in Madrid; this would be another way to spread the Gospel. We thought of what the Lord had done in Mexico in terms of the seven bookstores there. We prayed, "Lord, You did it in Mexico seven times, and we believe that You can do it here in this spiritually difficult country of Spain. You are faithful. You are the Almighty God. You have assured us from Your Word, over and over again, that if we just trust You and glorify Your name and ask anything in Your name, You will do it. So, Lord, we beg You, please allow us, for the sake of Your glory and those in Spain who need You, to open a bookstore."

God wonderfully answered prayer through Madrid's Christians. They were inspired and excited to see what God was doing. They caught the vision to open a Christian bookstore in their own city. They had the expertise, they knew the language, and they were able to facilitate the technical and legal aspects of the business of opening a bookstore. So through the church in Madrid and other small groups of Christians, the bookstore Liberia Victoria was opened. The English translation is "the bookstore of victory" and of course, victory is exactly what we have in Jesus Christ.

A portion of Scripture that comes to mind is found in I John 5:4 (NIV):

> …This is the victory that has overcome the world, even our faith.

That was the main message of the bookstore in Madrid. Even though this was a city in which it was difficult to speak directly about Jesus Christ, many people were coming through the door every day to buy a portion of God's Word, or receive free literature, or to freely ask questions about the Christian faith.

Scripture Posters in Subways

Later, we were exercised to put up posters in Madrid's subway stations that featured Bible verses, which we called "quotations." The posters referred readers to the bookstore if they wanted to know more about the book that had more information about these "quotations." When George Verwer first mentioned the possibility of putting Gospel posters in the subways of Madrid, a city in a country which did not allow open distribution of Christian literature, it seemed impossible. We began to pray about it and I must admit it was a challenge to my faith at the time. But God reminded me of what He had already done. The Lord allowed us, with the help of the local church to put up twenty-three Gospel posters throughout the subway system. The posters had verses like Romans 3:23,

> For all have sinned, and come short of the glory of God;

Romans 6:23:

> For the wages of sin is death; but the gift of God is eternal life through Jesus Christ our Lord.

…and Romans 5:8:

> But God commendeth his love toward us, in that, while we were yet sinners, Christ died for us.

In addition to putting the bookstore's address on the posters, we worded them such that people could find these great statements in one of the greatest books ever printed, and we encouraged people to go to the bookstore and buy the book, the Bible.

Certainly, without prior access many were reading these truths for the first time; equally probable was that the posters had a great effect on Madrid's subway riders. The local Christians were exceedingly happy about these activities. The people who came to Liberia Victoria to get literature and ask questions were referred to the local churches, not to our teams, and the churches began to grow. In the midst of a Catholic country, many people didn't even know about the existence of churches other than Catholic parishes, and they were thankful to discover them. Team members were inexperienced in so many ways, but our hearts were right in terms of wanting to make Christ known to others, and compelled by His Spirit of compassion, the hearts of thousands of people were touched.

As we wrote back and shared with our prayer and support partners what God was doing, they rejoiced with us and were greatly encouraged.

Heading for England's Youth

After I was in Spain about a month, George Verwer and I made plans to go to England to mobilize young people to spread across Europe and share the Gospel. The year was 1962. Most of the countries in Europe had little knowledge of the Gospel of Jesus Christ. The traditional Catholic church was in Europe, of course, as were the Anglican church in the British Isles and the Lutheran church in Germany, but overall these were not reaching out to the people concerning their own personal salvation. For countries like Spain, France, Belgium, Italy, and a few other European nations, Catholicism was one of the main religions. We knew that during the summer months in these countries, thousands of vacationing students traveled all over

Europe. The burden and vision that came to our minds was similar to that in Mexico. As we thought about how to reach the world for Jesus Christ, the Lord brought to our minds the learning experience He gave to us in Mexico.

Our hearts' desire was to go to England, speak in the local churches, and encourage young people to consider giving their summer months to a team to go across Europe and to spread the Gospel. The vision of Operation Mobilization was to work with and mobilize the churches of Europe. In the past, countries like England and a number of other European nations were great missionary sending countries.

The beautiful thing about most of the students in Europe at this time is that, unlike American tourists who travel with many suitcases and much paraphernalia, they traveled with the barest essentials, such as a small sleeping bag and a backpack containing necessities such as a toothbrush, washcloth, and soap. Also, the Lord burdened us to provide transportation for those who joined us from England to go all over to the continent and evangelize.

CHAPTER SEVEN

Send the Light: A Base in England

A Leader as a Servant

In February of 1962, George Verwer, his dear wife Drena, their son Benjamin, and I left Spain and headed to England in an old German car, a dark gray Opal. Since it was wintertime, the roads were icy and hazardous. We prayed for safety all along the way. When we entered France, we stopped in the city of Bordeaux, where a loving Christian family owned a shoe shop. They insisted on us stopping for a while and refreshing ourselves. I remember Brother Verwer asking me if I thought we should press on toward England, or maybe stay overnight in Bordeaux. Of course, wanting to be a good soldier, I said that we should press on. My mindset was, "We're in the battle. We're engaged in spiritual warfare. We can't tarry. We can't waste time." George graciously disagreed with me, and I'm glad he did because I really wasn't in touch with his wife and child's discomfort who had ridden in the back of the car. Even though there was heat in the car, it was uncomfortable traveling that distance cramped in the back seat of a car. It impressed me that George had used wisdom and balance in making the decision.

So we rested in Bordeaux at the home of this lovely Christian family. They provided food, a place to stay, and gave some money to encourage us on our way. The following morning we continued our journey. It was a precious time with George Verwer and his wife and son. The dialogue was priceless and it was a blessing to have the opportunity to travel with this dear brother, the leader and founder of the movement, initially called Send the Light and later Operation Mobilization. We talked about the burden on our hearts to respond to the Great Commission given in Matthew 28. We realized our human frailties and our ignorance of what it would take to go into other countries to spread the Gospel. We knew that we could only move forward with God's help and in the power of the Holy Spirit.

After a number of hours we reached the English Channel and took a ferry boat to the city of Dover in England. Once we drove our car off the boat, I reminded George that he was driving on the wrong side of the street! He, in turn, reminded me that in England they drive on the left side of the street. Not only do they drive on the left side of the street, the steering column in their cars is on the left side of the car. We had to make a conscious adjustment to our way of thinking, but it did not take long.

George Verwer had contacts with Christians in England and one of them had arranged for us to stay in Fulham, at 8 Tasso Road. It was an attached house, and in the wintertime it was quite cold. This one-family apartment on the second floor had a fair sized master bedroom and a relatively small kitchen like most English homes had. I had my sleeping bag, and I was setting up to sleep on the kitchen floor when George Verwer insisted that I take the bedroom. He said that he, his wife, and baby would sleep under the kitchen table.

At first I thought he was joking. But he was really putting into practice the portion in God's Word that exhorts us to esteem others better than ourselves. This is a revolutionary principle regarding relationships and it is found in Philippians 2:3:

> Let nothing be done through strife or vainglory; but in lowliness of mind let each esteem other better than themselves.

I was experiencing Brother Verwer ministering to me. It was genuine and it was really of the Spirit of the Lord. There we were, in the apartment, three whites and a black man, living out Christian principles which are, any way you look at them, revolutionary. The world does not think like that. In the world, leaders tend to think that they are the big cheese and that they should come first. This was not at all George Verwer's attitude. It touched me deeply. Here was a white brother giving the only bed to an African American brother while he and his wife and son slept on the floor. I reluctantly slept in the bed for a short time at George's insistence, and then we switched places and he and his family took the bedroom.

Observing a Model of Christian Marriage

The other thing that really impressed me when I had a chance to live close to George and Drena and observe their lives together was the manner in which Drena loved him and submitted to her husband. He wasn't tyrannical and her submission was an expression of love. It was very different from what I had witnessed in my own community as I grew up in Cincinnati, Ohio. I saw firsthand the truth of the saying, "Behind every great man is a great woman." As a result of the poor examples of marriages which I saw growing up, including that of my parents, I had decided I would not get married. My parents argued a lot, and in my community, I saw many families fighting, shooting, and killing each other. Some of these people called themselves Christians. As a young man, I was confused and lacked the knowledge that other communities—some rich, some poor; some white, and some African American—experienced these same kinds of problems. When I came to Christ, I decided to remain single and devote myself to the cause of Christ. I thought, "I'll give my life to this. What could be more glorious than preaching the Gospel? After it's all over, the Lord will call me home, and I'll be with Him forever and ever. Why hassle with getting married?" All I'd ever seen was disunity, division, and bickering in every family I knew in our community. One of the reasons I enlisted in the Air Force was to get away from all that strife and confusion.

I had to rethink my attitude toward marriage once I joined Operation Mobilization. I carefully observed the marriages of some of those in OM with whom I worked closely. Many of them had strong, loving, healthy relationships which were fulfilling to each spouse. Christ made the difference. These marriages were a testimony to what God can do in the lives of individuals who live according to His principles as set forth in His Word.

When we shared the apartment in England, I had a chance to watch George and Drena Verwer's marriage. I had a chance to observe and closely scrutinize both of their lives. I watched what he did and the way she responded. George Verwer was passionate about reaching the world for Christ, and I am sure that he would say he was far from a perfect husband, but I noticed that he was tender, loving, and considerate toward his wife. In turn, she submitted to him and was a Christian wife's example of love and considerateness. This was something I had never seen before. I observed many other good marriages in OM, and slowly I began to change my mind about marriage and to think that perhaps God had a life partner for me.

The Teamwork of Evangelism

We settled in at 8 Tasso Road and began to make contact with pastors and Christian groups. Many invited George Verwer to come and speak. Often he and I went together as a team. I would share my testimony and sing a gospel song and George would share the burden on his heart, not only for reaching other countries, but to challenge the local church in England to prayerfully consider reaching out in their own communities.

As was true in Mexico, George wanted to assure the local pastors that we would lovingly like to submit ourselves to them and their ministries, and help them in any way possible so that they could maximize their time going out and witnessing to people in the street. So often the local pastor and church leaders were bogged down with church activities in and around the church, and that really hindered them from going out in the streets and byways, witnessing to people and trying to help them see that Jesus Christ is the missing factor in their lives.

In several such churches I saw Brother Verwer helping with menial tasks like sweeping and scrubbing the floor and stacking the hymnals, and I had the occasion myself to help him. Pastors were thankful that our efforts freed them to witness and follow up with people as they had long dreamed of doing.

Before long, word spread that we were in the country and soon so many wanted George Verwer to visit their fellowship that he was not able to get to all of them. He asked me to take some of the meetings.

Opening Hearts and Minds with Christian Literature

During the few months we were in England hundreds of churches opened their doors to us, to share our testimonies and challenge them to join ranks in an assault on Europe with the Gospel of our Lord and Savior, Jesus Christ. In all the churches we visited in England, and later in every other country, we brought Christian literature with us. Much of this was literature from an apologetics viewpoint. Many people had never received such literature. They had received portions of the Bible, and that was powerful, but like myself before I accepted Christ, many had questions about Christianity in light of science and secular history. The books that we were burdened to distribute were mainly apologetics titles which referred to such inquiry. I think of the book *Science Speaks* by Peter W. Stoner, a mathematician and astronomer who simply testified that science had proven that many of the declarations in the Bible confirm the accuracy of science. One example is in Proverbs 6:6:

> Go to the ant, thou sluggard; consider her ways, and be wise:

When this portion of Scripture was written a long time ago, how did the writer know that the laboring ant was the female ant? This seems insignificant, but we found out statements like this give the Bible credibility to thinking students.

George Verwer and I as well as others at OM tried to be strategic in selecting certain books which confirmed that the Bible is God's Word from beginning to end. In addition, the distribution of books allowed us to create cash flow to sustain ourselves and this worked out well. We mentioned to the students as we challenged them during our talks that if the Lord led them to come on one of the teams, one of the tools they would use was the printed page, whether in tract, booklet, or book form. Books had a profound effect on the lives of the OMers themselves.

Foundational Books

When individuals were exercised to first join Operation Mobilization, we were challenged to read several books. One was *The Calvary Road*, by Roy Hession (1950). This book came out of an East African revival and stressed repentance and brokenness. These themes were particularly important to George Verwer and became crucial to OM because he was convinced that if Christians practiced repentance and were broken, the church would advance. Another book that we were encouraged to read in terms of challenging us toward a life of prayer and intercession was *Power through Prayer* by E. M. Bounds, originally published in 1912. The Christian life without prayer is not really the Christian life. When we think that our lives were salvaged, changed, empowered by the person of Jesus Christ, and realize the demonic forces that stand against the church and try to hinder everything that the Christian church attempts to do, the only way to withstand these onslaughts by the devil is by prayer. George Verwer and OM's leaders encouraged us to read *Power through Prayer* that we might be challenged to pray, since much of what we wanted to see done in the countries we were working in, and planning to work in, was humanly impossible. We certainly did not have the money or manpower, so the only thing left to do was to pray, fast, and watch God work.

A third book that was required reading was actually about our movement. Entitled *True Discipleship* and published in 1962, its author William MacDonald was the president of Emmaus Bible School for many years. William MacDonald was quite impressed with the zeal and determination of the young people in Send the Light. In the foreword of his book, MacDonald says:

> "This booklet is an attempt to set forth some principles of New Testament discipleship. Some of us have seen these principles in the Word for years, but somehow concluded that they were too extreme and impractical for the complicated age in which we live. And so we surrender to the chill of our spiritual environment. Then we met a group of young believers who set out to demonstrate that the Savior's terms of discipleship are not only practical but that they are the only terms which will ever result in the evangelization of the world. We acknowledge our indebtedness to these young people for providing living examples of many of the truths set forth here. To the extent that these truths are still beyond our own personal experience, we set them forth as the aspirations of our heart."

The young people referred to in this foreword are, of course, those in Send the Light, which later became Operation Mobilization.

In England, and later throughout Europe, we were continually reminded of the state of the church. The "chill" to which MacDonald referred was unbelievably and definitely what we experienced. Many churches were closing their doors because there were so few parishioners, and other church buildings were being used by Muslims as mosques. It seemed that huge numbers of people had become disinterested in the

Gospel of Jesus Christ. This cold reception to Christianity was, or course, heartbreaking to us.

At the same time it was a challenge to our own hearts. We knew that the Gospel is the power of God unto salvation and that reality is found only in Christ. Our goal was not to try to get people to come to the church or come to the Lord Jesus Christ for the sake of numbers or popularity, but so that they could experience the saving power, the joy, and the peace that comes when persons accept Christ as their personal Savior.

Youths in England Respond to the Call

As the Lord helped us to share the challenge, quite a few young people responded. They expressed their hearts' desire to join one of the teams during their summer break from school. They were ready to go to the continent and reach individuals with the Gospel. Most students had about two weeks, a fortnight they called it, to travel across Europe, and we challenged them to share the Gospel as they journeyed.

As we traveled throughout England challenging young people and seeing the swelling army of students who wanted to come along during the summer months, a question came to our minds: How would all these young people be transported? Many churches assured us of their prayerful support, and some adults offered their wisdom and their ministries to follow up on our talks and encourage young people to come.

The Blessing of Transport

Our principle was, and is, basically a principle of living by faith. The growing number of interested students meant that it would take thousands of pounds (British currency) to support them during that summer's crusade in Europe and provide transportation. We were exercised to do as we have always done. As we pursued God's will in our lives, knowing what it would take and knowing that He is faithful, we spent much time in prayer. As a result, information came to us about used trucks selling cheap; this information birthed a vision. For many years OM bought used vehicles and drove them all over the continent. God blessed the use of these old vehicles in a remarkable way. We were thinking in terms of trucks like the one we had used in Mexico and Spain, which we could use to transport both literature and students, as well as be a shelter from the rain. This time, we prayed to obtain more than one truck. We were blessed to be able to obtain about ten vehicles for the summer of 1962 at a very good price. Most of them were trucks, but a few were smaller vehicles, including an old ambulance.

We were encouraged because we realized that God was answering prayer so that we might pursue the burden and vision that He had given us. We were blessed to get trucks that while not new, were in good shape. Also, some of the students who were coming with us had mechanical abilities and could check the trucks out and assess their condition for intensive traveling throughout the continent. We rejoiced that we were able to get the trucks mega cheap. These were Bedford trucks—one of England's main products with a good reputation. The truck industry's technology and the integrity in England was number one in many ways and Bedford also had a top claim in the world in terms of its engine and durability. Of the trucks we purchased, one was assigned to travel in France, one to Spain, and three to Italy. As with the trucks used in Mexico and Spain, we cut windows in each truck's sides. Males and females would be traveling in separate trucks.

As summer approached, we had meetings in several of the local churches. The plan was to meet a team at a local church in London, take the team down to Dover and catch the ferry to the continent. Various groups were assigned to different countries such as France, Italy, Spain, Belgium, or Germany. These were countries where it was fairly easy for international students to travel. The Soviet bloc's nations were out of the question at that time.

Set to Go: A European Crusade

Students chose a country that would be of great advantage to themselves. For instance, if some of them were going to be working on a master's degree or doctorate where they would be required to learn a particular language like German or French or Spanish, they chose the country where they could practice using that language.

In all, about 200 young people responded to the challenge of the summer of 1962, and about ninety were from the United Kingdom. With such an army of young people, some regulations were necessary. We reminded ourselves that we were engaged in a spiritual warfare that necessitated a level of discipline which would allow us to be effective for God's glory.

After the orientation, we made it clear to the students that this was not going to be a vacation or sightseeing tour. Students were told that they would not be able to even bring cameras as we were not expecting them to spend hours taking pictures and traveling to historical sites. At this point some students dropped out, saying things like "Maybe we'll stay behind this time, but the next time we might think about going."

However, there were those who were of a different spirit. They had a real heart to witness for Jesus Christ. They saw the summer outreach as ideal and were willing to travel on their own at some other time to see the sights. Students who agreed with the principles and practices that we presented to them were free to come along with us.

Others, who felt that it would be impossible to live and travel as OM requested were encouraged to stay behind and not join the teams. It would be a waste of their time if they came. We found it wise to inform certain students that if they came anyway and decided to follow their own plan, OM members would ask them to leave the team.

This openness with interested students and their pastors and relatives, prevented trouble down the road and helped to facilitate close-knit units on the teams while enhancing our effectiveness when doing distribution.

Before leaving we found a discount warehouse for cheap canned foods and we bought large quantities of beef stew, potatoes, corned beef hash, peaches, and fruit cocktail. We would basically be living out of the trucks for the coming weeks. We would be in fellowship with local Christians in each country we visited, but our desire was to not be a burden on them. We made it clear to everyone on the team that we were camping out all over Europe, and everyone was challenged to bring sleeping bags. We had little portable cooking stoves, too. We planned to go to the center of most of the towns in Italy and France, to a public square or similar place, and fill our 5- and 10-gallon containers with water for drinking and cooking. We did research and knew that many cities in Europe had such a site and also had places where people could take a shower. We also knew that occasionally we would come upon rather inexpensive restaurants where the team would have lunch.

Breakfast was one meal about which we could be flexible and need not spend much money or time at all.

We were as ready as we could be for our first summer of evangelism with students in Europe.

CHAPTER EIGHT

Outreach in Italy and Switzerland

An Expanded Mission

I was with the team headed for Rome, Italy. Our operating base was in Rome, from which we would be going every day in different directions to many hundreds of villages. On the way to Rome we passed through other key cities in Italy, like Torino, Bologna, and Perugia.

Once we reached Rome we left George Verwer, his wife, and child in Rome, along with a girls' team that came in another vehicle so they could get our OM operations going there. Our general approach was to backtrack through Bologna, Torino, and other Italian cities, even when they were three or four hours' drive away. We distributed our literature in many villages on our way back to the cities, going and coming, and tried to establish contacts so that we could develop long-term relationships.

In some ways, our crisscrossing method of travel was the best way to see and experience a country such as Italy. We spent a lot of time in the villages with the local residents, in the marketplaces and restaurants, and we knocked on doors while practicing our Italian and experiencing their hospitality. The Italians are very hospitable people. Often when we went to their homes, especially in the summer months, they offered us a refreshing drink.

Evangelizing in Italy's Towns

I was encouraged to take the boys' team and reach out. For two or three days at a time we would leave Rome and travel by truck, camping out along the way and stopping in cities like Torino and Perugia.

Perugia is one of the oldest cities in Italy; some say it was there 2,000 years before Jesus Christ came. At the time, Perugia was a small city with a fort. Many of the cities in Italy have forts around them. I remember going to the cities of Genoa and Livorno, on the west coast, and the city of Pisa, where the famous leaning tower is. According to some accounts, Galileo dropped objects from the leaning tower to study the effects of gravity as the objects fell toward the ground. I had learned this in high school, but now I had this tremendous opportunity to actually see the Leaning Tower of Pisa and the surrounding area. We also visited Bologna, one of the larger cities in Italy.

On each trip, we had thousands of pieces of Christian literature in the back of the truck. We had our sleeping gear, our food, and our books and it was a joyous experience. The weather was beautiful during those summer months, with plenty of sunshine and practically no rain, and we enjoyed it immensely.

We would start our day at eight o'clock in the morning, go until noon, take a little nap, have lunch and go back out at about two until about seven or eight o'clock in the evening. At this time of evening in Italy, the custom was that thousands of people leisurely strolled through the center of town. This gave us the opportunity to share the Gospel with them.

After being out from the home base for about a week to eight days, we went back to Rome to regroup for a time of fellowship and orientation about any new information about the ministry, to bring in money that we may have received from donations for the books and to get more supplies of food. This time was mainly to fellowship and share with other team members about our experiences, and to encourage each other.

We also used this time to plan our strategy and coordinate it with the other teams working in Italy, as well as to make plans for the upcoming period of travel when we would again leave the base and go throughout the country.

Results Return with the Team

As a result of distributing literally millions of pieces of literature in France, Belgium, Spain, and Italy, many responded to the Gospel and thousands of people asked to study the correspondence courses. Near the middle of August we brought the teams back together to begin our return to England. Many of the students had to do this in order to return to school, and there were also some students from schools in America who had to return, too. Students had joined us from Biola University, Wheaton College, Moody Bible Institute, and other schools in the United States who knew about our work in Mexico and wanted to be a part of the challenge to evangelize in Europe.

We were careful to get students back by the last two weeks in August so they could make adequate preparation for enrolling in fall courses.

The following summer, even more students came over from America to join the teams, and we found it less expensive to charter a plane for them to come and go to the United States. This in itself indicates how much we received from the distribution of literature. The Lord blessed the nickels and dimes we received as people eagerly donated for books. While in Italy I remember distributing large quantities of one book in particular, by Billy Graham, published in 1953: *Peace with God: The Secret of Happiness*. In many villages, when I opened my book bag and shared books with individuals, they really grabbed this particular book.

The summer campaign was a tremendous experience and provided an opportunity to practice my Italian with individuals as I dialogued with them about the books and the Gospel.

Winter in London

After the summer crusades ended and the students returned to England for departure to their various countries or cities, after our own time of sharing and fellowship, we would discuss prayer burdens and plans for the winter months. Winter was an ideal season for individuals to spend time in their own local churches sharing with the pastor and the youth leader, dialoguing with the congregation's teenagers, and basically just sharing the vision of Operation Mobilization.

I remained in England with the Verwers. Often George and I went to churches and presented the challenge of reaching the lost masses of the world, and we reminded them of Matthew 28: God expects those of us who are Christians to reach a lost world with the Gospel. As I had the opportunity to watch the life of George Verwer from sunup to sundown, what he wore, what he bought, how he spent his money and his time, I was convinced that this young man was sold out to Jesus Christ, and it touched my heart. From all indications, he had the same intensity of desire to witness for Christ that I was experiencing in my own life. Some might call it fanaticism; we called it simply going all out for Christ.

After we returned to England, we spent most of our time in London. I was working out of the main office there and I was challenged during the winter months to travel to different parts of England to give a word of testimony. Every place we went, we were exercised and burdened to take books with us. To me, books were like an opportunity to experience a one- or two-week conference that featured different titles that people could curl up with in bed or a chair, anywhere really, and read Gospel stories. We distributed books containing the testimonies of individuals who had accepted Christ, books on the Christian life, and books on apologetics. People could read at their convenience and the books preached the same message that we did. We heard many testimonies from individuals who said that they first understood Christianity when they read a book that explained it.

The winter months were a bit slower; they were not as intense as the summer months. We spent our days doing some distribution at local locations, such as a supermarket, a subway entrance, or a sports arena where we encountered thousands of people. At night we had a time of fellowship and some of us were in a study program. We were also encouraged to leave London and join teams of three and four, visiting various churches in other cities in England, and that in itself was an education to me.

During one such encounter, I met an extremely wealthy family; apparently, they had made a lot of money from their import business in Africa. They lived in a very prestigious community. Their home was gorgeous and contained objects of ivory from Africa. Their children were in special private schools in England and they had really never been close to an African, or an African American, or any person of African descent. I was invited to have dinner with this family at their home and I felt just subdued by the love shown toward me.

At one point the daughter, about 14 years of age, came over to me after dinner and said, "Do you mind if I just feel the hair on your head?"

I laughed and assured her, "Yes, you can feel the hair on my head."

After she touched my hair, she smiled and said, "I've never felt the hair of an African."

And I said, "Well, today you did!" Everyone laughed, and it was clear that they knew I was just another human being, that the most miraculous thing was that my life had been changed by Jesus Christ.

Generosity and Hospitality

Another family, the Hooleys of Newtown, Macclesfield, Cheshire East, United Kingdom were members of a congregation that George Verwer and I visited. After we went to their church, the family approached Brother George and asked if I could stay in their home for a few days. He asked if I'd like to, and I said that I'd love to stay in their home.

The Hooley family showered so much love on me. It was like an injection. I felt very much at home. They had questions about my family and what I thought about the racial situation in America. I felt real liberty and freedom in sharing how I felt as an African American. I shared some of the things I had experienced, my own inner warfare with racism and how Jesus Christ had given me the victory. Having these discussions helped me talk about problems I was experiencing with racial issues so I could develop spiritually in these areas. I reminded myself that it was Jesus Christ who gave me victory and understanding in getting over those problems, and the Lord had prepared me to encourage and share with other people that Jesus Christ really is the answer to all of the issues in our lives.

This particular family not only provided a place for me to stay, but a few days after I was there the head of the house went out and bought me a beautiful suit. I think he must have seen the condition that I was in. It was not that terrible, but those of us on the team spent very little money on ourselves. We did have what they called a "Charlie," a barrel containing clothes that individuals didn't want, and when we were in need of a necktie or a shirt or a pair of pants or a jacket or a pair of shoes or whatever, we'd go to "Charlie" and see what we could find. We had some money for buying personal items, but since our hearts' desire was to spend money for the distribution and the production of Christian literature, we mostly spent it on the millions of copies of literature that we distributed.

The Hooley family not only bought me a suit and fed me breakfast, lunch, and supper every day, they gave me the key to their car so that I could drive around and see other parts of Newtown. After a week, I began to get uncomfortable living in all this lavishness. Although I'm saying this in a somewhat humorous way, after a week I was ready for more of a feel of the warfare in the battle to reach others for Christ.

Encouragement Builds Confidence

At times Brother Verwer had so many speaking engagements that he could not take them all. He asked me if I would take several for him. It was a humbling experience. It was not that I doubted my own capabilities or preparation, but it was difficult for me then and even now to explain how his request made me feel. George was sincere about asking if I would go and speak for him. These were not meetings with one or two people; often these were meetings with three or four hundred.

Again, my heart was touched by Brother George Verwer, the leader. He wasn't ego tripping on his own behalf. Over and over again, he would encourage not only me but many other team members to involve themselves in situations where they would be able to recognize and exercise their gifts. In many cases, it was the first time that some of us were encouraged to serve the Lord to our fullest ability. I learned much as God made it possible to speak at many churches in different parts of England and dialogue with local Christians across the country.

Mission Work in Switzerland

A few weeks after returning to England from the summer crusade of 1962, I met Brother Konrad Sonderegger who had been on one of the teams in France. I was challenged and encouraged to go with him to Switzerland and stay in his home. Once there we would be visiting different churches in Switzerland and challenging young people to consider spending the following summer in Europe on one of the teams.

Switzerland borders three major European countries— France, Italy, and Germany—and has four major languages: German, French, Italian, and Romansch. English is used to breach the divide.

Brother Konrad was a very loving, humble brother who spoke five languages: English, German, French, Italian, and Romansch. He lived in the city of Winterthur, in northeast Switzerland, near the border with Germany to the North, and Austria to the East. I was graciously invited to stay in his home with him, his brother, sister, father, and mother. All of them treated me so lovingly that I was dumbfounded. Even though I was a black man, it was as though I had been in their home all of my life.

Because of the many languages spoken in Switzerland, many of the college students travel in the summer to countries like France and Germany to learn these languages thoroughly. That way they are better prepared for work where they will be expected to know all four of Switzerland's national languages. Also, Italy, Germany, and France are just a few miles away so distance is not a problem. Even though the country is small, Switzerland has a broad international understanding among the people and perhaps this is a reason why I experienced such hospitality from the Sonderegger family.

Responsiveness Overcomes Culture and Language Differences

Brother Konrad knew many Christian groups, Christian camps and a Christian Bible School in Lausanne, Switzerland. Lausanne is on the west side of the country near the border of Germany and we attended a meeting at the Bible school. Brother Konrad spoke mainly in French and German. I gave my testimony in English, and he translated for me. Some of the students were surprised and happy to see the two of us, a white brother from Switzerland and an African American, testifying for Jesus Christ.

While there I met a white student from South Africa. He joined us for our car ride to another meeting. Along the way he looked in my face and said, "This is the first time in my life that I've ever sat this close to an African or an African American."

The Lord gave me grace and a sense of humor at times like that. I almost felt like laughing when many of my friends would have felt like fighting, but it was a work being done in my own heart. I believed that God was allowing me to experience that in preparation for future ministry.

I also traveled to other cities in Switzerland. The country had a very effective rail system. You could take trains to any part of Switzerland. The trains were warm, comfortable, and on time and took us to cities like Bern, the capital, and Zurich, the largest city. Many tourists came to Zurich and I saw many African students in Zurich as we had several meetings in that particular city. Once when I was in Zurich at the train station passing out tracts, a young man came up to me and asked me, "Do you really believe this stuff?"

I said, "Yes."

This particular young man had a dark complexion like me, and he quickly let me know that he was from Cuba and that he was a Communist. He observed my zeal as I rushed about passing out literature about Jesus Christ. So as to catch as many people as I could and give them our material I moved quickly among individuals leaving the train station. After a while the young Cuban took a tract from me. Still, he asked me again if I really believed the message in the literature that I was distributing, and I told him that of course I did.

He told me that I should consider becoming a Communist. He added that he could get anything that he wanted from the Cuban government and that he knew powerful people in Cuba, including Castro's brother, Raul. Today, Castro's brother, Raul, has taken Castro's place as the leader of Cuba. This young man, Raphael, was convinced that Jesus was not the answer to the problems in the world, and that instead, the world's problems would be solved when everyone had a proper job and deliverance from their oppressors. He was a committed Communist and impressed by my zeal. He was as dedicated to winning the Swiss to Communism as I was to winning them to Christ.

We talked for about an hour at the train station, and then I let him know, respectfully, that really I wanted to return to distributing tracts—I was not interested in becoming a Communist. I mentioned to him that what he saw and heard were my deep convictions that Jesus Christ is the answer to the need in human hearts.

Respectfully, he backed off and went his way, and the team of us went our way when we were finished distributing our materials. Still, I never forgot meeting that young man and the realization that he had come all the way from Cuba to Switzerland to be trained in a more profound way about Communism, the philosophy that he had embraced for his life. It was obvious that he was from the upper crust of Cuba's political strata, and in many ways the dedication of Communists and other groups put Christians to shame.

Not only did we travel from time to time to Switzerland's major cities, we also traveled up into the mountains during the winter months to the ski lofts where students came on the weekends to ski. I didn't know how to ski, and had no intentions of learning, but I watched these people come from many miles around to the Alps to ski. There and all over the country my experience with the Swiss led me to conclude that they were very friendly people. Many of them would ask Brother Konrad, the team's leader, if they could invite me to their home. Some of the invitations we accepted, but others we declined because we were too busy to accept.

Each time we went out to distribute literature, we carried books printed in German and French which we had bought from our depot in England. We also had contacts in Switzerland where we could get quantities of books. We did not actually sell the books; we would indicate to people that they could give a donation or make a contribution. This was because in some areas it was not legal to sell on the streets without a vendor's license. Konrad and I were able to generate thousands of Swiss francs to support ourselves in his home with his family.

A Challenge in Milano, Italy

Konrad and I were in Switzerland for several months traveling all over, meeting people and living in their homes. Then George Verwer, who was in England, mentioned that he was having a series of meetings in Milano, in northern Italy. He asked if we would come down for his weekend meetings in Milano to give our testimonies, have a time of fellowship with him, and share with the people the burden and plan that we had for reaching all of Italy with the printed page.

In the weekend series of meetings in Milano, pastors came from churches from all over Italy. George's message to them was that during the upcoming summer we wanted to come to Italy to evangelize in their areas. George added that we would be willing to do anything to help out at their churches so that they could maximize their time in going out to the local people to tell them about Jesus Christ.

Some pastors were a little offended by this offer. In so many words, they said, "We don't need you Americans coming to

Italy to teach us how to evangelize. We don't need you to supply us with literature; we can buy our own literature. You can go home, Americans. We don't need you here. We are Italians, and the task is left up to us."

We understood what they were saying, of course, but we assured them that we shared the same burden. We were not trying to do our own thing. Our goal was to work with local churches in order to fulfill the Great Commission. We were convinced that the Lord had burdened us to reach certain cities in Italy and we wanted to do it in fellowship with them. We assured them that all the contacts we made in their areas, and all of the names and addresses we gathered of people interested in the Gospel would be shared as we encouraged people to contact the local pastors. We were not trying to start a church of our own, or a movement of our own; we were trying to bring praise and glory to our Lord and Savior Jesus Christ. We had to obey Mark 16:15:

> And he [Jesus Christ] said unto them, Go ye into all the world, and preach the gospel to every creature.

Taking the Gospel Far and Wide

The brothers in Italy knew this portion of Scripture and it was wise to remind ourselves why we were doing what we were doing. So, as lovingly and graciously and humbly as we knew how, we assured all the pastors, even those that didn't agree with us, that by God's grace we would be coming to Italy in about four months: we would be coming with teams, we would be coming in vehicles, and we would be camping out all over the country. We let them know that we would have our sleeping bags with us and we would sleep in our vehicles; we would carry on crusades like we had done in Spain and in Mexico and in other countries.

Many of the pastors doubted that we could carry out a crusade that large. The scope of the crusade we presented to them made them doubt because we were talking about going over virtually all of Italy, including villages and major cities, with thousands of books and millions of Gospel tracts. They had never heard of such a thing. Also, many of us were much younger than they were, and they were skeptical, to put it mildly. One big question we kept hearing the Italian pastors ask us was: "Where is the money going to come from for such an operation?"

After we attended the weekend of meetings with Brother George Verwer, Brother Konrad and I returned to Switzerland to continue our ministry before the summer crusade of 1963. We were aware that many of the Italian pastors still doubted us but we did not doubt ourselves. We contacted students who had shown an interest. We encouraged them and gave them pertinent information that they would need to get to England and be assigned to a team that was going to Italy.

We were encouraged to see that as a result of our efforts, more than twenty students were willing to leave Switzerland and take part in the summer crusade. Also, while we were in Italy at the weekend meetings with George Verwer, we met a very beautiful young lady, Hannah Zack, a schoolteacher. She came to one of the meetings, and her mind was sort of blown when she heard what a group of students had planned to do during the summer months. She was a converted Jewish young woman and wanted to know if possibly she could join one of the teams. Of course we were happy about that and encouraged her to join. She later married an American, George Miley, and they became significant leaders in OM.

Konrad and I were in Switzerland for several weeks before being called back to England to prepare for the summer crusade in Europe. As we had done with previous outreach trips, we bought used vehicles, including trucks, at extremely reasonable prices. A major issue was how to feed an army of nearly 2,000 students from thirty countries planning to go on the crusade of 1963. We reminded ourselves of Jeremiah 33:3:

> Call unto me, and I will answer thee, and show thee great and mighty things, which thou knowest not.

Over and over, in my early Christian life, I had seen God do great things. As we had done the summer before, we bought canned goods from a wholesale distributor and loaded the trucks with these items of food. Once we got to the various countries, the teams supplemented these with fresh bread, milk, and fruit purchased on the trip, as well as jelly, coffee, and tea.

CHAPTER NINE

England: Operation Mobilization

The Difficulty of Missionary Work

By God's grace, summer of 1963 approached and we were on our way. Students journeyed to OM's headquarters in England from many countries in Europe, including Spain, England, Germany, and Italy, and many came from the United States. After orientation in England, we were able to charter a plane that came to us from America and which was less expensive for a group than reserving individual flights. All monies saved were used to help pay for the tremendous amount of literature needed for the teams.

God did remarkable things during the summer of 1963. It was not easy, and some teams were assaulted, arrested, and imprisoned, as well as left completely exhausted from sleeping in vehicles, but God proved Himself faithful. Many were reached for Christ and made commitments to Him. The huge numbers, about 2,000, of those on the summer crusade of 1963 were not repeated during other years in the 1960s, but much of the structure and strategy of Operation Mobilization was established at that time.

After the 1963 summer crusade, students again returned from all over Europe to England and departed to their homelands in time to continue their studies. However, Operation Mobilization lived on. In 1963-4 the first OM "year teams" were established. Teaching and training conferences on subjects like discipleship, human psychology, and how to work together were put in place. As OM expanded, regional centers were established and a Central Accounting Office and a Board of Directors was formed.

At this point in OM's history, OM was a "pay as you go" organization; the idea was to not have debt hanging over our heads. The Lord revealed His faithfulness by bringing in love gifts from all over the world to pay the bills and allow us to dream about going to ever more distant parts of the world. At times it seemed impossible to do this, but the Lord always helped us. We believed that the number one thing to do was to seek God's will and obey Him. He showed us what He wanted us to do and we would shout halleluiah! The bills were always cleared away. I remember once the bills went from $100,000, down to $75,000, to 50,000, to $25,000, down to zero and we were able to move on! Hallelujah!

Along with the victories, of course, were discouragements. One constant battle was with depression. I remember reading the testimony of Hudson Taylor after the Lord had burdened him to go to China. Brother Hudson expressed how difficult it was to understand why God would be sending him to China.

There was not a group of people going with him that was anywhere equal to the size he would encounter—millions of people in China—nor was there a way to truly prepare for the distances that would have to be traveled. The amazing thing I learned, and the insight into a very human part of Hudson Taylor, is that at one point he thought about committing suicide. That grabbed me. This man of God, who believed God and whom God used so mightily, wanted to take his own life? At first, this was hard to understand, but as I was engaged in spiritual warfare myself, I understood his feelings and the demonic activity behind the depression.

The need is overwhelming. When a person like Hudson Taylor, or even some of us in OM thought about going to these countries with hundreds of millions of people and their many cultures, languages, and religions, our efforts seemed so feeble. It appeared to be an impossible task. And humanly speaking, it was. We had to remind ourselves that we were sent by God, that it was His work, and that "The things which are impossible with men are possible with God" (Luke 18:27).

If you look at yourself and try to figure out how you're going to do something—especially something on a very large scale—you're going to get depressed. That's the devil's strategy. God does not want us to look at ourselves. He wants us to daily stay focused on Him and His work. As we pray daily and cry out to Him, "Lord, help us, Lord, strengthen us, Lord, broaden our vision, Lord, break us, Lord, teach us to trust You completely," the Lord proves faithful in all our verbalized desires.

An Upside of Missionary Work: Visiting Swansea Bible College

During our first year in England, 1962, Brother Verwer and I traveled all over England. One of the most memorable contacts the Lord allowed us to have in England was at Swansea Bible College in South Wales, England (the college has since relocated and become known as Bible College of Wales).

This college is so unique. It was founded by Rees Howells. Students were in attendance from England and many other countries such as Lebanon and the nations of Scandinavia. The basic textbook was the Bible itself. One of the most unique things about this particular school is that not only did the teachers and staff teach, but in their spare time they cared for the school. They were working in the gardens. They were patching the roof. They were tinkering with the automobiles and keeping them running by doing mechanical work on them. The students joined in and helped to do anything that needed doing. They avoided calling in outside help if at all possible. The faculty and student body was like one big family. They had dinner together. The son of the founder, Samuel Howells, was the president of the school. A large amount of his time was spent in his quarters praying for the school, the students, and for other factors related to the school so that the Lord might keep the school functioning for His glory.

We were greatly encouraged by this school. It appeared that 95 to 98 percent of the students were burdened, as were we, to use their lives for God's glory. We rejoiced when we realized that the president was fully behind our mission. He encouraged students to prayerfully plan to join arms with us to invade Europe with the Gospel during the summer months when they were free from school. We met and had fellowship personally with some of the staff members at the school. The thing that impressed me more than anything is that at Swansea each student and each faculty member had a specific and definite time to spend in intercessory prayer.

Another Plus: Meeting Fouzi Ayoub

It was at Swansea that we met Fouzi Ayoub, who was a Lebanese student at Swansea Bible College. Fouzi became one of my best friends. From the time we first met, our hearts really were bound together in the Lord. We talked freely and shared much with each other about our backgrounds. I had one or two opportunities to sit in his classes with him during our short stay at Swansea Bible College. After seeing and hearing about the practices of our group, Operation Mobilization, Fouzi was deeply impressed. His family was from Lebanon and had met many missionaries and missionary groups, and he sensed that our ministry was quite unique. He noticed that there were no so-called prominent leaders or Ph.D.s around, nor were there mission boards carrying out the ministry. Instead, there were a lot of seemingly insignificant individuals, including myself, an African American, being encouraged to take part in a white mission.

More significant than my encounter with Fouzi was when he met George Verwer and talked with him. I could tell that he could sense that this brother, George Verwer, was indeed different from any other Christian he had ever met. Even back then, in 1962, George was revealing his thoughts about the possibility of Fouzi leading a team to Lebanon, and perhaps later to other countries like Syria and Iraq and Saudi Arabia—parts of the world virtually untouched by the Gospel of Jesus Christ—especially since Fouzi spoke fluent Arabic and English. He could and would be a valuable addition to any team as we reached out to closed Islamic countries with the Gospel of Jesus Christ.

We prayed that somehow God might touch the life of this young man and give him a vision similar to ours. At first we didn't mention it to him, but we had no doubt that God was behind our meeting. Fouzi had only a few months before he was to graduate. He told me that he wasn't really sure what the Lord wanted him to do. He had met a lovely English girl, Wendy, whom he had fallen in love with and from all indications she loved him deeply. He wasn't quite sure, he told me, if he was going to remain in England and marry and settle down, or if the Gospel and the challenge that he had been hearing about all his life would encourage him to really launch out for Jesus Christ.

Putting Forth a Challenge: Join the Missionary Team

A few months later, George Verwer challenged Fouzi to take up the leadership in his own country of Lebanon and challenge young people to consider giving their lives for the service of the Lord Jesus Christ. George challenged me to prayerfully go with Fouzi back to his home country of Lebanon and work with him and assist him in any way that I could.

Brother Verwer and I spoke more about the possibility of joining Fouzi in his own country to help him in any way he saw I could help to challenge the young people of his country. Fouzi, of course, would be the leader. The next serious thought was: When and how would I get to Lebanon?

Raising the Stakes: Plans for Islamic Countries

During the fall of 1963, teams and individuals were being challenged to go to Turkey and Iran. These countries are Islamic states, and it was illegal to distribute Christian literature. It was also illegal to talk to Muslims about accepting Christ as their personal Savior because this would be considered proselytizing and there were strong laws and penalties against trying to convert Muslims to Christ.

And yet, Turkey, like all the other closed countries, was heavy on our hearts. We knew that there were not many Christians in those countries. We knew that Christianity, to a great extent, had many roots in Turkey, like the city of Ephesus and the other places mentioned in the book of Revelation. Turkey was saturated with Christian history before the Muslims took over. Yet somehow the church had been almost entirely wiped out by Islam and there were very few Christians in the entire nation. Our teams had the names and address of a few of them, and as we prayed about how we were going to reach a country like Turkey, the thought came that maybe one or two individuals could enroll in the University of Istanbul, and affect a witness for Christ in that way. They would simply enroll in school, and during break time between classes, in the coffee shop or the study hall, try to make Muslim friends. Over time, eventually they could share the Gospel with Turkish people.

Many Christians in our home countries did not think this was a very good idea. They said it was a waste of time, and insisted that the Gospel should be presented in a more direct way. As we scrolled back in our own minds about the history of Christianity in those countries, we saw that very little had been accomplished. As young believers, we reasoned that new tactics should be prayed about and developed in terms of reaching a nation like Turkey. We dreamed of Christian bookstores in Istanbul, Turkey, like those the Lord helped us to raise up in Mexico and Spain. Mexico and Spain were difficult countries, and we reasoned that if God did it in Mexico and Spain, He could do it in Turkey.

CHAPTER TEN

A Journey for the Lord in Eastern Europe

Evangelism by Train

Dale Rhoton and Roger Malstead were the first Operation Mobilization team members to go to Turkey. They rented a flat; one enrolled at the University of Istanbul and went to classes, and the other taught English. They prayerfully initiated their ministry. Later their wives taught English. After being there for several months, there were prayerful considerations for one or two more students to join them. The plan was not to send for a big group because it would be too conspicuous.

During the fall of 1963 after that year's summer crusade, plans were made for several of us to travel over land, dropping off one or two team members in Turkey to join Dale and Roger. I was deeply impressed with the wisdom, strategy, burden, and heart-filled desire on the part of our leader, George Verwer, to encourage those of us who were burdened for evangelizing in those parts of the world to plan for such a trip. We decided to take the train from London all the way to Istanbul, which was relatively cheap. We would be going as tourists and smuggling as many Bibles into Turkey as possible. Betty, a sister from England, John Carling, Rodney, and I were going to Turkey and then on down to Lebanon.

The trip from London was very educational. The train got on the ferry at Dover and came off the ferry on the other side of the English Channel in France. The train hooked back up, we got back on the train and headed to Eastern Europe. I'd never dreamed of an experience like that. Actually, there were many, many times while I was in Europe that I thought about returning to the United States. Each time, George Verwer would come and challenge me to prayerfully consider extending my time in Europe to be active for Jesus Christ. And seeing how the Lord was working with his leadership, my heart greatly responded and I stayed. I ended up staying for almost eight years without coming home once.

As the train moved through closed Communist countries such as Yugoslavia and Bulgaria, we were burdened for the lost. We had wondered how we could distribute some literature in those closed countries as the train passed through them. Before we left England I'd shared with the brothers about the possibility of taking small packages of literature printed in the language of the people and taking the packets with us on the train. We reasoned that at certain stations the train would stop to let people off or pick people up. Those stops would be for short periods of time—15 minutes, 30 minutes, or maybe an hour. During our planning sessions in England we thought, well, when the train stopped in those countries, if we had literature for that particular country, I could get down off the train, go to the tea shop (there always seemed to be one steps away from the station), pass out the literature, and quickly walk back to the train and get on before the train left.

At first I thought the idea was foolish. What if I got off the train and got arrested? When the train left with my team members, I would still be stuck in Italy, or Bulgaria, or Turkey. But as I scrolled back in my mind back to Alaska, and to my promise when I dedicated my life to the Lord that I would be willing to do anything, by life or death, to make Him known, I went ahead with the preparations to distribute literature in these Communistic and Islamic nations.

We had many suitcases and about twenty pieces of other luggage for the teams we would be meeting in Turkey, including supplies, Bibles, and literature. This was another reason we took the train; one vehicle wouldn't be able to carry that much. So we carried it all on the train. Just as we envisioned it, the train made brief stops to take on people and let people off; there were restaurants close to the platform. I distributed some literature on the platform to the limited number of people near me. I did not walk up and down the platform giving out literature. I did manage to walk in the nearby restaurants. Being an African American, people were kind of shocked and looked at me wonderingly. I smiled at them and extended the tract in my hand, and they always grabbed it. They must have been thinking, "What on earth?" By the time they read the first or second page, I was out the door and headed back toward the train.

Once I was back on the train I felt somewhat relieved. If anything were to transpire after that, the other team members would know about it and be able to assist me. By God's grace, I was able to do this in Yugoslavia and also do the same thing in Bulgaria as we went by train through that country. We made several stops, and each time I would leave the train carrying the small packages of literature in the language of the people, go into the coffee shop, and again people would look up and see this black man and wonder who I was and what I was up to. Again, they took the tracts as I offered them with a smile, and then I headed back to the train.

The Joy of Planting God's Word

Each time the train pulled out we rejoiced because we knew that we had planted God's Word. I was rejoicing, too. We had planted God's Word, and we reminded ourselves that God's Word will not come back void; whatever it is sent to accomplish, it will accomplish. God promises in Isaiah 55:11:

> So shall my word be that goeth forth out of my mouth: it shall not return unto me void, but it shall accomplish that which I please, and it shall prosper in the thing whereto I sent it.

We reminded ourselves that our distributions in these closed countries were not just an expression of so-called human wisdom or strategy, but that even passing out tracts on these one-time occasions, God would honor our hearts' concern for the people in those nations to hear and receive the Word of God because once the seed is planted, it will bring forth fruit.

Consequences: Arrested in Turkey

For a great part of the trip, things went well as we executed our plan in Italy, in Yugoslavia, in Bulgaria, and then we entered Turkey. As we pulled into the station in Turkey, before we got off the train, several secret policemen came and arrested all of us!

We were shocked and asked the policemen, "What did we do?" They reminded us that we were distributing Christian literature in the few towns in Turkey before we got to Istanbul, which was illegal. They removed all of our bags from the train, loaded them onto a hand truck, and took all of us to the police office at the train station. There were a total of four of us: myself, John Carling, Betty, and Rodney. The secret policemen separated us and interrogated us.

"What," they asked, "were you going to do with the literature? Where are you going in Turkey?"

We told them that we were passing through Turkey and that we were to meet friends in Turkey, which was true. We were supposed to pick up a Volkswagen from our friends in Turkey and drive it all the way to Lebanon. We also assured the policemen that we were students, not missionaries. We were just students on a practical learning tour of some countries, just making notes as we went through and that was why we were taking the trip.

After glancing through our literature, they expressed concern about some of it, especially the tract which stated that if you want peace or joy, it's to be found in Jesus Christ. But they took it from a political perspective, in terms of individuals not being happy with their country and government, and if people weren't happy and didn't have peace, the policemen thought that the literature could provoke thoughts of a riot or a revolt against the government. Of course, that was the farthest thing from our minds; we hadn't even thought about anything of that nature, but that's how they perceived it.

While we were being interrogated, our friends discovered that we were in Turkey and came to meet us. They brought the van for us to use, took out their personal items, and left the items we planned to take to Lebanon. Once again we assured the officials that we were just passing through and meeting our friends. Thankfully, after a period of about a day and a half, they released us.

During that time, though, I was somewhat apprehensive. It was my first experience being arrested in a Muslim country. I don't think I showed that I was nervous, but there was one police agent who pulled me aside. The other team members were all white, and he pointed to his skin, which was dark like mine, patted me on my back, and assured me that everything was going to be okay.

I think he was trying to tell me, "You're black, I'm black. I'm a policeman and because of my authority I'm trying to assure you that nothing serious is going to happen to you, so don't fret." I was surprised, but I just smiled at him at him and said, "Of course, I know that this is a wonderful country." He took me back to the group and I relaxed somewhat.

Finally they decided we were free to go. They decided that we were not a threat to the government; we were just students traveling. Turkey was a popular destination for tourists, including students. Thousands of students came through Istanbul and other parts of Turkey with backpacks and bedrolls like we had. And since we definitely were passing through because we had not applied for visas or other forms of residency, we were not a threat to the government.

Distributing Tracts: Invitations to Correspondence Courses

As we had planned to drive from Istanbul all the way down to Lebanon, the team in Turkey had prepared hundreds of pieces of literature in the Turkish language that we would pass out on our way through Turkey. The literature mainly comprised correspondence courses in the Turkish language; people could write to an office in Germany and enroll in a correspondence course to study more about the Bible.

After our friends helped us put our bags and other luggage in the Volkswagen van, we went to a local restaurant, had a bite to eat, and were on our way. Our friends went back to their apartment. We decided not to go to their apartment lest the officials who were still watching us think that we might be making plans to stay in Turkey. We proceeded on our way.

Going east first, we went through the city of Ankara, Turkey. We stopped to pick up fresh bread, yogurt, and fresh, sweet fruit of the season. I remember eating delicious tangerines and apples. After leaving Ankara, we headed south toward Adana, a city on the southern coast. We had large quantities of Turkish literature, so during the evenings and at night, we stopped in small villages and distributed letter-sized envelopes with Gospel tracts in them and information about correspondence courses. We distributed at night when we thought we were not being seen, on our way to Lebanon.

Arrested Again and Again

Before we started distribution in these small towns, we would drive around in the town and determine the best way to get out of the town quickly if we had to, and the best way to distribute the tracts. Sometimes it was wise to put the literature on the windshields of cars if no one was watching at night, or put them in mailboxes before we exited the city. At first we tried that during the day on our way from Ankara to Adana, but just as in Istanbul, we were apprehended, arrested, and taken to jail in a small town between the two cities. At the jail, we were asked about our plans for the literature. Our story, of course, was that we were just passing through.

We mentioned that we were on our way to Lebanon, so after being held for a day and taken separately in a room and questioned, the police were convinced we were just students passing through. Fortunately, we were allowed to keep the literature, so we continued on our way again, going southward through Turkey to Lebanon without losing our supply of tracts.

The third time we were apprehended in Turkey we were a bit apprehensive, of course. We were distributing literature in Adana when the secret police arrested us. We waited at the police station, not knowing really what they planned to do, but our hearts were comforted by the fact that God had promised to always be with us. He says in Hebrews 13:5b,

> ...I will never leave thee, nor forsake thee.

Those might sound like trite words to some, but whenever the Word of God came to our minds, it put our hearts at ease. We knew that our Lord was observing everything and had ordered everything to happen the way it was happening that we might learn to trust in Him. At times like these, I thought about how I had never planned to stay with OM more than a few weeks, or a few months at the most. The thought would always come to my mind, *"Well, Hoise, you've had such a tremendous experience, but it's time to go home. Let somebody else do it."* And of course that thought was directly from the devil, appealing to all my fleshly, emotional feelings of wanting to see my parents, and wanting to see old friends and do familiar things. The forces of the devil were strong, appealing to my emotions.

Communicate with God and Be Thankful

One lingering thought was, "Where's my wife, Lord?" I often felt that I was not in a position for God to reveal my wife to me and I needed to return home in order for Him to do that.

Usually in a matter of minutes, the Spirit of God reminded me that He was in control: all I had to do was to continue to obey Him and He would work out all things in my life for His glory. I was thankful for the continuous presence of the Spirit of God, even in a police station in Turkey, far away from my family and friends.

Again, we were released. We thought we might start doing the distribution at nighttime, where we wouldn't have the confrontation with police officers, and in the next town we did just that. We waited until it was very, very dark. In some of those smaller towns they only had electric lights on the main street; the rest of the city was dark, so we commenced our distribution. In some cases, we stepped out of the Volkswagen bus to put some Gospels in mailboxes. We had our sleeping bags and Bibles and Gospel tracts in that bus, and there were three of us traveling, myself, John Carling, and Rodney (Betty had gotten out in Istanbul to minster with the team in that city).

Spiritual Warfare and Roadblocks

So we continued to distribute the literature, and in this one particular town at night, we saw that a policeman was on foot, watching us. We thought it would be wise to signal to everyone to get back in the van and exit the city as soon as we could. We did just that, but then we saw another car pull up and pick up the policeman that was on foot. We sped up as fast as we could and turned off onto a long road alongside a farm. We drove real deep onto that road in the darkness and turned our headlights out. We decided to sleep there and began to bed down. Just in case they followed us there and asked why we were trying to evade them, we could tell them that we were just students traveling through, and had turned off the road for the night to sleep.

Some Christians later had trouble with that. They thought that we were not being honest with the police. But we believed that our position was for the Lord and we were making decisions based on the fact that we were engaged in a spiritual warfare with the enemy. The tactics we were using were for God's glory; we felt they would be approved of by the Lord.

In another Turkish town going south we stopped in during the day. We thought we'd exercise faith and undertake the same type of distribution but do so during the day. However, we were immediately stopped by the police. We felt that they may have heard of our distribution in other towns and had set up a kind of roadblock. While the road was not actually blocked, from all indications they were looking for our little brown Volkswagen bus.

Police agents arrested us and took us into the police station, where they took all of our items out of the bus. They ordered a court trial for us, and the following day we were taken before the judge to answer the charges lodged against us for distributing literature. We thought for sure that this time we might get some jail time. On our second day of incarceration, we were taken before a judge again. It was made clear that we should stand at attention, and the judge began to question us.

He asked, "What had you planned to do with the literature? Were you distributing this literature for political reasons? Or were you distributing it because you were trying to tell people that they can really find happiness and peace by reading this literature?"

When the judge put it that way, we began to smile; it seemed as though he knew the deal and knew what we were doing. For a moment we were happy about that, but he quickly told us, in strong words, to wipe those smiles off our faces. He reminded us that we were at attention. Of course, we stopped smiling. He scared us.

During the day and a half of our arrest, a representative working with an oil company in the area had been contacted to help on our behalf. He was a Syrian businessman. Throughout our incarceration we were insisting on seeing someone from the American embassy, but no one came. The man with the oil company had been contacted to vouch for us and be our advocate; he was to speak on our behalf in the place of an American embassy official. We wanted him to assure the judge that we were just a group of students who were traveling through the great nation of Turkey in order to experience its culture and learn from its people and that we had no political motives whatsoever in what we were doing.

Unexpected Kindness

Meanwhile, court was recessed for an hour or two and one of the policemen took me personally to a side room. I must admit to a little bit of fear in my heart. I thought, "Why is he singling me out from the others?" To my amazement, the policeman had prepared a cup of tea and some cookies for me. He was very kind and although we didn't converse, he seemed to be trying to say that he was sorry for the treatment my team and I were receiving and that he and his fellow policemen hoped that we had not gotten a poor impression of their country. He was offering me tea and cookies because he wanted to show Turkish hospitality, that unlike the way blacks were treated in America, they were hospitable to blacks. I was dumbfounded, but at the same time I was feeling good about being a black person.

The following morning, the Syrian from the oil company came and told us that we had been set free. Released from jail, we loaded up our Volkswagen bus and headed toward

Lebanon. Once the van was packed again, our Syrian friend urged us not to stop until we got out of Turkey. Apparently, he had heard about our activities in other cities on the way to that particular little town, and he graciously told us that we were not to stop for such activity until we were out of Turkey, lest we be incarcerated for a longer length of time.

Perhaps because of his words, we carefully went through everything to make sure that we had gotten back all of our possessions. Everything was there except my Bible. We went through our personal items several times to make sure, but it was clear that someone had stolen, of all things, my Bible. Even though I felt the loss keenly—it was my personal Bible, I used it all the time and underlined and wrote notes in it— we rejoiced that a person in this closed Muslim country had a copy of the Word of God. Here we were distributing portions of the Bible in secret in a nation that was void of God's Word, and someone among these individuals found one Bible and wanted so desperately to read and study it because they didn't have access to such literature, that they stole my Bible. It was a day of rejoicing as we got into the Volkswagen bus and drove toward the mountain range that we had to cross over, down into Syria, and down toward Lebanon.

Heading for Lebanon: A Merciful Outcome

We headed toward southern Turkey; in order to maximize our time getting to Lebanon, the three of us, John Carling, Rodney, and myself, took turns driving.

One night when John was driving, we went over a small bridge which did not have any side barriers. It was just a flat slab of concrete on a river bed. John dozed briefly and the wheel of the Volkswagen went off the side of the bridge. The van plunged 30 feet into the bed of a river. I was sleeping and awakened with a shock, wondering what in the world had happened that we were in the bed of a river with the Volkswagen turned on its left side. There were two of us in the front seat and John was under me, because my body had shifted to the left from the van going over the bridge and falling on its side.

We managed to get untangled and climb out of the Volkswagen. We were very thankful that there was no water in the river bed because we would have been history. The Volkswagen would have been submerged, we would have been totally disoriented as to where we were or how to get out, water would be gushing in, and we would have been gasping for breath to keep from drowning. Fortunately, none of us was seriously hurt. Rodney had a few scratches on his head. I had an abrasion on the left side of my body, which I still have today.

As we were standing around in the dark trying to get our bearings, a family came running toward us. They had heard the sound of the crash, which to me indicated it may have happened several times before. They asked if they could help and when we explained everything to them, the father of the house beckoned for us to come with him.

We gladly followed him. This was also during Ramadan, the Muslim holy time of the year when believers fast during the daytime and eat well at night. They prepared food for us. We feasted on what they call *chapattis,* which are somewhat like tortillas, small pieces of curried goat, yogurt, and tea. We really enjoyed it. The father in the family informed us of a United States Air Force station in the same town. It wasn't exactly a base, but there were military personnel, and he encouraged his son to contact them and tell them that there were some American citizens in dire straits who needed help.

A Wrecked Van Gets Towed: Praise God!

Fortunately, the next morning, several Air Force personnel
came. They brought a tow truck that was able to pull the
Volkswagen out of the bed of the river without too much
trouble, or too much additional damage, and they took it to
the Air Force compound. We were shouting hallelujah, thank
You, Lord. We were just so thankful that we were not injured
and there were individuals who could help us in such a way,
especially since we had almost no money. God was truly to
be praised. The soldiers took us to the compound and gave
us a place to stay. They assured us that we could have some
meals, but at the same time they indicated that we should make
contact with others who could facilitate our departure from the
compound as soon as possible.

Fortunately, our brother Fouzi Ayoub was in Lebanon and
had heard about the accident on the radio. He knew that it
must have been us, because he was expecting us in a few days.
Brother Ayoub was an extremely loving brother. He was Arab
and he would give his life for you. We didn't know it at that
time, but he had immediately prepared to come and meet us in
the town and at the Air Force compound.

A Plan: Hitchhike to Lebanon

Meanwhile, the three of us in that little town on the Air Force
compound were thinking and praying as to what would be our
next move. We were not sure if we should attempt to drive the
van to Lebanon since it was not in the best condition. None
of us spoke the Turkish language, or Arabic, so our hearts'
desire was to make contact with Brother Fouzi and see how he
would advise us. We agreed that I should try to make my way
to Lebanon by hitchhiking.

Back in the early 1960s, foreigners hitchhiking in those parts of the world didn't usually find it very difficult to get a ride. People wanted to dialogue with foreigners and often they wanted to show visitors that they were friendly. So, after one night at the Air Force compound, I took my sleeping bag and since it wasn't very cold, I dressed in a rather thick sports jacket, wool shirt, and a pair of thick denims. I started hitchhiking southward in Turkey going toward Syria, and then to Lebanon.

When I got to the town just before the mountain range, I wasn't sure whether I should go to the left, the right, or straight toward Syria. I managed to ask people, using sign language and a few Syrian words the direction to Syria. Many of the people that I came upon at that junction thought I was on a pilgrimage to Mecca. They were quite excited. One family ran into their house and came out with a big portion of meat, bread, and raisins. I was about to say thank you, but no, thank you, and they were indicating that I'd need the food for the trip to Mecca. They were being hospitable and it was important to accept their hospitality. So I gladly received the food and smiled at them. They waved me off, and I was on my way.

When Night Falls, Will Faith Arise?

I had left the Air Force military compound early afternoon, and it was about two or three in the afternoon as I was passing through the junction where the family so graciously prepared a snack for me to have on the way. Encouraged by the hospitality, I continued to hitchhike going south in Turkey, toward the Syrian border on my way to Lebanon. But nightfall quickly fell and with no ride to pick me up, I continued to walk. It wasn't a strenuous walk, but it got very dark. There were no streetlights and in spite of the darkness, I kept walking, telling myself that I was going to press on by faith, as a soldier of Jesus Christ.

Then a man came on a motorcycle. He stopped the motorcycle right in front of me and gestured very strongly for me to get on it. I was scared. I thought he may have heard about some of our Christian activity in some of the towns behind me and wanted to take me for questioning. Many doubts came to my mind and I was hesitant to get on his motorcycle, but he was gesturing very firmly to get on. So I thought maybe if I didn't get on he would hurt me, so I sat on his motorcycle and we drove off.

I was still scared. I didn't know where I was going, and I was thinking that no one would know where I was, and maybe no one would ever hear from me again. All of a sudden I shouted as loud as I could, "Help!"

Of course, I was shouting in his ear. He turned around. It scared him. But he kept driving and after a while I settled down. I remembered that God was always with me, no matter what. It is amazing how the Spirit of God is able to give us peace in any situation. He promises in Isaiah 26:3:

> Thou wilt keep him in perfect peace, whose mind is stayed on thee: because he trusteth in thee.

I wasn't sure if it was the end of my life or not, but my heart was comforted by the Spirit of God applying the promises of God. So I went on the motorcycle to where the man was taking me.

He took me to a small village, to the door of a home. The head of the house came to the door, and he and the man driving the motorcycle exchanged a few words. He headed toward the entrance and when he gestured for me to come in, I followed him. He directed me to a place to sit while he and the head of the house continued to talk.

As they spoke they looked at me. When I was alone traveling in such countries, I purposely would always carry a book or a magazine. The purpose was to pretend that I was reading in case I didn't want to talk to someone for whatever reason in that particular country. In most of the countries we were in, we were not supposed to be doing what we were doing, and that was why sometimes I didn't really want to talk.

This time, I had a copy of *Reader's Digest* magazine with me. It was a small, pocket-sized magazine that I could carry with me, so I pretended to be reading it while the two men talked. After about ten minutes, about five other men came to the house. They began obviously to talk about me; it seemed that they were discussing my situation and why I was hitchhiking. I got the impression that it was really a court of the elders as is typical in Muslim countries in towns where there needs to be a collective judgment on some issue or some person. It was possible that in this part of Turkey not many strangers visited or were forced to hitchhike. Evidently, the council decided that I was not a threat and should be treated with courtesy and hospitality.

Hospitality Becomes a Challenge

Shortly afterward, a young pretty girl, maybe about 16 years of age, brought me a bite to eat with some tea, and rolled out a mat for me. The head of the house gestured that here was a place for me to sleep. What they had been discussing, apparently, was that I was probably on my pilgrimage to Mecca. They wanted to comfort and encourage me, and help me to continue my journey by giving me food and a place to lay my head.

The other five men left the owner's home. The owner came back as I spread my sleeping bag on the mat, and in the young girl's presence he gestured back and forth from me to the young girl, indicating that if I wanted to, I could have her for sex. In about one millionth of a second, the devil showed up. The devil was putting things in my mind like well, how nice this is. None of your friends are here, you're in a village that you know nothing about, and the father of this young girl is offering to give her to you for the night. No one will know about it, you've never had sex before, and this will be an ideal opportunity. The father was not pressuring me, and the girl was showing a posture of submission. All I had to do was say yes, but in that one millionth of a second, the Lord encouraged my heart, gave me strength to fight against all my bodily desires, rebuke the devil and say strongly in my own heart: No! No! No! No! No!

I cried out, *"Lord, help me."* In a gesture to the father like I wanted to sleep, I put my hands upside my head. He consented and gave a sign to the girl to leave the room, and then he left. I got in my sleeping bag and played dead for the first several minutes. Before I knew it, I was so tired I fell off to sleep.

Testing the Heart

A blessed portion of Scripture regarding temptation comes to mind. It is found in I Corinthians 10:13:

> There hath no temptation taken you but such as is common to man: but God is faithful, who will not suffer you to be tempted above that ye are able; but will with the temptation also make a way to escape, that ye may be able to bear it.

As is eternally true, the Lord proved His faithfulness to me; He did not allow me to be tempted above that which I was able. I was in an isolated place, and the devil tried to convince me that since I would never see these people again and my Christian brothers would never know, this would be the ideal time to have this new experience of sex. It was a true test of my own heart. That one millionth of a second was a difficult struggle. My whole body was crying out to submit, to give in, to try it, and I am so thankful that God delivered me from this temptation. I realized that my life had been changed by Jesus Christ, and I would have been dead before now if over and over again I would not have relied on the Word of God to help me in my Christian life.

I slept like a log and woke up very early in the morning. Soon after I got up I saw the young girl. She had taken the *Reader's Digest* I was carrying and was trying to read it. Once she noticed that I was awake, she put the magazine down quickly and ran out of the room. Shortly afterward her father entered. He saw that I was out of the sleeping bag, had rolled it up, had my Bible and was trying to read it during my morning devotions. He encouraged the lady of the house to bring in hot flatbread called *roti* and a cup of tea so I could be on my way. I thanked them for their gracious hospitality.

Saving Grace: Believing the Bible

Before I left, a man stopped by who could speak English, and I discovered that the man on the motorcycle had most likely saved my life. The English speaking visitor told me that there was a snowstorm in the mountains; if I had proceeded on up into the mountains, I could have been overcome by the severe weather and froze to death. This is why the man had been so insistent on me getting on his motorcycle. This was my personal angel. It reminds me of the verse in Psalm 34:7:

> The angel of the Lord encampeth round about them that fear him, and delivereth them.

This experience in Turkey alone was enough to write a book. We were delivered from the police over and over from the very day of our arrival in Turkey. We were arrested and incarcerated several times. We had a fairly severe accident that caused our van to roll over into a river bed. People gave me rides and food along the way, and then I was saved from almost certain death in the mountains by an angel on a motorcycle. Instead of yelling "help," I should have been praying. After that series of experiences I did begin to pray more. But my fear and shouting revealed a very human side of me and a reminder of the criticalness of trusting the Word of God and trusting in the Lord Jesus Christ.

I knew that I had to stay close to the Lord as we are reminded to do in John 15:4-5:

> [4]Abide in me, and I in you. As the branch cannot bear fruit of itself, except it abide in the vine; no more can ye, except ye abide in me.
>
> [5]I am the vine, ye are the branches: He that abideth in me, and I in him, the same bringeth forth much fruit: for without me ye can do nothing.

I was learning in a practical way to believe the Bible. Not only the Bible, but I was learning from the lives of my brothers and sisters in Christ, the ones with whom I was traveling and ministering. It was a great encouragement to see their trust in the Lord and their courage as they reached out to those that knew not Him as their personal Savior. As I saw the way God worked in Turkey, it helped me to renew my commitment to continue to allow the Lord to use me for His glory.

After I had partaken of the snack they gave me before leaving, the head of the house pointed me toward the road leading to the mountain range. He assured me that the Turkish/Syrian border was just over the top. He said it wouldn't be very long; I could get to the border before nightfall. It was not a big border with a lot of traffic by trucks; it was a very simple customs post where individuals, trucks, and cars came through on their way to Syria from Turkey or from Turkey to Syria.

CHAPTER ELEVEN

Syria and Lebanon: Carrying Out the Burden and the Vision

Border Customs

I was traveling alone after the accident in Turkey, hitchhiking southward to Lebanon, on my way to where our brother Fouzi Ayoub lived. Fouzi was supposed to meet us in Lebanon, but our journey was interrupted because of the accident. As I mentioned, we did not know it but Fouzi had heard about our accident and was making his way to the Turkish border.

I approached the Turkish/Syrian border and came to the customs post. To my surprise, the customs official asked me if I was with a group that was involved in an accident. I was a little apprehensive about answering because I thought perhaps he had heard about our distribution of Christian literature and the several times we were incarcerated in Turkey. I had visions of him calling officials and saying, "We caught him! He's right here." I was slow to give him information. I did let him know that I was with the group. He completely surprised me, because he told me about Fouzi Ayoub, our friend in Lebanon who was on his way to find us at the Air Force base.

Border Gratuities: Fouzi Arrives from Lebanon

The customs official said that Fouzi had come to the Turkish border and was pleading to be allowed to enter without an official visa so that he could make contact with his friends. He wanted to see that they were well and cared for properly and he needed to facilitate getting his friends together and helping them to return with him to Lebanon. The customs official negotiated with Fouzi: if he would go into the town and buy the official one or two dozens of fresh fish, it would compensate for the official's time spent helping to facilitate permission for Fouzi to enter Turkey. Fouzi assured him that would be not a problem.

From the time we met Fouzi in England, both the OM leaders and myself had experienced him to be an extremely loving, gracious, and compassionate brother who loved the Lord. He knew the Word of God and was burdened for his country of Lebanon and other Arab countries. So the leaders of Operation Mobilization challenged him to prayerfully consider leading the team in Lebanon and Iraq as well, another country which was heavy on our hearts.

Fouzi was ecstatic about the possibility. He knew the choice could be very dangerous for him; Iraq was a Muslim state and an Arab coming and talking about Jesus Christ would be ten times more dangerous than for foreigners. They could write foreigners off, cancel their visas and send them back home, but they might want to kill an Arab. So, it encouraged our hearts that he was willing to invite us to come under his leadership. Fouzi wasn't the type of person to dominate or dictate. He was a very gentle, loving man who gripped the hearts of Christians and non-Christians alike.

I was delighted to hear that Fouzi was in the area and had gone to get some fish. This meant he would be back presently. The thing that really blew my mind is how God orchestrated the precise timing of our arrivals at the border. I had no idea that he'd be coming through there. If I scroll back in my mind I can see that when I was rescued from going through the mountains by myself and taken back to the village to be with the family, God was delaying me so I could meet Fouzi. God controls everything and works it out for His own pleasure— that's what I was experiencing with this situation.

It was a meeting with precision timing: Fouzi was coming all the way from Lebanon to the border, and I was on my way from Turkey to Lebanon. God brought us together. There's no way that I can explain that. Our hearts were encouraged because God already knew what was on our hearts in terms of reaching lost people. He helped to bring cohesiveness to our activity in order to carry out the burden and vision we had. It was just astounding. And I was so happy.

God Has His Way

So I took a chair in the customs office to wait for Brother Fouzi to return. Sure enough, he comes bouncing in the door with some fresh fish for the customs official. We greeted each other very warmly. He was surprised, I was surprised, and he was greeting me in Arabic and English. We embraced each other with a warm hug. We melted in each other's arms with thanksgiving and tears. We wept for a few seconds, realizing that God had really saved us from that accident, saved us from the jail experience, and God only knows—we certainly didn't—whatever else we were protected from. Anyway, there we were.

I scrolled back in my mind to our discussions in England as we talked about what was on our hearts for Lebanon and Iraq and Syria and some of the surrounding countries. It was almost indescribable, but there we were in tears, embracing each other. It was like saying, "Yes Lord, our hearts' desire is still to do Your will, and we are willing to do it together by life or death."

The customs official was happy to get his fresh fish. He allowed Fouzi to proceed to Turkey and gave him a margin of time to come back through the border, and of course, to bring him some more fish. Fouzi had decided to order a taxi. In countries like this, a taxi was like a bus; people may not have a system of public transportation to go to different locations, but a person could hire a taxi for a nominal fee to take them where they wanted to go.

Fouzi hired a taxi, and we asked to be taken through the town where we had experienced the accident and on to the U.S. Air Force compound. When we arrived, John Carling and Rodney were ecstatic that I came back safely and Fouzi was with me. They hadn't known that news of the accident was broadcast on Lebanese radio; when I left them they were simply praying for me and for my safe hitchhiking trip to Lebanon. They didn't know how long it would take. They had limited funds with them. Fortunately, Air Force personnel had assured them that they could stay there until I returned. And there we were, back in a shorter amount of time than they expected, and of course, we all were just simply amazed and very happy.

After a short time of prayer and thanksgiving and praise, we thought we would make an effort to take the damaged Volkswagen bus and limp slowly, not at the speeds of 60 to 70 mph as we had done before, but with much lesser speed to Lebanon. The left side of the van, the driver's side, was really smashed, but fortunately the engine was not damaged, the steering column was not damaged, and the body was intact and able to hold our belongings. We headed toward the Turkey/Syrian border and were allowed to go through to Syria. And of course, the customs official got more fresh fish.

The fact that Fouzi spoke fluent Arabic made the trip so much easier from that point on, and we traveled well. We were comfortable and full of joy. We bought little snacks along the way. In most of the little towns we passed through, we bought fresh bread and butter, yogurt, and fresh fruits. Along the route were many inexpensive fresh fruits which were in season. When we arrived at the Syrian/Lebanese border, the customs officials had a lot of questions about the damaged vehicle we were in and they wanted the registration papers to prove ownership, which we had. Also, they wanted to know the connection of Brother Fouzi, an Arab, to the rest of us Americans.

"Why is an Arab traveling with Americans?" the customs officials asked.

We explained our purpose. It was an occasion in which we could share with them openly what we were about and what we were doing. We saw it as an opportunity to witness to them about Jesus Christ, as well.

They were happy and they were not happy. They were happy to see a black American, two white Americans, and an Arab, all living and sleeping together in a van. They were happy to see that this was possible. But they weren't happy that we were distributing Christian literature and preaching and telling people about Jesus Christ. Some Muslims teach that all unbelievers, including Christians, are infidels. Also, some Muslim extremists teach that infidels should be killed.

Safe Arrival in Lebanon

Thankfully, the customs official just a few steps away at the Lebanese border was very friendly. He insisted on traveling with us from the border all the way to Fouzi's home in Lebanon to prove that we were who we said we were and that we were going where we said we were going. This was fine with us because it enabled us to get past the Syrian customs officials. Actually, we were happy that the Lebanese customs official would be in our midst because he would get a chance to experience us as a group of Christians living together.

By God's grace we arrived at our destination in Lebanon about a day later. Fouzi's father was a certified public accountant; we went to his office first to let him know that his son had returned safely. We shared with him that the customs official was with us and was a bit dubious about letting the van go and giving us clearance, unless he was sure that we were who we said we were. It seemed to boil down to the fact that the official wanted a gratuity, not fish, but something to show appreciation for his service in facilitating and helping us to get to Lebanon. Fouzi's father understood, of course. He whipped out a roll of Lebanese liras and rolled off about two or three hundred. Soon the customs official was happily on his way back to his post at the Lebanon/Syrian border.

All four of us, Fouzi, John Carling, Rodney, and me proceeded on to Fouzi's home. Fouzi had made plans for me to stay with him, his father, and mother at their apartment. Arrangements had been made through the pastor of the First

Baptist Church for John Carling and Rodney to stay in the homes of two Christian families. We would be in very close proximity so we could meet every day for prayer and distribution and we could visit churches and share the burden and vision. We also asked for prayer as we went about the city of Beirut, making contact with Christian groups, distributing Christian literature, and making plans to visit Christians in other parts of Lebanon and in Syria.

One of the additional blessings in terms of meeting the Christians in the Baptist church in Beirut, Lebanon was a businessman who had a body repair shop. We called him ND. He was a very warm, happy person who smiled all the time. ND's joy was obvious. You couldn't come anywhere near his home without him preparing a meal or a snack for you. His wife was so charming that she would put you to sleep. This is no exaggeration. We were humbled by their love and I personally think it was yet another way that the Lord God Himself was encouraging our hearts.

The Lord knew that we didn't have much money, and He knew that we were involved in telling people about Himself, which could be dangerous. Throughout the campaigns in Europe and all the way through Turkey, the thought came to my mind many times to cancel everything and return to America. I wanted to forget about the hardship, to say nothing about the thought of working in Arab countries where my life would be in danger for even talking about Jesus Christ. These were the human feelings and temptations that the devil would keep in my mind all the time.

At times it was so discouraging to be in countries with which we had no familiarity about daily living. We didn't have proper water to drink at times, or a proper place to take a bath.

Good old America would come to mind and I was thinking, "Let me out of here! I'm going back home!" But God didn't allow that to happen, and in Lebanon with Brother Fouzi we were experiencing encouragement in our hearts with the cordial, warm, friendly hospitality of Lebanese Christians.

Brother ND looked at the van and assured us that he could fix it. We asked him how much should we start saving for in order to pay the bill, and it was clear that we had insulted him. We didn't mean to insult him, but he said to us, "How dare you think of that? You are my brothers in the Lord. The Lord has gifted me with this business and here's a situation where I can give service to you, so please, please, allow me to take care of this."

We were speechless, dumbfounded really, so we submitted by God's grace.

The Van Is Fixed and the Work Begins in Lebanon

Since he lived in the city, Fouzi was well acquainted with the pastor, his family, and the people at the local First Baptist Church. We were encouraged to have several meetings with the church's young people. We shared our testimonies and experiences traveling in Europe and witnessing, and we tried to encourage and challenge them to come out with us to do the same thing in their own city and their own country. Some of them had never even thought about it and had never been challenged. Of course, they were a bit hesitant because they realized it could be dangerous. But they thought about it, and one or two did come with us for a day or two of distribution.

In the coming weeks we continued to have fellowship with the congregants at Fouzi's church. They really appreciated and loved our presence. One weekend, they took us on a tour of different parts of Lebanon. They took us into the mountains where there were big, big cedar trees. Scripture tells us how King Solomon had his men to chop down many of those big cedar trees and float them down to Israel to use for building Solomon's Temple. Lebanon is full of biblical history.

Go Out into the Street and Spread the Word

However, as much as the tour provided fascinating glimpses of Lebanon, we were not there as tourists. We focused mainly on evangelizing. On several occasions as we were distributing Christian literature on some corner in Lebanon, Muslims would come and engage us in conversation about the literature. Before the conversation was over, they would be tearing up the literature, threatening our lives, but with his command of Arabic, Fouzi would hold them off, calm them down so we could get in our van and leave the area as soon as possible.

We did take a side trip, to visit Aleppo in Syria. It was just outside of Lebanon up the mountainside. Aleppo is a very old city, and it has a famous street called Straight Street. When the apostle Paul was converted, the Lord told Ananias to go and find Paul on Straight Street. The Scripture says in Acts 9:11:

> And the Lord said unto him, Arise, and go into the street which is called Straight, and inquire in the house of Judas for one called Saul, of Tarsus: for, behold, he prayeth.

This street is an extremely long commercial street with all kinds of shops on both sides, but it was wonderful to have an opportunity to see a biblical street mentioned hundreds of years before—and being able to see it and distribute Christian literature along it was indeed an experience.

While there we met some of the Syrian Orthodox Christians who were very loving. Many of them had dark complexions just like my own, so I felt especially comfortable and at home.

After seeing that some of my clothes, the pants and shirt, were a little frayed, they had pity on me and had a suit made for me. One of the men in the Syrian church was a tailor. He took my measurements while we were in Aleppo for a few days in Syria and he made a suit for me which I shall never forget.

After spending time in Aleppo and sharing the burden and vision with the Christians there, we encouraged their hearts. They lived in a Muslim community where daily they could sense threats hanging over their lives for everything they did concerning the person of Christ. We also shared with them that we were praying and thinking about going to Iraq and of course, we needed their prayers as we planned for that trip. They assured us that they would be praying for us, and we assured them that we would be going back to Lebanon first, and at some time in the future we would be coming back through Syria, but we would not stop at their location since we did not want to draw the authorities' attention. They were happy about that and assured us they understood. They stood with us in prayer, and we returned to Fouzi's home to continue the ministry in Lebanon as well as to keep praying about going to Iraq.

Going Out Across the Middle East

As we were making preparations in Lebanon to go to Iraq, Fouzi took us to visit some Christians in Amman, Jordan and Israel. Brother Fouzi was born in Israel and in his late teens the family moved to Lebanon. It was a historical event for me to visit the Garden Tomb in Israel. Christians in both countries assured us that they would be praying for us as we were planning to venture into Iraq.

Rodney Scott had planned to visit and spend time with another mission while he was in the Middle East. He did not plan to go with us to Iraq. He was with us in Turkey when we had the accident and then came to Lebanon, but he left the team in Lebanon and went to be with the other mission.

In Lebanon, we met an Arab missionary who was married to an English lady, a very lovely couple. He warned us to take it easy in Iraq because we could be killed. Of course we could understand his fear and caution, but we had thought about all of that before we determined to go to the ends of the world to share the Gospel, so we were ready for whatever we had to experience in Lebanon and any other Muslim country.

I learned a lot in Lebanon, under the leadership of Brother Fouzi, living in his home and eating at his table every day. His mother lovingly prepared us breakfast every morning. We normally ate lunch out because we were visiting churches and making contacts and we didn't come back to Fouzi's home at noontime. When we came back in the evening, there was always a well-planned meal for us.

Other than his parents' bedroom Fouzi's home had one other bedroom; he and I slept in the same bed. That was quite revolutionary. Think of it. An African American in the Middle East with a converted Arab who had experienced the revolutionary work of Jesus Christ in his own heart, and we were sleeping in the same bed. It was a daily reminder to me of the grace of God and the love of God, how He was challenging us to take that message to the world.

During the later part of our stay in Lebanon, Fouzi, John, and I curtailed our visits to various churches in the cities and surrounding villages, because we wanted to spend the time in concentrated prayer for our trip to Iraq. Many of the Christians lovingly tried to discourage us. They felt that it could be a one-way trip, and in our hearts we, too, sensed this possibility. There were a few Christians in Baghdad and Iraq's surrounding cities, and we had the names and addresses of these Christians. We were planning on visiting them first, but we wanted to really make sure that John, Fouzi, and my own hearts were really bound together in the person of the Holy Spirit.

Who's in Charge?

I remember a personal breaking-point experience in Lebanon. There was no question that Brother Fouzi Ayoub was in charge. He didn't labor over that fact with John and me. One evening, I recall that Fouzi was trying to orientate me and instruct me in terms of what he expected me to do in the coming days to prepare for going to Iraq, and my attitude was not what it should have been. I felt that since there were only three of us going, we should have equal leadership.

I was dead wrong. I was trying to convince myself that we all were being led by the Holy Spirit, but a leader like Fouzi was critical. He understood the culture and spoke fluent Arabic; it was foolish of someone like me to think of going into a country like Iraq, where I did not even speak the language, and expect to be effective for the Lord.

Fouzi picked up that I was resistant; I was not listening to his instructions and was not writing them down. He lovingly and graciously rebuked me. He said, "Hoise, you're not listening to me. You're not listening to me. Here we are praying together, planning to go together to Iraq, and your attitude is not what it should be."

I was defensive. I said something like, "I'm spiritual just like you are. Yes, you're the leader, but we have our own thoughts about how things should be done."

I realize now that my attitude was totally unacceptable for the situation. Fouzi was hurt but I continued to have a bad attitude. I thought, "Well, you know, if it's going to be this way, maybe I shouldn't go." What a terrible thought. We had prayed about the journey for months. And there we were, in Lebanon, planning to go, and the devil worked me into having a disrespectful, disagreeable attitude about my part in the group. That's all that the devil wanted—to cause chaos. In a situation like that the devil eats us alive.

Hindrance: Uncooperative Spirits and Racism

Brother Fouzi went to the next level. He strongly rebuked me. "Brother, you're not in the spirit. Your attitude is not right. Here we are thinking about going to Iraq and it's dangerous for us to even think about going to Iraq with an attitude of disunity."

I heard him clearly, but I still didn't give him a positive response. The thing that the Holy Spirit used to break and crush my own stubborn, proud, rebellious heart was that Fouzi came to me and apologized.

We were out in the evening walking and talking and praying, and the thing that really gripped my heart was that he came to me. We stopped in the park and sat down. Tearfully, he apologized for talking to me the way he did. He was telling me that he didn't really mean to talk harshly to me; he loved me in the Lord. He put his arms around me and held me. Before it was over, we both were weeping almost uncontrollably.

The Spirit of God had worked in my heart. The Spirit of God said, "Hoise, you're so proud and unbroken. I died for you on the Cross because I love you. It has been Me who has brought you brothers together, you, Fouzi, and John, to be used to perform a burden that is on My heart. I have told you in Matthew 28 to go into all the world and preach the Gospel. You know that one of the factors that weakens Christian missions is disunity and the lack of brokenness and lack of love amongst the brethren. Here you are, showing disrespect and a non-cooperative mind and attitude concerning what's on My heart. Fouzi Ayoub, like you, belongs to Me, and I desire above everything else to use each of you to further My Kingdom."

About another twenty minutes passed and Fouzi and I were weeping so uncontrollably that we could hardly talk to each other. But we were holding each other, in each other's arms. I cannot put into words the powerful spirit of conviction, love, and forgiveness that we experienced that night. I doubt that I ever will be able to put it properly into words.

The history of missions tells the unfortunate story of Christians being their own worst enemies. Books could be written about American and English missionaries on the field not cooperating and going after each others' necks. This aspect of Christian missions is often not mentioned in books; nevertheless it is true and is often a major hindrance to the work of God. Such divisions are also stumbling blocks for new Christians and non-Christians who are watching Christians closely.

Christians are flesh and blood; we are not perfect, and the devil uses every device he can to divide and conquer. There is strength in unity and weakness in division. In several countries there was a big question about me as an African American with a white mission group. Some spoke somewhat openly about it even though there was not a full conversation on it. Many watched our team to see if the concept of unity was working. One of the most revealing of my very first experiences when I met George Verwer was his love and compassion for all people. Color, ethnic background, or nationality did not change his loving response to them in the body of Christ.

And that was a great challenge, of course, in the midst of racism all over the place, in every country, and in so many churches. Someone has said that the most segregated hour in America is at 11:00 AM on Sunday. There is much the Lord desires to do in the church and in the world through His people, and racism is a great hindrance.

Preparing for Iraq

That particular night John Carling was not with us. He was staying with another lovely family from the Christian church in Lebanon. While there he was picking up Arabic pretty readily. The people loved him. He was receiving the same loving experience in that particular home, and he enjoyed it. He was the only one in that home that was getting all the love and attention. Had he been with us, he would have been receiving one-third of the love and attention, but as it was, each day we met, he was ecstatic. He had a lot to share about how the Lord had spoken to his heart and what he had learned from being with the family.

Before we left, a few churches and a few believers came to us very lovingly and assured us that they were praying for us as we prepared to go to Iraq. As I mentioned, in the Arab world, the Christians know of each other in every country. We got the names and addresses of Christians in Iraq with the understanding that it would be for our use only. They were to be memorized by Fouzi because he spoke Arabic and not ourselves because we might have carelessly given the information to some political officials or enforcement officers. Officials might visit those Christians' homes later on and cause a lot of havoc, disruption, and persecution.

One of the items we planned to take with us to Iraq was oranges. Lebanon produces beautiful oranges for all of the

Mediterranean area, and often an orange is eaten after every meal. Since we were going into the desert, it was advised that we also take lemons with us in case we got into a situation where we might get very thirsty; lemons ease thirst and compensate for water until you can get some water. So we took a good quantity of oranges and lemons with us. We also took packets of dried fruit like peaches and apples to munch on; if we couldn't find a good, safe restaurant, it was easy to carry these packets with our sleeping bags.

Our luggage was loaded with Bibles and Gospel tracts in Arabic. This was the greatest risk of all. If they caught us with this literature at the Iraqi checkpoints or inside the country we could be arrested, and who knows what could have happened to us inside a country where we would have no contact with the outside world. Our plan was that if we were ever separated for a day or two, three at the most, we would contact the American Embassy immediately.

The Volkswagen bus had been given to Brother ND in Lebanon and he was repairing it for us. We were thinking that we would be gone for about ten days and by the time we returned, the van would be repaired free of charge. Our plan for getting to Iraq was to take a local form of transportation, mainly the bus.

CHAPTER TWELVE

Iraq: Checkpoints, Prayers, and Thanksgiving

Arrangements for Iraq

The time came for us to leave Lebanon and go to Iraq to distribute Christian literature. After careful consideration, it was decided that Fouzi would go one day ahead of us, and not be with us Americans in case his presence caused border officials to be suspicious. Fouzi felt that we wouldn't have any problem getting on the bus, a black and white American, as tourists. Iraq was a country that many international tourists visited.

We agreed to meet in Iraq's ancient city of Baghdad where we would be staying at the YMCA. The YMCA was an international hotel with tourists and many foreigners. We had postured ourselves as tourists as part of our plans. We had obtained the addresses of several Christians and Brother Fouzi had written them before leaving Lebanon, explaining what was on our hearts. One or two families wrote back and told him to not even think about coming or contacting them. So of course, he scratched those, but there were several other families that encouraged us to make contact with them upon our arrival.

We started out from Lebanon on a Monday. The church had a special time of prayer for us on the Sunday before we left. Many in the congregation were concerned and really burdened to pray for us, because they realized what can happen to two Americans. At this time, anti-American and anti-Western feeling was strong; Muslim states would definitely not look favorably toward Americans distributing Christian literature. In some places doing this could bring the death sentence. We had considered all of that and we were prayerfully going forward in Jesus' name.

There was no one coming back from Iraq with reports of what God was doing in this country, nothing of that nature at all. At times, we were a little apprehensive and of course the devil tried to discourage us and get us to change our minds. Perhaps this subconscious fear was behind my disagreement with Fouzi in Lebanon. The devil could have been trying to use me to sabotage the entire trip because he knew that God had a plan. Fortunately, my commitment was to the Lord and I admitted in my heart that God had brought us together and that He had raised up Brother Fouzi to lead us. The next issue was submission, which I did with the help of the Lord.

A Bus Ride and a Desert Checkpoint

The bus had reclining seats and was very comfortable. We passed through Aleppo, Syria and traveled through the desert.

Another important piece of equipment on that bus in addition to its seats was a long, 4" thick cable to use in case the bus got stuck in the desert and needed to be pulled out.

Going through the Arabian Desert was quite an experience. One of the families on board was a young Arab man who had married an American woman. He had three children with him and had just finished his Ph.D. in electrical engineering in California. He was returning home and his children were young. His American wife seemed to be coping very well. We began to talk about different subjects. He asked us what we had to eat. We told him about our dried apples and peaches and grapes and raisins and bread and yogurt. He seemed somewhat annoyed that he and his wife hadn't prepared in such a way.

I asked him if he would like to have a pack of apples for his boys and he said quickly, "Oh, yes, I'd love to have that." So I shared some of my food with him and his family, which was a turn of events from previous occasions when others shared their food with me.

We made good time. Some of the sights in the desert were educational. But one sight was especially heartbreaking. The bus made a stop at a small village and we saw several families standing behind a wall. Within minutes, the villagers put about five children who appeared to be about one to two years of age in front of the wall. At first I thought that they had put them out there to beg for money or just to say hello, but then I realized that they were really marketing the children—selling them as slaves. I didn't say anything, but I was astounded that in this day and age, human beings were still being sold into slavery in the desert on the way to Baghdad. My heart ached that both they and the people who sold them might be set free by the very Jesus who said in John 8:36:

> If the Son therefore shall make you free, ye shall be free indeed.

Of course, as we went toward Baghdad, my heart was more burdened to reach people, many of them who were bound into slavery, that they might be set free by the Gospel of Jesus Christ. I am certain that God intended us to see this tragic sight in order that we might deepen our resolve to evangelize.

Before we got to Baghdad, we came upon a border checkpoint in the desert. We had traveled all through the night, and when the bus stopped at the checkpoint we got out and went to the restroom. Officials observed out of the corner of their eyes; not necessarily being suspicious, just being observant, and of course we were praying that they would not look into our bags. We had started praying about that before we left Lebanon and many of the Christians praying for us were praying that the Bibles and tracts would get into Iraq. The worst that could've happened was that they would take all of the literature and tell us, "We can't allow you to take these items into Iraq with you, but if you want to continue without it, you can go on." This would also have meant, however, that we would have been followed by the secret police. They did not look into our bags, though. We breathed a sigh of relief and got back on the bus.

Arriving in Baghdad

In a few hours we arrived in Baghdad. Brother Fouzi was there waiting for us, smiling. Our hearts were so happy that the trip had gone as well as it had, and we were so happy to see Fouzi. Customs officials in Baghdad were concerned about our bags, but they were distracted from the bags containing the Bibles and tracts by the fruit that we were carrying.

The officials expressed concerned about the unusual quantity of oranges and lemons we had with us; they worried that we may bring some infestation into Baghdad through the fruit from Lebanon. They said they had to confiscate the fruit to make sure that there was no contamination and no fruit pests being brought into Baghdad. Fouzi tried to assure them in Arabic that the fruit was not contaminated. "Why can't we take our fruit?" he kept asking.

The officials kept saying "La'a, la'a," which is "No, no," in Arabic. After a while, it was obvious from their tone that they were indicating that Fouzi should stop arguing with them. Fouzi translated what they finally said: "Well, you can come back tomorrow and check and see if the fruit is here."

We had to give up the fruit; of course, it would have been ludicrous to go back the following day—we knew there wouldn't have been any fruit. Perhaps our fruit provided a feast for the officials and their families and friends, or perhaps they did throw it away. Anyway, the Lord gave us grace, and we thanked Him for the Bibles and tracts getting through with no restrictions. On reflection, the fruit was a small price to pay for the literature getting through. We took our bags and proceeded to the YMCA.

The people at the YMCA were cordial and friendly. They were happy to see foreigners and I always noticed a special gesture of friendliness from them that suggested: *"Welcome, you African American. We've heard about the racism in America and we want you to know that you are welcome in our country."* Of course, I used that sentiment to the max, and my OM brothers didn't feel uncomfortable with it; they knew what was going on. They felt that it was a plus for the team and for its functioning.

After arriving in Iraq at the YMCA, we had a really special time of prayer and thanksgiving. We thanked God for our safe arrival. We had prayed about this trip for months, years, actually, and thousands of other Christians were praying for the three of us in Iraq. Many of them knew what was on our hearts. Some thought it wasn't safe to go to Iraq, and others felt that we would be lying if we didn't tell the officials what was in our bags. We were convinced that we had to obey the law of God if it conflicted with the law of man.

We took extra rest that day after the bumpy ride through the desert. The following morning we made contact with several Christians in Baghdad. One was a Christian barber. All three of us went to have our hair cut. Also, we could leave some money for the work in Iraq because as is true in other Muslim countries, Christian businesses were boycotted. Muslims would not go to a Christian to have their hair cut. Christians were not even supposed to exist but by God's grace the Christian barber was carrying on.

He shared his testimony with us. He said that when he came from Syria, he lived in a very remote part of Iraq where he had a little farm. When he lived there he stood outside and prayed five times a day because people observing him from a distance would be impressed that he was a good Muslim praying five times a day. He knew that certain people were watching him and if he was not seen praying five times a day, it would arouse suspicion. Fortunately, after getting situated in Baghdad and learning the city, he made some friends and was able, to a certain extent, to melt into the culture.

The other fortunate thing for the Christian barber was that he did not have to marry a Muslim woman. He was able to marry a Christian; the marriage had been planned by a group of Christians in Syria. His overall testimony was about the faithfulness of God preserving his life every day, the miracle of God providing him with a Christian wife in the midst of a Muslim culture, and the way that God continually strengthens them to live out their faith in such a culture.

At times, we experienced a small glimpse of what life was like for the barber and others in Iraq. People would come up to us and ask, "Are you Muslim or are you Christian?"

We smiled and said, "We're Christians." We got different reactions. Some people accepted our statement of belief, some people frowned at us, and some frowned, turned their backs and walked away. We had planned in every such situation to testify to the fact that we were really Christians, individuals whose lives had been changed by Jesus Christ. We knew that in Muslim culture we were considered by some as infidels, and as such, deserving of death. We had prepared ourselves and were determined to be truthful and open about our faith.

Biblical History Comes Alive in Iraq

As I mentioned, our strategy was to meet and visit Christians in Baghdad, but we planned to visit the city of Babylon also. This is the city mentioned in the book of Daniel. God used the book of Daniel greatly in bringing me to Himself and at the time of my conversion in Alaska, I never dreamed I would ever visit Babylon. But here we were.

Since we had declared ourselves tourists, we had to involve ourselves in tourist-type activities to make it seem like we were actually tourists. We also planned to go to the city of Nineveh, about 100 miles north of Baghdad. Nineveh is the city featured in the book of Jonah where Jonah spent three days and three nights in the belly of the great fish as he tried to avoid obeying God and preaching to the Ninevites. We wanted to visit Nineveh, but time wouldn't allow it, so our itinerary included plans to visit some historical sites in and around Baghdad and go to Babylon itself.

We were happy as well to visit with the Christians with whom we had made contact before coming. They made us feel very comfortable. They fed us very well. Our strategy, even before doing any distribution, was to meet these families and we appreciated the fact that they were willing to show hospitality toward us. Once we arrived in Baghdad, they entertained us by fixing a meal for us. Even though we all knew the potential for risk by offering us a meal, they seemed unconcerned about that. They created the impression to all that they were just being hospitable to some visitors to their nation.

Risks Taken for Christ in the Middle East

However, they did want very much to share their testimonies about their experiences as Christians in a Muslim country. As we sat around their table talking, as was true in Lebanon, we heard many stories about Christians who had suffered and lost their lives in Iraq for the cause of Christ. Just as in Lebanon and other closed countries, some of these families were engaged in professional work but their underlying motive was to reach their coworkers for Christ.

The Christians we visited in Baghdad talked to us for hours about the history of the country. Quietly and softly, they spoke about the political situation in the country. They warned us not to mention anything they shared with us to anyone else. They pointed out that if the authorities suspected that we had political or religious interests in coming to Iraq, or any interest other than as tourists, we would probably have been apprehended and questioned and not allowed into the country.

Something else that they shared with us involved the southern part of Iraq, a marshland where Arabs lived. This swampy area was somewhat isolated from the mainland for many years; the inhabitants were believed to have come to Iraq from Yemen and their complexions were dark like mine. Some of the Christians in homes that we visited didn't hesitate to point out that they were happy that as an American black man I was visiting their country. John Carling understood this and he had no problem with it. Brother Fouzi greatly understood it, and it was a great boost to me to feel that I was loved and accepted by the people in Iraq. Their hospitality was such that they gave us food to take back to the YMCA so we could have a snack later, and they sent us off with much encouragement and prayer.

We spent three days with the Christians as they wined and dined us. The wine in Iraq was fermented fruit, a part of Arab culture, and even though we didn't drink wine normally, we drank a small glass with these Christians. The Bible exhorts believers to take whatever is set before us as long as we can eat or drink it with a clear conscience. We were offered wine in Spain also, but they used to mix the wine with carbonated water, so we could just ask for *aqua gaseosa,* carbonated water. But in Iraq that was not the case, and as we felt comfortable, we drank the wine.

Each day we came back to the YMCA from the homes of various Christians. We spent time in prayer and planning and packed our literature, including Bibles, for the upcoming evangelizing. We also discussed how we were going to distribute the literature. We knew that in closed countries visitors are often watched, stalked, and followed, however discreetly, by police and other officials. One exciting thing about the upcoming visit to Babylon was that one of Baghdad's local Christians and his wife planned to go with us as though they were tour guides. We were happy that they were coming with us because their presence was bound to be helpful.

Learning about Babylon

So it was that on the fourth day after we got to Baghdad, we left early in the morning for the two-hour drive going south from Baghdad to Babylon. At the time I did not know that the city of Babylon was founded by Nimrod, a son of Cush, who is mentioned in Genesis 10:6.

Babylon is mentioned prominently throughout the Old Testament, especially in the book of Daniel. King Nebuchadnezzar of Babylon was used of God to punish the Israelites and take them captive. He was also the king who put four Hebrew boys into a fiery furnace, and he was punished with insanity for seven years because of pride. This insanity was foretold by Daniel when Daniel interpreted one of Nebuchadnezzar's dreams.

Babylon was also famous for its beautiful Hanging Gardens, one of the seven wonders of the ancient world. God said that even though He used Babylon to punish Israel, He would, in turn, punish Babylon for its wickedness. God said that not only would Babylon be destroyed, it would never be rebuilt. The prophet Jeremiah says this in Jeremiah 50:39-40 regarding Babylon:

> [39]Therefore the wild beasts of the desert with the wild beasts of the islands shall dwell there, and the owls shall dwell therein: and it shall be no more inhabited for ever: neither

shall it be dwelt in from generation to generation.

[40]As God overthrew Sodom and Gomorrah and the neighbor cities thereof, saith the LORD; so shall no man abide there, neither shall any son of man dwell therein.

There we were hundreds of years later in Babylon. The river Euphrates was still flowing through Babylon and the city was still not inhabited. That afternoon in Babylon an entourage of about four Mercedes stretch limousines came near to where we were and a very tall black man stepped out of the first limousine. His skin was extremely dark and there was an air of royalty and dignity about him. He cast his eyes over all the ruins of Babylon. Seconds later, his security men emerged from the other limousines; they carried Uzi machine guns and stood around him, protecting him.

We stood there wondering who on earth this man could be. We asked the tour guide, "Who is this man?"

He said, "This is the great, great, great, great, great, great, great, great (I forget just how many greats) grandson of King Nebuchadnezzar."

We almost collapsed with amazement. Here was a distant relative of a ruler of one of the greatest empires in history. This ruler was profiled in both secular and biblical history and had a profound influence on God's people, the Israelites. I was in his city and seeing one of his descendants, and suddenly I realized that none of the history books had ever mentioned that Nebuchadnezzar was a black man. It was quite an experience. Now many modern historians acknowledge that the Chaldeans and some other ancient peoples mentioned in the Bible were black people, but this is a recent phenomenon.

Someone raised the question as to why it was important to have direct, firsthand knowledge that Nebuchadnezzar was a black man. Well, black people who live in a racist and oppressive society and are continually bombarded with negative images of themselves need positive images. We also need to know about our accomplishments in history. There is a feeling of pride and a feeling of joy when a black person discovers that he or she has been a part of a certain portion of history and they are fortunate enough to discover it. It's difficult to put into words.

Apparently, this man had heard the story of his great, great, great, great, great, great, great, great grandfather Nebuchadnezzar and it may have been hard to believe. He probably wanted to see this for himself. We never found out what city or what country he came from, as the security guards kept us far from him. The tour guides didn't get the information from him, either. But here he was, in Babylon and evidently he was quite well off financially. It wasn't too long before the prince from the lineage of Nebuchadnezzar got into his limousine and was driven away. No one was allowed to leave the site until after he left.

We were convinced that God allowed us to visit the city on that particular day and at that particular hour. Just as the Bible prophets had predicted, the city was not inhabited, goats were dancing on the ruins of the city, and the Euphrates River was still flowing through the city. As we settled down from the excitement of our experience, we wondered aloud if we were really experiencing what we thought we were experiencing. We also expressed great joy as we witnessed the truth and historicity of the Bible. This made us even more determined to take upon ourselves the high honor of making known the living God.

We stayed in Babylon for a day and then went back to Baghdad. We dropped off our brother who had graciously played tour guide at his home and returned to the YMCA. We made plans for commencing literature distribution to occupy the remaining days we would be in Iraq. As before, our itinerary included a time of prayer before we set out, and we decided on a general direction in which to go in the city.

Strategy: Tourists Spreading the Gospel

Fouzi had partly planned that himself and gave us instructions. Our plans for distribution in Baghdad were that we would go three separate ways in the early morning, about nine o'clock when people were on their way to work. We also carefully mapped out our area of distribution and plotted a direction to escape or run if we were followed or chased. We agreed not to reveal the identity of the other team members, which for me included Fouzi and John.

Our distribution strategy was to put a little Gospel tract about Jesus Christ in mailboxes. The tract was in Arabic in a small envelope and had an address for a correspondence course, so that those who were interested in studying the Bible could write outside the country and ask for the course. They could also write to the same address to get additional material such as other tracts, or they could ask questions about the Bible and the Christian faith. The correspondence allowed people to have a confidential dialogue about Christianity. This was important because if family members and friends in an Islamic culture become suspicious about a person's interest in Christianity, it could have extremely dangerous consequences. By writing in, a person could carry on their own secret investigation. This strategy worked well in many closed countries.

Circulation: Bibles, Mailboxes, Shops and Windshields

The Bibles we had with us were only given to people who showed a personal interest after we had talked to them for a period of time. At the YMCA, we would have tea in the lobby and strike up conversations with people about the Bible. Some of them expressed a desire to have a Bible and we were happy to be in a position to give them a free copy of the Bible in Arabic.

As we went out to put Gospel tracts in mailboxes, we noticed that in some of the larger buildings housing five or six families, we could go in and close the door behind us, and no one could see what we were doing. In these instances we felt fortunate; we would put the tracts in the mailboxes and leave and the tracts were not out in the open.

When we went in a store to buy a few items to take back to the YMCA with us, we used these opportunities to also leave Gospel tracts on the premises. If we met one or two people on the street that we felt had a welcoming attitude toward us, we might extend a tract to them. We also left tracts on the windshields of parked cars, knowing that we could be stopped and questioned. Of course John Carling and I didn't speak fluent Arabic, but we learned a few Arabic phrases meaning, "It's free," "Good morning," "Thank you" and "You're welcome." Sometimes when people saw that we spoke one or two words of Arabic, they stopped and read the material, and by that time we moved on, out of their sight.

One day I was distributing the literature I had with me after making one or two stops in apartment buildings and stopping in one or two stores. I didn't buy too much at each store so I'd have an excuse for visiting more shops. Once outside again, I saw a man walking down the street. From a distance it seemed that he recognized that I was a foreigner and was an African American.

Welcome or Not?

He began to smile like so many had done just before saying, "You're welcome, you're welcome, you're welcome," in Arabic. He was telling me that I was welcome to his country. I felt that he was friendly so I extended a tract to him. I gave him the tract and said, "It's free" and "good-bye" in Arabic.

I began walking. As I looked back over my shoulder, I saw that he was reading the tract, and as I looked back again, he began to follow me. I began to walk a little faster. He began to walk a little faster. Then I began to trot and he began to trot. I was scared so I turned the corner and ran until I came to a dead end. I was really scared and I thought, "Oh Lord! This is it. This is curtains."

But then I started figuring out a way to get past him without getting hurt, and without him calling other people to stop me or help attack me. I stopped casually in the street. It was a broad walkway really, not actually a street, with apartment houses on each side of the walkway. I took a booklet out of my bag and pretended to read. I had decided that when the man got close to me, I would dash past him before he could grab me or stop me or say anything to me. I would take him by surprise and rush past him so fast that he would be confused and scared and probably think I was trying to attack him. My goal was just to get out of there.

The closer he got to me, the more my heart began to pound. I was so scared. When he got to within about 30 feet, I became even more frightened. I realized that if something happened to me John and Fouzi probably would never hear about it. All kinds of thoughts came to my mind. Maybe the man was with the secret police and would call in reinforcements. Maybe I would be put in a dark jail and never heard from again.

None of this happened. As the man approached me, I was shocked to hear him say in English, "Do you have more of these?" He was referring to the Gospel tract.

I said, "Yes, you can have all of them. Take this one, take this one, take the Bible, take it all." I needed all the strength I could muster to keep from collapsing. I was truly amazed: here was a man who apparently had been looking for Gospel literature for so long but had never been able to find it until now. Not only that, he spoke English.

I didn't want to speak too much English to him, of course. He may have had questions about who I was, where I came from, or what my plans were. I would have developed a serious case of amnesia had he started asking questions.

Recapping the Week: Encouraged

After that experience I made my way back to the YMCA and told Fouzi and John about it. We had a time of prayer and thanksgiving that nothing serious had happened, that no one had followed us or come to the YMCA to contest our activity. Our hearts were encouraged in terms of the amount of literature we had distributed in apartment buildings, stores and shops, on parked cars, and to the one or two people to whom we had given literature while on the street.

We had been in Baghdad for about a week. We were told that a Christian Protestant service was being held at the YMCA on Sunday, so we attended just to see what was going on. Several individuals gave their testimonies, but their words were extremely philosophical. They were not centered in the Word of God. After the service at the YMCA we returned to our rooms, and we prayed and planned in preparation for the coming Monday.

The plan for Monday involved the same strategy in terms of distribution and going out in three different directions. First, though, we did something quite unexpected for a group of evangelists.

CHAPTER THIRTEEN

Opposition and Grace

Visiting a Mosque

We had a special time of prayer after the church service at the YMCA during which Brother Fouzi shared that he was burdened to visit the main mosque in Bagdad the next day. He said that he prayerfully and humbly wanted to speak to the main imam on duty and share the Gospel with him. In many Muslim countries tourists are often invited to visit local mosques to study the architecture, culture, and history of Islam in the country. Such visits are often used as a way of promoting and putting a positive face on Islam to foreigners. For example, our Muslim friends here in America have a program where they invite Christians to come and visit their mosque. Fouzi felt that we could visit the main mosque and hopefully get a chance to witness to the main imam.

On Monday, the following day, we went to the mosque after midday prayer had ended. We took off our shoes as we entered the mosque, clearly looking like tourists. An imam graciously approached us. He was cordial and humble in his mannerisms, greeting us in Arabic. He really put us at ease. Fouzi responded in Arabic.

Then Fouzi gently began to ask a few questions about Islam and the mosque. Another imam emerged from the dark shadows of the mosque and joined his fellow imam in the discussion. He could sense as we did, some tension between Fouzi and his fellow imam. The second imam began to say loudly, "La'a," which means "NO" in Arabic. When the first imam allowed Fouzi to speak a few more words, the second imam began to say very loudly, "La'a, La'a." The first imam tried to tone his fellow imam down a little with a gesture so that Fouzi could say a little more. He seemed mature and somewhat patient as he listened to Fouzi who was speaking Arabic. I did not know exactly every word that he was using, but I knew that it was the Gospel because I'd heard it interpreted several times before.

Strong Opposition

I could tell that Fouzi was sharing in as gracious and humble a way as he knew how and not in a boastful, proud, or haughty way. I felt pretty sure that what was upsetting the imam was the fact that these infidels had the audacity to come into the mosque with their blasphemy.

Still, the first imam encouraged Fouzi to continue. Fouzi continued sharing his testimony and portions of God's Word that he had memorized. After a few minutes, it became too much and both imams began to say strongly and loudly, "La'a, La'a." By this time I was trying to slip on my shoes without even untying them. I was nervous. The imam picked up that I was nervous because even though I did not jump up and run out of the mosque, I was trying to get to the doors as fast as I could. We had prayed about it before going, of course, but here we were in Baghdad, in the mosque and with two imams upset with us. We could have expected such a reaction, but in the flesh, I was responding in a fearful way. Fouzi also realized that the opposition he was picking up indicated that all three of us should remove ourselves from that mosque as soon as possible, which we did.

We went back out into the city, and began our usual evangelizing, heading in three different directions. At about four o'clock we ran out of tracts and, as we usually did, met at a prearranged location and had supper. Sometimes we sat in a tea shop and tried to initiate conversations with Muslims so that we could continue to witness and maximize our time in Baghdad for God's glory. After the incident in the mosque, we evangelized, met up later and had a word of prayer together, thanking the Lord for the opportunity to visit the mosque, first of all, and for the fact that the imams gave us an opportunity to share the Gospel message. Once we said we were Christians they could have immediately insisted on us leaving the premises, but the Lord didn't allow that. He allowed us to give the full Gospel message inside a mosque, inside Baghdad, Iraq. Anyway you look at it, this was a divine blessing from God.

When we returned to the YMCA, we gave thanks for a day of safe distribution, we encouraged each other in the Lord, and we took part in our individual interests, whether it was reading a book, writing a letter, or just simply getting rest. Before lying down, as was our custom, we prayed and planned our strategy for the following day. On the Tuesday after the mosque incident, we went out for distribution as usual in the morning and planned to meet in the late afternoon at the YMCA.

An Official Request: Leave

In the late afternoon when I returned to the YMCA, I was in for quite a shock. Fouzi and John were in the room, and in their midst was a government secret service official. As I opened the door and looked into the room, I quickly became aware of the situation. The official gestured for me to come on in, come on in. I was trying to ascertain, within seconds, if Fouzi and John were okay or if I should try to run back out the door and get help, but his gestures were gentle. The expression on Fouzi's face was also gentle, and he encouraged me to enter. As I did so, the secret service official informed me briefly but clearly that the government and its agents had been watching us closely every single day that we'd gone out.

The agents had gone behind us and examined the literature that we placed in mailboxes and on the windshields of cars, and left in local stores. He let us know that the distribution of such literature in Baghdad was illegal. He said that this was a governmental offense and that neither he nor the government could assure our safety in Baghdad for more than twelve hours. We understood that he was telling us to leave the country within twelve hours.

Well, we were happy and shocked at the same time. We were shocked that they had followed us all along and had known what we were doing each day that we had been in the country. They knew that we were not tourists, we were distributing Christian literature, and we were engaged in the activity of proselytizing Muslims, which carries a death sentence. We were happy that he was open and candid enough to let us know, but at the same time rather than arrest us, give us time to leave the country. He did it very diplomatically and calmly, which kept us calm; we appreciated that and we let him know that we would do everything possible to obey his suggested timetable.

Hasty Departure from Iraq

As soon as he left our room in the YMCA, Brother Fouzi immediately began arranging for a taxi to take us all the way from Baghdad back to Beirut, Lebanon. We could have taken a bus but we did not want to take a chance on a bus; Fouzi wanted to engage a more private form of transportation. We had traveled from Lebanon to Iraq by way of a bus, but we did not feel comfortable going back the same way. As had happened elsewhere, Baghdad had taxis that individuals could rent for travel fairly long distances. After making those arrangements, we started our journey the following day in a private taxi going back to Beirut. In accordance with the warning of the secret police, we left Baghdad in less than twelve hours.

The route was through the desert where the soil was very hard. We were reminded that sometimes there are sandstorms in the desert, and large quantities of sand can shift, perhaps blocking the road, but there was a way of dealing with that so there was no need for us to be concerned.

Protect the Sheep

As we were on our way to Lebanon, the taxi driver saw a herd of about fifty sheep. Since it was Ramadan, the holy month for Muslims, he wanted to buy a small sheep to take home with him. He beckoned to the shepherd and indicated that he would like to buy one of the smaller sheep. The shepherd shook his finger vigorously and said, "La'a" meaning, "No, no way possible, don't even think about it." The taxi driver stopped the car and gestured to the shepherd again and the shepherd spoke even louder, shouting, "No, No." By this time the shepherd was about 50 feet from the car. He came closer and made sure that no one tried to grab a sheep. He was like the good shepherd, protecting his sheep.

Then the cab driver got out of the car and as he approached, the shepherd pulled back a layer of his clothing and put his hand on his dagger. At this point, we were a little apprehensive; we were hoping the driver would get back in his car. We did not know what would happen next. The thought went through my mind that I might have to jump behind the wheel and drive off with the taxi. It was clear that the shepherd was prepared to do whatever was necessary to protect his sheep. Fortunately, the driver got the message and backed off. With his hand still on his dagger, the shepherd watched as the driver got into the taxi and drove off. We were relieved.

This shepherd's protectiveness reminds me of Jesus. Jesus reminds us that He is the Good Shepherd, in John 10:11:

> I am the good shepherd: the good shepherd giveth his life for the sheep.

Returning to Lebanon

We were thankful as we went toward Lebanon. After about ten hours, our main stop after leaving Baghdad was Aleppo, Syria. We stopped in Aleppo briefly but did not go to our friend's place that we had visited before going to Baghdad. Finally, we went down the mountain into Beirut, where we went immediately to Fouzi's home. His parents were overjoyed to see us, and the three of us spent hours sharing our experiences. They were happy that we got back safely; they were delighted that the Word of God went out, and they were grateful that we had a chance to visit some of the Christians in Baghdad.

Fouzi's parents were sitting on the edge of their chairs listening to the testimonies of Christians in Baghdad, including the Christian barber. They gave God special thanks for our escape from the secret police in Iraq. But for His grace, we could have spent years in an Iraqi prison or been sentenced to death for our activities. After we finished sharing with Fouzi's parents about our experience in Baghdad, John Carling joined the family that he had spent time with before. Later in the week at church we shared our experience again and the result of their prayers for us while we were in Iraq.

OM Asks for a Return to England

After being in Lebanon for approximately a month, headquarters in England indicated that they wanted me and John to return to England. This was normal in terms of the overall ministry of Operation Mobilization. After evangelizing at a distant location, the movement was back toward Europe where we would attend a conference and regroup. Also, we could share with other students, our home churches and our supporting churches what God did in Turkey, Lebanon, Jordan, Israel, and Iraq.

John and I were saddened that we were going to leave our brother Fouzi in Lebanon and return to Europe. We had grown close and our hearts were bound together as a result of our fellowship and experiences; now two of us had to leave and go back to Europe.

A Stop in Istanbul: Avoiding the Secret Police

A Christian brother by the name of John Ferwerda who had been ministering for years in Lebanon and Jordan, was planning to drive back to Europe. It was arranged for me to get a ride with him from Lebanon back to Istanbul. Once there we would meet for a brief time with the Christians in Istanbul and connect with one of them who was thinking about traveling through the Scandinavian countries and going back to OM's headquarters in England. It was possible that I could get a ride to England with this person. The Lord gave us a safe trip from Lebanon back over the mountains through the same territory where I had hitchhiked and the same villages where I had been arrested with the other team members in Turkey.

We didn't get out of the car in those towns. We went through kind of fast, with our faces covered lest someone recognize us and arrest us for reentering the town. We were praying. We reminded ourselves that we were engaged in a spiritual warfare, and we had to exercise wisdom. We were careful and the Lord helped us. We got back to Istanbul and met with the team members confidentially at nighttime. We didn't want to be noticed by the police, draw attention to ourselves, or put the team members in jeopardy.

While we were in Istanbul this time, I got on a city bus very early in the morning, and I saw one of the secret policemen who had detained us at the train station the first time we came through the city. At first I tried to pretend that I didn't see him, but he was looking directly at me and the astounding thing was that he was smiling at me. He was the one who, when we were detained that first time, pulled me to the side, pointed to the color of his skin, pointed to the color of my skin, and assured me that everything was going to be okay. The official continued to smile at me on the bus and we went our separate ways without incident. I knew that God was continuing to protect me as He had so faithfully done and would continue to do.

An Adventuresome Hitchhike to England: God Covers Us

On our second day in Istanbul, I was faced with the prospect of finding a way back to England. The anticipated ride did not work out. Several options were discussed. There were buses leaving Istanbul going to Europe. Also, my Christian friends in Istanbul contacted a trucking company to see if I might be able to arrange a ride on one of their trucks going through Europe as far as Germany, but there was no space. I expressed a desire to hitchhike back. I really wanted to challenge myself to hitchhike back through Bulgaria, back through Yugoslavia, back through Italy, back through France, and into England. I had my sleeping bag, a small pouch to carry some sandwiches, and a bottle of water. My shoes were in good shape. I had a pair of denim-like trousers and a shirt that would be durable for several days.

So I was on my way. Once I got outside of Turkey, the Lord helped me to hitchhike all the way back to England. I did get some rides along the way, especially in France. Two African men gave me a ride through France to the English Channel. I learned from them, during the course of conversation, that they were businessmen who had been smuggling diamonds in France.

As I made my way back to England, I was so thankful as I scrolled back in my own mind and realized that there were no serious cases of illness during that time in the Middle East. I think now how an appendicitis attack really could have upset everything and altered all the plans, but that didn't happen. Some of the food that we ate could have caused problems but it did not. On the contrary, the food was delicious and none of us got a sick belly. The Spirit of God covered us and kept us well so that we could continue to do His will.

CHAPTER FOURTEEN

Customs and the Evangelical Call

Seasons of Underground Missionary Work

Once I arrived back in England and had a time of regrouping and praying and sharing, I was graciously challenged to prayerfully consider going to Yugoslavia to do ministry with a special team. We were operating in an underground posture, going in as tourists to do similar work that we'd done in other countries. It was in late summer of 1964 that I was asked to go with two other brothers to Yugoslavia.

When I first went to Europe to join one of the crusades, I really had in mind staying only a few weeks or a few months at most. But when I met so many college students—candidates for Ph.D.s in science and history and biochemistry and all the arts and professions—and these young people had experienced Christ as their personal Savior like myself and believed in the

Bible as the Word of God, I was challenged to remain with the group.

We examined the Bible critically in the light of secular history and historical documents. We found that the basic subject in the Bible from the beginning to the end was about Jesus Christ: He was sent to help man pull off what God had desired for him to pull off when God put him on earth. Some of these students were from so-called closed countries like Yugoslavia and Czechoslovakia, and one young man was from Russia. Their hearts' desire was that they might be used to spark a spiritual revolution in their own countries.

Trieste and the Yugoslavian Border

During that summer of 1964, we were encouraged to contact Dave Bormann, who was in the city of Trieste in the northeast corner of Italy, on the border with Yugoslavia. Dave Bormann was on one of the teams in Europe before he met his wife Lidia in Spain. They married and moved to Trieste because one of the countries we had been praying for was Yugoslavia. It was a Communist country that didn't allow any Christian activity. Our hearts' desire was to take the Gospel to the uttermost parts of the world as commanded by our Lord and Savior Jesus Christ.

One could sense the burden on Dave Bormann's heart. He knew that he could not do any open ministry in Yugoslavia, but he positioned himself and his family as near to the country as possible to prayerfully consider somehow, some way, of facilitating the Gospel message being distributed in Yugoslavia. He was able to make contact with two or three Christian families in Zagreb, Yugoslavia. These families had a long history of Christianity.

Depending on the danger and the political situation in their city, some of these families were open to contact with Christians outside the country, and some were not. In many cases, it was much too dangerous to extend an invitation to outside believers to come and do undercover ministry.

Dave Bormann had made contact with a Christian I will call Dr. B., who lived in Zagreb. Dr. B. was very excited about the prospect of a group of students who desired to make Christ known in his country. There was another Christian man in Yugoslavia, who I will call Mr. T.; at this time, he was a political official in a high office. He did not want his name to be associated with any foreigners because it might jeopardize his life or his position with the government.

Zagreb: The Strategic Edge of Blackness
The strategy, as in other closed countries, was for three of us to go as tourists to Zagreb during the summer months when thousands of people were allowed to visit a Communist county like Yugoslavia for the sake of bringing in money, but only if they came as tourists.

We planned to visit Yugoslavia's historical sites. There also were youth hostels where students who were hitchhiking or passing through the country could spend the night inexpensively. I was approached to prayerfully consider going to Yugoslavia mainly because I was an African American and had dark skin like some people already in Yugoslavia. It was a country that allowed Africans and others to study at their universities.

This idea was never verbally expressed, but I knew and everyone else knew of the opportunities that my dark skin offered in breaking down barriers where some of my white brothers were not able to penetrate a country with the Gospel.

At times I was ecstatic knowing that I had this particular advantage and could be a more effective witness for Jesus Christ.

One day while shopping in the local marketplace, we met two African students who were studying at the University of Zagreb. I was pleasantly surprised to see Africans in Yugoslavia. They were friendly and we began a lively conversation. They graciously invited us to come to their dorm on campus to meet more of their African friends.

We were happy to get such a personal invitation to visit campus and we went the following day. We met about fifteen of their friends and spent time having lunch and talking in the cafeteria and also in some of their dorms. The Lord allowed us to develop a close relationship during those few days we were in Yugoslavia and we went to the campus about three consecutive days at lunchtime.

Evangelizing amidst Communism

We learned a lot from the African students about their academic experience in Russia before coming to Yugoslavia. They were invited to Russia because at that time the Communist Party was making a strong bid to recruit the best and brightest among students as future leaders of their countries so that they could influence the youth toward communism.

These students were from different parts of Africa, but mainly from Sudan. The Russian government went as far as trying to persuade them to take young Russian women as wives. These were young women who were not just expected to be housewives cooking and cleaning; they were brilliant scientists, engineers, educators, lawyers, and politicians. We were also told that the Russian government had programmed the African students to learn Russian in six months before being sent to a Soviet bloc country like Yugoslavia. Even though Russian is an extremely difficult language, these students mastered it in six months and continued their communistic orientation in Yugoslavia.

As we talked with the group, we were amazed to discover that several born again Christians were in their midst. One was a Methodist pastor. They understood exactly what we were doing in sharing the Gospel, and they applauded and encouraged us. One of them said he had never seen a white and black Christian ministering together in a foreign country.

We understood that the reason the students seemed to have embraced communism was to take advantage of educational opportunities and technical skills, and the promises for material goods such as heavy equipment and tools they and their countrymen could use in their countries when they returned. Some of them shared with us confidentially that they had no intention of propagating Communism when they returned to their homelands. They told us that in a few years they would be leaders in their countries and they invited us to visit. Even though it appeared on the surface that all of these students had embraced communism, it became clear once we dialogued with them that some of them were simply using communism as a strategy to further the development of their own countries. The three days spent sharing and discussing issues with the African students was like a semester in Soviet-African politics.

Dr. B. invited us for a time of fellowship in his home. At lunch we sat and talked and had the opportunity to share with him some of the places we had visited. He encouraged us to come on Sunday and have fellowship with them at their underground church. Mr. T., the other Christian man we knew in Zagreb was also a part of this church; he realized that we had no political agenda and were not involved in activities of the

CIA or governmental agencies, and so he also invited us for lunch and a time of fellowship in his home several times.

Learning about Bakht Singh

At one of the underground church meetings an elderly lady came to me and asked if I knew Brother Bakht Singh, an indigenous minister in the nation of India. I mentioned that I'd never been to India. I told her that I'd heard his name but had never met him. She went on to relate to me how she had read one of his books and it had such a spiritual impact on her life, in terms of the joy she experienced and the encouragement to study God's Word, that she had several copies of the book mimeographed. At that time they didn't have computers and printers and all of that. The government was in control of the local press, but they did have mimeographing machines. She had Bakht Singh's book mimeographed and circulated in the underground church in Zagreb, and also in the city of Rueka.

With much excitement, she shared with me how the Christians also had experienced the same spiritual encouragement and joy from reading the book that she had shared with them by Bakht Singh.

Learning about Christians' Struggle amidst Repression

In Yugoslavia, as in other closed countries, when local Christians begin to sense that they can trust visiting Christians, they begin to open up and share with them about intimate problems in their church and their country which they normally wouldn't share with other people.

The people we met by going to the underground church told us that the government didn't really like Christians visiting and seeing the state of the country and the social situation, because in the past some Christians had returned home and disrespectfully criticized such governments' treatment of Christians. The result of this criticism was more repression of the church, and this, in turn, made it even more difficult for local people to live and function as Christians.

One of the things I experienced individually, apart from my other two brothers with me in Yugoslavia, was when Dr. B. and Mr. T. took me to surrounding villages where small groups of Christians lived. I wondered why they took me and not the other two brothers. When I asked my hosts they said, "Well, it would be better if they did not go because we are sure that the secret police are following us, and it is better if they are not with us."

It was true that the secret police really were following us. We couldn't easily tell who they were, but on a few occasions they were distinct in their activity, and Dr. B. and Mr. T. were understandably fearful that the OM brothers with me might get information, take it back to America and share it with reporters, and bring even more oppression upon the church.

I was acutely aware of the freedom we have in our own country and the danger these Christians experienced every day as they attempted to live their lives for Jesus Christ. My hosts also shared with me that there were Christian groups in the West that wanted to donate money to the small group of Christians in Yugoslavia, but their government made it very clear that this would not be allowed; any donations would be confiscated. It was discouraging to both the underground church and the church in the West that donations could not be received for the church in Yugoslavia.

Once when I was at Dave Bormann's home in Trieste, an OM couple I knew very well, Ron and Nan George, were in a serious automobile accident in September 1964. I had met Ron George when I first went to England before he met Nan, an American girl. They had gotten married. At this point, they were on their way back to Europe to regroup with those in Operation Mobilization who came together to prepare to go back out in the fall. But Nan had broken her neck in the accident and she wasn't able to travel by car, so they had to be flown to England. We were rejoicing that in spite of the seriousness, God protected Ron and Nan and they were not killed in the accident. They are still serving the Lord as of today.

During our week in Yugoslavia, I was locked out of the youth hostel one night. If you were not in the hostel by 11:00 they locked you out. I was late coming back, and was locked out. I tried to explain to the authorities that since it was only 10 minutes past the scheduled hour, I should not have gotten locked out. They simply said it was rules and regulations and they suggested I go to a hotel. I didn't have money to go to a hotel, but it was summertime and there was a beautiful park near the hostel that had benches. So I thought, well, I am used to roughing it; I've slept in the back of trucks in Mexico and throughout Europe, so I'll just sleep on the bench until morning.

To my surprise, after stretching out for a few minutes, a policeman came and reminded me that I had to sit up, I could not lie down. I was quite surprised and tried to explain what had happened, but he made it clear that if I did lie down, he would arrest me. So I sat up through the night, my head bobbing to the right and to the left and in front of me. But the Lord gave me grace. It wasn't too long before the sun came up, and at 8:00 I was able to return to the hostel, wash up and get ready for my day with the other two brothers.

Followed—Not in a Good Way

We were systematically followed in Yugoslavia. It got to the point that during our last few days in the country, we could actually look in the faces of the secret police and smile at them. We said good morning, good afternoon, and good evening. I was impressed that they were pleased to know that our activities were not political. We were not trying to bring down the government with our evangelizing, and they were just doing their jobs. They were really very friendly, and it could be that they were familiar with Christianity.

Before leaving Yugoslavia, the elderly sister I met previously asked that if I ever met Brother Bakht Singh, to please share with him her testimony about his book and how her life had been touched by his writing as she mimeographed and circulated it in the underground church. She asked me to plead with Brother Bakht Singh to consider coming to Yugoslavia and ministering to the Christians there. I told her that I wasn't sure that I would ever see him, but there was a possibility I might get a chance to go to India, and if I did, of course I would convey her message. She pronounced the Lord's blessing upon us as we left the country to return to Trieste in northeastern Italy and Brother Bormann's home. We reported to him about all that happened in Yugoslavia.

The Annual Conference in England

I returned to England from the spring 1964 tour in Turkey, Lebanon, and Iraq, and the brief excursion in Yugoslavia in summer 1964, and attended the annual conference. It was the practice of Operation Mobilization to have a conference in the fall, after the spring and summer campaigns in various countries. The purpose was to regroup and reunite with all the teams coming back from across Europe.

We rejoiced over what God had done, shared with one another what was learned, and encouraged each other about our shortcomings. We reaffirmed our commitment to prayer and the importance of reading the Bible and our dependence on the Spirit of God to use us to accomplish His work in the world.

Also, we prayed over a map of the world. There were so many parts of the world that were unreached. We prayed for direction as to where the Spirit of God wanted us to go. Often, as we looked at the map, we wept over the lost souls in the many unreached areas. It was heartbreaking to think of the millions of individuals who had never heard of Jesus Christ—living in darkness, knowing nothing about the peace and joy that only Christ could give, and facing an eternity without Christ.

We cried out to God, "Lord, show us how we can reach them with the Gospel." We had such a burning desire in our hearts to tell them. As relatively young people, we could have been frustrated and overwhelmed with the enormity of the task. We could have thrown up our hands and said, "Forget it; we'll go back to doing what we were doing before. We'll go back home and live an easy life and give up on this seemingly impossible task of reaching lost souls for Christ."

The Spirit of God would not allow us to do this.

Not knowing a country's native language was always a barrier to sharing the Gospel, and it was always our strategy to try to contact believers in the countries who spoke the language. In some of the closed countries, there were very few contacts to identify, and the fear of discovery and persecution made the evangelical call even more complicated.

PART THREE:

Extending Horizons and Heading Home

1965 - 1969

CHAPTER FIFTEEN

Prospects for a New Experience

A Year on the Road, Spreading the Gospel

As we prayed about the unreached masses of the world, the nation of India kept coming up. Operation Mobilization had a group of young men led by a team member named Greg Livingstone. He had gone to India several months before the annual conference of 1964, and his heart was challenged and burdened. After he came back to England for the conference, he cried out for help for the hundreds of millions of people in India, which is about one-third the size of the United States with over three times the population.

Greg and his wife Sally, together with Ron Penney were among those in the first of two OM groups to start the long overland journey to India from Europe. Others included Frank Dietz, who had been recruited from the Chicago area, and

Gordon Magney who had been at Wheaton College in Wheaton, Illinois and who had evangelized in Spain as well. They traveled in a Volkswagen to Turkey and then picked up a large Bedford truck, one of the trucks OM had purchased cheaply.

As a result of Greg Livingstone's cry for India, the challenge was presented. Who would prayerfully consider going to India for a year? India was a long way from England. There would be hardships. It was an expensive undertaking and at times there undoubtedly would be a shortage of money. As we were being fashioned into good soldiers of Jesus Christ, India was certainly an ideal place for this fashioning; it was an ideal place to exercise our faith.

The decision was made to send another small group to travel overland in two trucks to India. The women would be in one truck, and the men would be in another truck. These were used trucks that Operation Mobilization had purchased in England but they were in excellent shape. The trucks were a direct answer to prayer. We now had a reliable means of transportation to travel a tremendously long distance. Also, the trucks had space for Christian literature, canned food, sleeping bags, personal belongings, and extra parts for the truck such as tires.

We cried out to the Lord to help us to find an inexpensive way to get to India and He answered the prayer, as He always does. A verse which comes to my mind is Philippians 4:19:

> ...my God shall supply all your need according to his riches in glory by Christ Jesus.

Preparations for India

Some did not think that it was wise to drive used trucks across the continent to India. Indeed, some of the older missionaries among us had never considered such a thing and they thought the idea was ludicrous and crazy. I must admit that at times we did, too. More than once the thought occurred to us that some of our plans were not normal. But then we looked at the Word of God and realized that living by faith is not normal. We decided to take the word of the One who created the entire universe and believe that He would help us pull His will off for His glory.

After much prayer, I felt strongly that God wanted me to be a part of this second team going to India. And so I joined those of us who spent much time in preparation, gathering the specific items that we would need. I was to be one of the drivers; we established a route through England, France, Italy, Yugoslavia, Bulgaria, Turkey, Iran, Afghanistan, Pakistan, and then into India. Joining me in the front of the truck would be Ron Penney, a brother from England. He and I were forming a really close bond. I had met him a few months before. His mother had a grocery store, as mine did, and like many other students Ron heard the challenge to march out for Jesus Christ, and he did just that. He had gone to India with Greg Livingstone and the first group and now he was on his way back.

Also with us were Ray Eicher and Christa Fisher, who later married and became close friends of mine, and Sister DF, who later married PC, who was with the first group to go to India. DF and PC spent many years with Operation Mobilization and ended up laboring together in Afghanistan until Brother P's death a few years ago. As of this writing, DF is still in Afghanistan and God is greatly using her for His glory. Brother Mike and Audrey Wilshire also were on the team in the truck I was to drive.

As we had done to prepare for previous journeys, we bought cases of canned food from a discount food distributor, and we had cooking stoves as well as our sleeping bags, literature, and personal belongings. The men had a three-ton truck and the women had a four-ton truck. We called the women's truck Dennis the Menace because we could put in so much literature and other items, transport students in the back of that truck and still have plenty of room for the women. After we loaded the trucks, we had a time of prayer and headed south to Dover to cross the English Channel and go across the continent toward India.

The Long Drive to India

By God's grace, things went smoothly. We had funds for gasoline as we went toward India. Each truck had about three drivers, who took turns for three-, four-, or five-hour shifts, sleeping in the back afterward and then relieving each other. The shifts and places for going off-duty were very conducive for reading, relaxing, and studying, and for joining the other passengers in singing praises to the Lord and praying for the other teams heading to other parts of the world. As we passed through towns and villages, we observed people through a window we had cut in the side of the truck.

We were very careful as we drove through the closed Soviet bloc countries of Yugoslavia, Bulgaria, and Turkey. We drove straight through Turkey; we didn't stop except for gas. We didn't want to be detected and identified as the same group that had come through several months before distributing Christian literature. We certainly did not want to be detained and have our tour and plan completely interrupted by drawing attention to our group as we moved through Turkey.

We stopped in Iran where we had a small team already in place. Iran was not as hostile as Turkey at this time. The Shah of Iran was in power and he was liberal toward Christians compared to the period after the Ayatollah Khomeini came to power. OM was able to function fairly well in the nation of Iran. In Iran we were able to rest, bathe, and refresh ourselves. After spending several days in Iran, we prepared to move on toward the nation of India.

After we left Iran, the next country was Afghanistan, where we stopped for one evening in the city of Mashhad for a meal. Vendors served food along the road such as hot beans and rice which we felt was safe to eat.

God's Faithful Steering through the Khyber Pass

One of Afghanistan's main routes was the Khyber Pass, which linked this country with Pakistan. On each side of the Khyber Pass are high mountain ranges, and many of the people still used camels and donkeys for traveling. Many of them lived in little mud huts. It was an ancient scene in a modern world. Alexander the Great used this route when he moved his army through centuries ago. He took them through this mountainous road all the way down to Secunderabad in India, and afterward, it is said that Alexander sat down and wept because there were no other countries for him to conquer.

In the back of the truck when I was not driving, I had time to reflect on what was happening. It dawned on me that I was traveling the same route as Alexander the Great, not on a horse, not on a donkey, and not on an elephant, but in a used Bedford truck. It blew my mind. I was thankful that Jesus Christ, the faithful one, had burdened our hearts to even dare such a trip. As we planned to do, we left the Khyber Pass and drove south to

Karachi, Pakistan instead of driving directly south to Delhi in India because we wanted to visit a Christian family in Karachi.

By God's grace the trucks held up. There were one or two mechanics with the trucks in case there were problems. If something mechanical had gone seriously wrong, we knew we could send a message back to England and have the OM staff forward parts to a pre-established address, but none of that happened. We believed it was the result of prayer and God's faithfulness. We praised God as we moved toward the city of Karachi. Once there we looked up the Christian family, introduced ourselves, and freshened up a little by taking a bath before crossing over into India.

Populous Byways

As we made our way down through Afghanistan and Pakistan, I saw more people than I have ever seen in my life. We passed a continuous line of people walking along the side of the highway, carrying things on their backs, carrying things on carts, carrying things on their heads, carrying things for miles and miles and miles. Imagine millions of pedestrians along a major highway in the United States, walking for miles and miles—that is what we witnessed as we drove through Pakistan, right into northern India.

We had the names of many believers to contact once we got to Delhi. Before we left England we contacted a Bible school in Delhi and were confident that we would meet with those Christians. They would advise us, entertain us, and refresh us. Indeed, when we got to Delhi and met the Christians from the Bible school, they were encouraged to see young people attempting to believe in the Lord and making it as far as India. They were astounded at the stories that we shared with them, and they wore expressions of amazement as they looked at the

Bedford truck and realized it had made it all the way across Europe to India. A bit later, the truck holding the women's team arrived as well. This truck was delayed because it could not go under as many bridges as ours could, but by God's grace, both trucks made it to India.

The Long Journey Completed: Arrival in Delhi
Once we got to Delhi in India and regrouped, rested, and had a brief time of celebration, we plotted our course for going to the different cities in India. The advance team led by Greg Livingstone was eager to assign each of us to a team. There were usually ten to fifteen members on the team, including local Christians and Operation Mobilization members. At that time, most of our team activity was in and around Delhi in northern India. Each day we were encouraged to move out in a truck among the masses. Any direction we went, north, south, east, or west, we covered a distance of forty to fifty miles a day. Because of the density of the population, this meant that each day's trip took us to ten to fifteen villages.

When we got to a village, we would go to the center of the village and start speaking from the back of the truck. Local Christians would join us and translate what we said. Hundreds of people gathered around our truck. When they saw us coming, many who were at work in their fields would stop and come running toward the truck. After we spoke we handed out preprinted portions of the Bible, tracts, and information regarding Bible correspondence courses which we had stowed in the back of the truck. At each stop our interpreter encouraged our foreign members to give their testimony. After about an hour spent like this, we then drove on the larger roads and distributed literature to homes where individuals were not free to come to the center of their village. After about an hour we moved on to the next village, as instructed by our brothers from the local church.

On most mornings we covered five to seven villages. We had plenty of literature in the back of the truck. Often the local brothers would plan for the team to finish the last village of the morning near the home of a church member or good friend who had lunch prepared for the team. Because of the intense heat, the team rested for three or four hours from midday until twilight. Then we would start evangelizing villages again until dark. Often in the evening, the teams would have a meeting at the makeshift Operation Mobilization Center that Greg Livingstone and others had set up or in one of the villages where people desired an extended time for dialogue and question-and-answer sessions about the Bible.

CHAPTER SIXTEEN

India and Nepal: High, Far, and Wide for the Gospel

The Visa Challenge

The terrain from Delhi to Calcutta is called the Indus Valley. Most of our evangelism during our first few months in Delhi was along this valley, in the shadow of the Himalayan Mountains. Some of the major cities our team evangelized across northern India were Agra, Kanpur, Allahabad, Varanasi, Patna, and Calcutta. In Allahabad we stopped for a few hours at Allahabad Bible School. The school's principal, Rev. Rabe, was happy to meet such enthusiastic young people engaged in intense evangelism. He encouraged us greatly.

One situation that we faced during our travels in India was the constant requirement to renew our visas. The government refused to give long-term visas to missionaries and as such, we were in a somewhat troublesome category. The government's policy made it clear that the time for allowing or welcoming missionaries was over; it was felt that the people of India did not need foreign missionaries because they had their own religions of Hinduism, Buddhism, Islam, and several other minor religions. The government was very reluctant about giving long-term visas to anyone who would be coming to India for the first time for the sole purpose of being a missionary.

It was not very long before we realized that our visas would expire soon. We had only spent the first few weeks of our stay in North India. As the time drew near for me to renew my visa, the leaders thought that Kathmandu, Nepal would be the best option in terms of time, distance, and cost. Kathmandu, northeast of Delhi, was only a two-hour flight from Patna, India but the cost for the flight made air travel out of the question. The other option was by bus; its winding, steep route up a mountain would take an entire day. This was strategic, not only in terms of cost but also in terms of witnessing. Practically everyone on the bus would be interested in what this African American would be handing out during the trip.

Kathmandu, Nepal

Fortunately, Operation Mobilization had key contacts in Kathmandu, Nepal who could help facilitate visa renewals. Our bus left early in the morning and when we reached Kathmandu in the evening, our team was waiting for us with a few of the local believers. Most of the people in Nepal were an Asian-Chinese mixture. It was a wonderful experience to meet a group of Christians high in the mountains of Nepal.

We were not able to speak the Nepalese language, but there were interpreters in the fellowship, and we could tell from their smiles and hugs that they were warm and loving. Their affectionate greetings stimulated my heart to the point that I wanted to sing, dance, and shout "Hallelujah." I was thankful that God had given me a strong body to walk the hills of Kathmandu. As I did so, I realized that most of the people with whom I had contact had never seen a black man. Indeed, this is what the world needs in Christ and that is why we dedicated our lives to taking the Gospel to the ends of the earth: we felt that only the Gospel of Jesus Christ can foster the type of unity that our team was experiencing.

It only took a day to get my visa renewed in Nepal. After almost a week spending time with the Christian contacts in Kathmandu, I booked myself on the bus going back down the mountain to India.

Southern India and Bakht Singh's Leadership

When I returned from Nepal, George Verwer thought that I and a team could be used in southern India under the leadership of Bakht Singh, an indigenous church leader in that part of India. Actually, the assemblies that we had worked with in Delhi were also under Bakht Singh's leadership. Part of the decision to go to southern India involved a change of our literature. Unfortunately, the truck to which I was assigned was full of Hindi literature; we didn't want to take it south with us because most of the people in that region did not speak Hindi. They mainly spoke Tamil, Telugu, Malayalam, and several other languages. Colleagues encouraged us to leave the literature in Varanasi at the place of an evangelist named John and then proceed to Hyderabad, a city at the crossroads of North and

South India. Teams evangelizing in the North could continue to use the Hindi literature stored at Brother John's.

Meanwhile, we headed to Hyderabad, a metropolis where we were going to set up one of the main centers for the teams in India. We would be working in Hyderabad with Bakht Singh, a former Sikh from the Punjab. By the time Operation Mobilization came to India, Bakht Singh was a well-known evangelist all over India. He was greatly used of the Lord to establish over 300 New Testament-style Bible assemblies throughout India.

Assisting the Missionary Center in Hyderabad

Before OM began its efforts in India, Bakht Singh had already founded a missionary center, or compound in Hyderabad. He was a very godly man who knew the Word of God, held firmly to the biblical principles of the first century church, and preached and taught tirelessly the Gospel of Jesus Christ. Brother Bakht Singh and his coworkers planted probably the fastest growing evangelical churches in India. From 1940 to 1960, Brother Bakht Singh became very widely known in Europe, America, and Canada. He often spoke at Christian conventions in Toronto, Canada and in Chicago.

God gave wisdom to George Verwer, the leader of our group, to put the Operation Mobilization teams in subjection to such local leaders as Bakht Singh. We were grateful that Bakht Singh's group agreed to allow us to work alongside them. They did not have to do that. We learned that many groups had approached Bakht Singh and requested permission to minister with him; after much time in prayer, he would let them know that it would not be convenient for them to come.

One thing I did learn about Brother Bakht Singh was that everything he thought about doing, he prayed about it first. I also learned that all of his activity was bathed in prayer. Before he left for a meeting, he would pray. When he arrived at the meeting he would pray. During the meeting, he would pray, and when he returned from the meeting, he would pray and give thanks for answered prayer. If you were a part of the group going with him, you were a part of this frequent prayer.

I learned that there was great wisdom in the way that he ordered his life, seeking the Lord's guidance in every aspect of his life and ministry. He waited upon God in order to know God's specific plan. I was amazed at the great and mighty things that God accomplished through this humble, unassuming man. He was truly a man of prayer and faith, and he proved the faithfulness of God by his life because he trusted God for his every need. Many Christian missions, both then and now, make appeals for funds publically, but Bakht Singh made his needs known only to God. God honored his faith by providing for his every need throughout his life. God used him to do an amazing work in a country that was experiencing the threat of many challenges, including idol worship, overpopulation, and poverty. I am convinced that his life of faith was second to none. He is among the great heroes of faith like Hudson Taylor, George Mueller, D. L. Moody, and Billy Graham.

Bakht Singh Helped with Growth in the Lord

In light of the glorious ministry of this beloved man of God, I am deeply humbled and thankful for the opportunity to have been at his side all over India and nurtured by him spiritually. I count it an extreme privilege to have been allowed to minister side-by-side with him. I am so glad that through his personal encouragement I was able to grow in the Lord. This was another example of how God touched and orchestrated my life beyond description. To think that at one point, I was contemplating not even going to India! Not only did the Lord send me to India, He sent me to a ministry with a truly godly man and my life was deeply affected. I am forever thankful to my loving Lord and Savior, Jesus Christ.

George Verwer often spoke gratefully of the love and acceptance Bakht Singh had for Operation Mobilization. In other countries, when people heard about what was on our hearts about missions, they often were not too excited once they met the leadership and some of the students. They thought that we were still wet behind the ears and needed a lot more training before we even thought of going out to do foreign missions. We were greatly encouraged by the mission and church groups like those of Bakht Singh's.

Bakht Singh had heard about the testimony of these young people in Operation Mobilization and about how God was using them, and he was encouraged to see how God was working. I think he was most impressed with the simple way that the team exercised faith and the simple way we were living.

Ground-Level Missionaries

Even though we were foreigners, we did not operate like most missionaries. It was obvious that we did not have money to have cars shipped to us from foreign countries, and we did not live in enclosed compounds away from the people to whom we were supposed to minister. This was similar to Jesus Christ who was always accessible to the people. In many countries, the local people told us that they were not attracted to a group of people who claimed to have such a powerful life-changing message and yet stayed behind walls and fences instead of sharing that message. It did not seem logical to them. It did not seem sincere. We heard of some cases where missionaries were among the people for years and years and never learned to speak the language of the people, so there was no one-to-one communication. Is it any wonder, then, that there were no converts after many years?

Bakht Singh was a very wise man. He realized that the young people of OM were serious about their faith. I believe he must have thought: *My goodness, these young people have come this far overland, and they are living in the back of a truck. They are willing to sleep anywhere, they're willing to eat any type of food given to them and they're not insisting on their American diet to be served to them.*

It is an extra burden for the local Indian church when an American comes and he says he can't eat the food, he has to have certain dishes such as eggs and sausage, and the Indian host—being hospitable—has to go throughout the village or maybe a distance to get that specific type of food. This is to say nothing about the summertime when there's no ice cream around; yet some missionaries feel they can't function without it. In an active ministry such as that of Bakht Singh's, catering to foreigners' tastes can be an expensive, tiring drain and can slow down the faith work of a ministry like that of Bakht Singh's. It is no wonder that the local people rejoice when outsiders adapt to their food, customs, and ways of doing things.

God Kept Telling Me about Bakht Singh

The first time I heard about Brother Bakht Singh, I was a student at Moody Bible Institute. Late one Sunday evening, Billy Graham was speaking over the radio. He spoke from the passage in Acts 13:22 where David is called a "man after (God's) own heart". He mentioned that he had met a man named Bakht Singh in India, and he was impressed that Brother Bakht Singh was truly a man of God, a man after God's own heart. Dr. Graham commented that Western missionaries said that Brother Bakht Singh was a "lone wolf" who labored for the Lord all by himself. Seemingly, he wanted to work apart from missionaries and other church groups. But actually, as I discovered when I worked alongside him, he felt called of God to be active in an indigenous movement, training Indian Christians to reach their own. Before I went to bed that night, I prayed and asked God to make me a man after His own heart.

The second time I experienced the impact of Bakht Singh's ministry, I was still a student at Moody Bible Institute and I was sitting in the lobby of the men's dormitory when I saw a man from India going out of the building. For the rest of the day, I heard students discussing the anointed man of God who had spoken at chapel. It was quite unusual for me to miss chapel, but for some reason, I was not at this particular chapel service where Brother Bakht Singh spoke. The students were impressed with how thoroughly he knew the Bible and commented about his challenge to study the Bible, like no other book, for their entire lives.

The third time I heard about Brother Bakht Singh was in Beirut, Lebanon, with Fouzi Ayoub and the Operation Mobilization team. Pastor Bulos Haddad of the First Baptist Church in Lebanon asked me if I had ever met Bakht Singh of India. I told him that I had heard of him, and he began to share with me how the Lord had sent Brother Bakht Singh to Lebanon to minister to them on two different occasions and God had used him mightily in their midst.

The fourth time I heard of Brother Bakht Singh was in Zagreb, Yugoslavia. I had gone to Yugoslavia with two other brothers to spy out the land for future evangelistic invasions; Yugoslavia was then under Communistic control. We had the names of certain Christians, and we visited the only church in the city that the Communists allowed to function. After the church service one Sunday, an elderly sister came to me and asked if I knew of Bakht Singh of India. I told her that I had heard of him but had never met him in person. I mentioned that I was hoping to visit India in a few months, and was looking forward to meeting him. With tears in her eyes, she told me that she had read one of his books, and that her heart was deeply blessed. She shared how difficult it was to obtain Christian material under Communist rule; she had made mimeographed copies of Bakht Singh's book and circulated them secretly to believers in the underground church. At another meeting, she pleaded with me to ask Brother Bakht Singh to please prayerfully consider coming to Yugoslavia.

Later, while in Hyderabad, India, I did indeed have the opportunity during early morning devotions to share this woman's request with Bakht Singh. I told him about my visit to Yugoslavia, the impact his book made on the Christians and their deep desire for him to come to minister to them. At the time, he simply said that he would pray about it. A few months later, Brother Bakht Singh left his missionary compound in Hyderabad, India for meetings in the United States and Europe. It was not until he returned to India that I discovered that on the way back to India, he made a stopover in Yugoslavia. He shared about the blessed time of ministry he had among the believers in Yugoslavia. He told us that the Yugoslavian believers were warm and loving and rejoiced greatly because of his visit. He said that the Communist government, in an unusual move, had not only granted him a visa, but had also given him complete freedom to speak whenever and wherever he liked. Each meeting was so full that the believers were encouraged to stand in order to maximize the space. Brother

Bakht Singh was greatly used in that country to declare that Jesus Christ is the Savior of the world.

A Truck Driver in Hebron

When Brother Bakht Singh visited Yugoslavia, I had only been in India for about five months. Fortunately, I was assigned to the Operation Mobilization team ministering in Andhra Pradesh, in Hyderabad at "Hebron," the main assembly and compound in India where Brother Bakht Singh stayed, and the base from which he prayerfully directed all of the assemblies in India. I was privileged to be asked to stay at Hebron, and to work and travel with the OM team out of Hebron.

Each morning we were encouraged to go out from Hebron with the Indian brothers for open-air ministry. The used trucks which miraculously and only by the grace of God made it across the continent, continued to function in India. While in Hebron I was responsible for driving the OM truck assigned to Hebron. Not only did we use this particular truck to distribute tons of literature in different sections of Hyderabad, but we also drove it to hundreds of villages in the surrounding areas.

Each season, Brother Bakht Singh and the leaders at Hebron would plan crusades in other parts of India, from Kashmir in the North to Kerala in the South. We traveled the entire length and breadth of India, distributing thousands upon thousands of pieces of literature, Bibles, New Testaments, Gospel portions, and tracts in the language of the people of the region. Sometimes, there were as many as forty people in the front, back, and sides of the truck. The sisters would sit on one side of the truck, and the brothers would sit on the opposite side. This was truly a "church on the move."

In each village or city we visited, we held Gospel meetings in the street, or in the home of a local believer. This is how many assemblies were started under the leadership of Bakht Singh, this great man of God. He used hundreds of Bible verses, which he had memorized, in a single sermon. He was a prayer warrior who often spent whole nights on his knees in prayer, and he was a man of tremendous simple faith, who believed God and took Him at His word. Under his leadership, everything the team did was bathed in prayer. On all of the crusades, and for four years, Brother Bakht Singh kept me close at his side.

We were helped greatly by the discipline in devotions, prayer, and study of the Scriptures. Brother Bakht Singh led by example. He was up at five o'clock in the morning for family devotions. On the compound at Hebron, there were young men in training for the ministry and Bakht Singh expected them to come to each morning's family devotions during which he gave a devotional thought. Afterward there would be a brief breakfast, and the team would go out to evangelize the people. There was an advantage in getting started early, when it was relatively cool. Late in the afternoon, if it was summer, the temperatures would climb to 100, 110, 115 degrees; it was wise to avoid those times in the day for very much activity.

Distributing Tracts among Thousands and Thousands

When we went out in the morning in the truck, the country is so densely populated that you could go to one portion of a city such as Hyderabad or Secunderabad, which is next to Hyderabad, and you could have an open-air meeting with preaching and passing out Gospel literature and Gospel packets to thousands of people passing right before you. Or, you could stay there for an hour or two, go to another part of the city and distribute literature to thousands more. At first, it was almost unbelievable to see so many people. It was like a huge sea: swarms of people seemed to come out of thin air and out of the ground. I had never seen so many people at one time. The population of India was really something to experience. At the time, I think India had a population of over 650 million people. Now over a billion people are in India. In Hyderabad, where the main language was Telugu, we had Gospel portions, Bibles, tracts, and correspondence courses to pass out to people who had never seen such literature about the Bible in their language. Day after day we went to different parts of the city distributing thousands of pieces of literature and holding open-air meetings where individuals preached and gave their personal testimony.

I had the opportunity to do that countless times. After we thoroughly hit the city for several days, we went to the surrounding areas. We would go to one village, and cover the whole village in about an hour, bombarding it with literature. As we did so we included information about correspondence courses that individuals could write in and receive so that they could study the Bible at home. We also included addresses where they could come to any of the assemblies under the administration of Bakht Singh and the believers, and learn more about the Word of God. The advantage of going in the morning, besides avoidance of extreme heat, is that we could reach many of the people before they went to the fields. The people lived in small mud huts and they went to the fields about six o'clock in the morning when it was cool.

Ministry in the Fields and Villages

In many cases we would drive on the roads in the fields and preach. Many gladly received a portion of the Word to take home, read, and study. Often we planned a one- or two-day journey where we extended the ministry to villages in and around Hyderabad, sometimes going as far as 50 or 55 miles away in order to reach the masses. In each village we entered, the people would rush to see what this truck had to offer with these people in it. Some would stop their work and come in from the field with their shovels in their hands to see what was being given out, which was mainly a free Gospel booklet. Since the people were curious and came to us, we didn't have to go down every little footpath and road to reach a village. Practically the entire village came to see our big Bedford truck, which to them might have looked like a vehicle from outer space. It certainly drew the people.

Using a battery-powered speaker at our disposal, a local brother would present the Gospel in their language; there was an interpreter for me. Many people were shocked and surprised to see and hear this African American all the way from the U.S. coming to visit them in their little, seemingly insignificant village in India. After spending 30 minutes in a village with the truck surrounded by local people and us passing out hundreds of pieces of literature as fast as we could, the local brother explained to them in their language what the literature was about. If the literature was a correspondence course, the team provided details about the course, such as where people could send away for it and where they could contact believers in local assemblies.

That was the other beautiful thing about our relationship with Brother Bakht Singh. We could direct people to local assemblies, no matter where we were, and not to America or to some foreign missionary center.

When I arrived in Hyderabad with the team, one of the leading Operation Mobilization brothers was Brother Peter Durham from South Africa. He and I often talked about our relationship in the Lord. Here we were ministering together, waging war in Jesus' name, and he came from a society where blacks and whites were almost not even allowed to look at each other, where there was an unbelievable amount of hostility between blacks and whites and yet, because of Jesus, we loved each other.

Enrolling at Allahabad Bible College

We continued to face the problem of needing to renew our visas every few months. If Operation Mobilization team members wanted to stay in India, each member had to go outside the country to renew his or her visa every three months. This was extremely expensive, so we were encouraged to prayerfully consider enrolling in a local Bible college or secular university as students. In most cases, the government found favor with that strategy because we'd have to pay the school for room and board (and therefore an Indian agency or organization obtained money from us "outsiders") and while we were students we would not officially be missionaries.

I thought of the Bible school in Allahabad, India. The principal of that school, Reverend Rabe, had previously encouraged us to apply to study there. He knew of Operation Mobilization's vision and was trying to help us stay in the country. So I applied and was accepted to study at Allahabad Bible College for one year, in 1965-1966. I took courses in Hinduism, which was extremely helpful, Islam, cultural studies about India, and the Christian church in India. After Jesus rose again, He told His disciples in Acts 1:8:

> But you will receive power when the Holy Spirit comes on you; and ye shall be witnesses unto me both in Jerusalem, and in all Judea and in Samaria, and to the uttermost parts of the earth.

In an Apostle's Footsteps

After the Holy Spirit descended upon the disciples, they blasted the Gospel throughout the earth and turned the world upside down. It is believed that the apostle Thomas brought the Gospel to India. At the seminary in Allahabad, I learned that there are two theories concerning how Thomas came into India. One theory says that he came through the Khyber Pass, through Pakistan; the other theory says that he went first to Kerala in southern India. Because of the schools established by the Christians and the high literacy rate, the theory of the apostle's southern route has more credibility than the northern route theory.

Even today, Kerala is the most literate state in India. Most of India's political and government officials are from Kerala, and they routinely speak English in addition to their native dialect. A famous monument to Christian history in India is St. Francis Church in Kerala's Fort Cochin. Originally built in 1503, it is the oldest European church in India. Over the centuries, the church was controlled by the Portuguese, Italians, Dutch, and the British. The Franciscans, the order founded by St. Frances of Assisi, controlled the church for more than a century. The literacy rate and quality of life in this part of India are a direct result of the influence of Christianity.

Rewards of Study at Allahabad

One of the blessings of studying at Allahabad Bible Seminary was that during the summer months I was allowed to travel around India and learn about the culture and people. At Allahabad we had contact with a pastor named John, who lived in Varanasi. The city of Varanasi is the center of an extremely important Hindu pilgrimage called the Kumbh Mela which is held every twelve years. Millions of Indians come from all over

India and the world for the special religious events, including dipping in the Ganges River in order to be, according to Hindu belief, cleansed from sin.

When I finished my courses at the Allahabad Seminary, I wrote to Brother Bakht Singh and asked him if he would be gracious enough to allow me to come back to Hyderabad and more or less enroll in "assembly-ology." This was a somewhat humorous way of expressing the importance of what I would learn while at Hebron, Bakht Singh's base, but he understood exactly what I meant. He graciously invited me to return to Hebron, with George Verwer's permission, to continue the ministry. After rejoining the team, I jumped in with both feet. The team was still immersed in its evangelism.

The Bonds with OM and Bakht Singh

One of the great blessings and opportunities that came with the fellowship with Bakht Singh and the local assemblies was the loving care for Operation Mobilization team members. They always readied a place for us to sleep and wash our bodies. They prepared food for us morning, noon, and night. The believers at Hebron washed and pressed our clothing, and local believers in the area took it upon themselves to take care of the trucks' mechanical aspects. This included cleaning, oil changes, and tire repairs. The love and fellowship that we experienced from Bakht Singh's group was an amazing blessing to each of us.

In addition to his hospitality, Brother Bakht Singh was a tremendous strategist in terms of planning outreach evangelism, not only in Hyderabad, but in many cities all over India. He arranged meetings in major, faraway cities like Vijayawada, Solapur, and Bombay (now Mumbai). When such meetings were planned, Bakht Singh would have us transport him and the other believers to the specific location. By using our trucks it saved him and the local assemblies thousands of dollars (rupees, in Indian money) on plane and train fare for himself and the people he often took with him. We were also able to provide great help to his ministry by transporting their personal items, such as suitcases and hundreds of pounds of literature. Some of this literature was later sold by the assemblies to help support their ministries.

When we spent a few days in Vijayawada, we branched out and covered the cities of Guntur, Eluru, Rajahmundry, Terali, and Madras, which is on India's extreme southeast coast. While spending a few days in Madras, we hit the cities of Vellore (where one of India's major medical schools is located), Ambur, Kolar Goldfields, Tiruppattur, Chittoor, and Tirupati. Amazingly, as we traveled the highway to the cities and villages there was always a constant stream of people walking along the highway. There were small donkeys, loaded down, small carts carrying people, and people carrying their personal belongings on their heads. I had to drive very carefully and slowly.

A Distinction in India: Color

One of the factors that kept me greatly energized was I saw a great many people who were black like me. I had never been in a country where 90 percent of the people were black-skinned like me. This was not the case in Spain, Italy, France, or England. The people in Iraq, Lebanon, and Syria came close in skin tone, but the people in India were my color. It wasn't until years later that I realized the positive, affirming effects of this on me.

The believers traveling with Brother Bakht Singh from place to place in the truck were simply ecstatic. They were experiencing different parts of India and learning, as were the OM team members, so much about the different dialects and customs in other parts of India. The teams of women, transported separately, came along so that they could minister to women. Everyone was clearly excited to get up each day and go from place to place, experiencing a warm and loving reception from the believers. There was opposition also, of course, but during this period Hindu extremists were not as active as they are in India today. Also, we were moving fast. Often we were gone from an area before opposition could gather.

The OM Trucks and Team Members Traverse India

We moved fast and we covered a lot of ground. We found ourselves led to go to Bangalore, a major city from which we went to the cities of Mysore, Tiptur, Tumkur, and Hassan. We drove on to another major city farther south, Madurai, and from there we went to Viruduragar, Rajapalaiyam, and Pudukkottai. We then went farther east to the city of Mangalore, and farther south to the city of Trivandrum. By God's grace, other Operation Mobilization teams in India were carrying on the same type of spiritual warfare with their used Bedford trucks. It was obvious that God had given George Verwer great wisdom and vision when it came to the trucks. We had supporters who were mechanics stationed to the North in Delhi. If the trucks encountered any serious mechanical problems we were to send a telegram or make a phone call and soon the mechanic was on his way in another vehicle or by plane to take care of the problem.

Once I'd finished the year at Allahabad Bible School and rejoined the team at Hebron, time whizzed by, especially with all of the travel throughout India, and again I needed to renew my visa. Brother Bakht Singh knew about it, and fortunately, there were men in the assembly in Hyderabad who worked in the immigration office. I remember one dear brother, George

Butt, an astute government official. His two sisters were medical doctors. He and I grew close in the Lord.

Concerning my visa, he said, "Brother, don't worry about anything. The Lord has you covered. We will take your visa and passport to check and see if you can get an extension since you work among the assemblies. You should not have to interrupt your work to go outside the country." Brother Butt took my passport one day and when he came back from the immigration office, I had a four-year visa for India.

I was jumping and shouting, "Hallelujah, thank You, Lord!!!" I no longer had to go outside the country every three months to request a renewal for my visa. This was truly in the plan of God because as things worked out, I was in India four of the nearly eight years I was overseas with Operation Mobilization.

Sky-High in the Himalayas: Kalimpong

Brother Bakht Singh's ministry was not only confined to the main continent; it also extended to Kalimpong, a city high up in the Himalayan Mountains. It borders Nepal, which in turn borders China, and a group of believers in Kalimpong encouraged Bakht Singh to come every year. In the early days of his ministry he was invited to those areas, and his ministry was so fruitful, so encouraging, that people begged Brother Bakht Singh to come back.

In 1968, I was encouraged to come with the team to Kalimpong. What an experience! Before we left Hebron, I was informed that we would be taking a train to Calcutta, and then taking another train to Kalimpong, high up in the Himalayans. I did not say anything, but I wondered how in the world a train could go up the Himalayan Mountains, which have a very high elevation. Being a student and new in the country, I just wanted to wait to see how it would happen.

When we got to Calcutta, I saw that there was a system of small trains that looked like big toy trains. Relatively few people could fit in each coach; one coach had barely enough room to hold the approximately ten brothers and sisters in our group. The train reminded me of the miniature Lionel trains my father bought for me when I was a little boy of about 8. I can remember lying on the floor for hours as my train ran around and around on the track on the floor of our home. I was privileged to have such a toy in our home in the ghetto community where we lived, and I played with it until my knees were sore. It was hard to obey my father when he told me to stop playing with my train and go to bed.

When our train in Calcutta started, the "chug, chug, chug" of its engine echoed in the valley, and it finally began to wind its way up into the Himalayans toward Kalimpong. We left early in the morning and after about eight hours we reached a plateau. It was a beautiful day. All along the mountain and as far down the valley as we could see, there was green foliage. We could see Nepal, a small country that exists on one of the Himalayan peaks.

As we reached the heights of the Himalayan Mountains, with the hypnotic views of surrounding valleys, we could look over into China to the North, Burma (now called Myanmar) to the East, and Kathmandu, Nepal to the West. When we arrived in Kalimpong, the believers were waiting for us and greeted us warmly and affectionately. Even though it is in India, the people in Kalimpong had Chinese features, an indication of the proximity of Nepal to China. I was so happy to meet these believers. I found it difficult at times to put into words what I was experiencing as I fellowshipped with groups like these beloved Christians. I was not able to speak their language, but we had an interpreter in our group and we communicated a lot with looks, smiles, and hugs. Needless to say, most of them had never seen an African American dark-skinned man.

An Egalitarian Approach to Ministry

The believers in Kalimpong had a week's worth of meetings planned. Brother Bakht Singh was the main speaker for the meetings, but he always took up to four other brothers to speak and share in the ministry. He would ask some of the leaders from the assemblies in Madras, Bangalore, Mumbai (formerly Bombay), Delhi, Calcutta, or Hyderabad to come along. This was one of the beautiful things about his ministry; he did not try to dominate the meetings. He would lovingly encourage leaders from other areas to give a word from their perspective, to share what God had laid on their hearts, and to burden the believers to pray for them in their corner of the vineyard. Some of these leaders had studied under Bakht Singh at Hebron and been sent to other areas. Some were truly gifted in what some call "breaking the bread of life," that is, speaking and teaching from the Bible. Their gift for expounding on the Word of God in a clear and powerful way was no doubt from the Spirit of God.

When I was in Kalimpong, I met some young men who were students at a college in Burma. They had come a long way to take part in the meetings. I was encouraged to know that in an area where there were very few Christians, God had planted seeds in the lives of young believers to carry the flame to those dark areas where Jesus Christ was not known.

We were encouraged to get up early in the mornings and go out and distribute literature and reach people in the paths, roads, and winding routes in the mountain. After the morning meetings and outreach, we would come back, have something to eat, and take a short rest. It was not as hot in the Himalayan Mountains as it was in the lowlands, so we did not have to take as much rest from the heat of the day. We were back out in the streets early in the afternoon, taking every opportunity to reach these people in this breathtakingly beautiful part of the country.

Giving Testimony Outdoors

When we stopped to give testimony an entire congregation would gather at key sections where several roads met. I was encouraged to give my personal testimony and preach the Gospel of our Lord and Savior Jesus Christ as a brother translated for me. At times I was gripped with the fact that here I was, an African American reared in the ghetto of Cincinnati, Ohio and saved in Fairbanks, Alaska, preaching high up in the great Himalayan Mountains. The thought was almost overwhelming and my heart was in a constant state of praise and thanksgiving.

In the open-air meetings on the streets, members of the group would stand on the corners and pass out Gospel literature. Many people took the literature, stopped and read it, and then they stood at a distance and just observed the ones who were passing it out. They had not experienced individuals declaring themselves to be Christians, and they were curious. Many of them engaged the brothers and sisters in conversation who could speak the language from the local church. And sure enough, in the evenings when the meetings were held, many of those same people came to the meetings and sat and listened to the glorious Gospel of Jesus Christ.

After the street meetings each morning, we invited all who stopped for the open-air meeting to come to the local church for the main gathering each evening. There was never an evening meeting where there was not at least one person who gave his or her life to the Lord. This in itself was worth the whole climb into the mountains. I was thankful that the Lord had given me a strong body and legs so that I could walk the paths of the Himalayas. I will never forget the joy I experienced.

The local church was thankful that we came and helped them with evangelism because they did not have the necessary manpower. They were involved in other things at the church, and by God's grace, those of us who were visiting were able to relieve them of some of their daily chores that were keeping them from going out for evangelism. That was a part of OM and Bakht Singh's strategy.

With the visitors from Bakht Singh's assembly, and the one or two of us from Operation Mobilization, we would go out, singing as we went and playing musical instruments such as a portable harmonium, a small organ. Some of the believers had other instruments of metal, which they would pluck or beat on, and we created a joyous, harmonious sound as we went to the center of the city of Kalimpong to preach the Gospel. When people saw these foreigners, including an African American, they came by the hundreds and we gave loving invitations to all to attend the meetings, held in the home of local Christians. The home was a concrete building, well structured, with a first and second floor. There were spacious areas for chairs to be arranged, and if there was an overflow, mats were placed around the building where people would sit and listen. A loudspeaker or megaphone was used so everyone could hear the messages.

A Multi-Cultural Seminar on Wheels

On the third day when we were in Kalimpong, we went to a place where water was coming out of the side of the mountains through the rocks. The men went to one area and the women went to another. The water created a stream which flowed down the mountains and as this fresh, clear water came through the rocks, we took off our clothes down to our underwear and cleansed our bodies. It was a nice, cool morning in the mountains and the experience was so refreshing. Not only were our bodies clean, but the believers at the assemblies took it upon themselves to wash and iron all of our clothes. It was a humbling experience being in the midst of those loving Christians.

One interesting aspect of the ministry was talking with people of different religions, including Hindus, Buddhists, and Muslims. They had many questions. Many of the local Christians were astute in the different Asiatic languages and religions, even more so than some seminarians. These believers lived with the people and rubbed shoulders with those who practiced these religions; they knew the history of their faiths and their practices, and they were able to use relevant and urbane illustrations in conveying the Gospel. The entire experience was a seminar on wheels to me. I was learning an incredible amount, much more than in an hour's introduction in a Bible college. I had never been offered a course with this type of in-depth information about the Hindu, Buddhist, and Muslim religions; I was witnessing people practicing their beliefs and going to their temples, ashrams, and mosques.

CHAPTER SEVENTEEN

Crisis and Compassion

Kalimpong: A Naturally Beautiful Seminar

We were living in a house that was erected, as were many nearby houses, on the side of a mountain. The pass leading to the house was very narrow. You could get there in a very small car, but in order for one car to pass, the other one would have to pull off the side of the road somewhere, or into a crevice. Mostly, the narrow road was for pedestrians, carts, and donkeys.

As we looked out from the front of the house, we faced a deep valley, about 25 miles across. All along the side of the mountain above the valley you could see hundreds of small homes. They were like dots along the ridge of the mountain. Since this was a steep, elevated mountain, it was not possible to build large homes, so the people built small homes that clung to the side to the mountain, with narrow paths and walkways.

Because of the beauty and the cool temperature, areas in Kalimpong were highly sought after by vacationers in that part of the world. On sunny days, it was so beautiful. The mountains were green, and the rooftops of the houses were different colors such as green, red, brown, and orange, making for a picturesque scene. Surrounding the homes were rice paddies, low-lying areas where people grew their own food on the mountainsides. That's how the people survived, by the millions, and seeing this about people we knew practically nothing about, was another grand seminar for me.

Don't Put Off Salvation

In the evening of about the fourth day while we were in Kalimpong, a terrible catastrophe happened. It got very cloudy in the mountains. The clouds were hanging very low and it began to rain as it had the previous three days, but people came to our regularly scheduled meeting. Actually, it had rained, off and on, for three full days, but the meeting was being conducted as usual, and the house was full. That evening it began to rain, and rain, and rain, and rain, and rain. Even though it rained so heavily, the people were alerted early enough so they brought their umbrellas, raincoats, and ponchos, and they stayed until the meeting was over, around 11:00 pm.

At about 12:00 midnight, we heard a loud boom of thunder, a roar in which everything shook, and then it became calm. Everyone, including the local people, thought that whatever happened, it was just thunder, thunder with vibrations. We really didn't know what happened. We went to bed and slept. We were guests and we didn't want to show any signs of fear.

But in the early morning hours we heard crying. People were weeping and telling each other about the catastrophe that had taken place overnight. There had been an earthquake and massive mudslides. The local people told us that since the Himalayan Mountains were comprised mostly of soft dirt, some rock, but mostly dirt, after the hours of rain, when the earthquake happened, the mountain gave way. Homes and people simply slid down the mountainside and were buried in the massive mudslides.

When we heard about the earthquake, we got dressed and went as a group up and down the road outside the house. We found out that homes near where we were staying were covered with mud. Some of the people who had thought about coming to the meeting, and didn't come, lived in homes that were destroyed; the people were buried inside their houses by the mudslides.

I thought about the message. A few nights before at a meeting, the speaker lovingly encouraged people to not put off salvation. He reminded everyone that it was important to embrace salvation that day because we never know what is going to happen. As God reminds us in II Corinthians 6:2:

> ...now is the accepted time; behold, now is the day of salvation.

It reminded me of when I was in Alaska and I heard the Gospel message for the first time. It was so clear, and I was challenged with the issue of deciding whether to accept Jesus Christ but I had a desire to put it off. I was thinking that I would do it next week, maybe next Sunday when I would have on a suit and tie. I'm thankful that God did not allow me to put it off. Had I put it off, it could be that I would not have been in India, or to all the other countries where the Lord allowed me to go and bear testimony for Him.

Natural Beauty Contrasts with Devastation

I was stunned as I stood on our side of the valley, looked across at the other side, and saw that the hundreds of beautiful homes I had seen before were gone. The little homes with the orange, green, red, and brown rooftops were gone! We walked for hundreds of yards. There were homes buried in mud with relatives digging frantically with their hands trying to get their relatives out. We pitched in, of course, with what help we could.

All around where we were staying, mudslides had washed homes down the mountain. We were thankful and humbled that the house where we were staying was not washed away by a massive mudslide. Within hundreds of feet of that house, to the left, to the right, to the North and South of us, houses had been taken away. We could easily have been buried by a mudslide and we had no explanation other than the saving hand of our Lord and Savior Jesus Christ.

As we surveyed the damage we went to a site on the mountain where we had seen the rice paddies. Fortunately, none of them seemed to have been affected. Thousands of rows of them were along the mountain, still in place. This suggested that at least there was the possibility of farming and crops to come for the people.

A more serious concern and one of our first questions was that the Papacy Bridge, the main bridge over the valley from the mountainside which connects upper Kalimpong to the lowlands of India, had been wiped out. Once word reached us that the bridge was gone, our next question was: "How will we get back down to the lowlands of India?" I must admit I wasn't nervous at this particular time because I was taking my cues from the local believers and listening to what they were saying, especially Brother Bakht Singh. Truly a man of God, he was rattled by nothing. We were rejoicing that we were alive; there was no level of anxiety at all.

The enormity of the situation was just dawning on us, and we were simply trying to help the people around us. Some of us took shovels for a few hours or so and tried to help those whose homes had been buried in mud. Others tried to comfort ones whose homes had been wiped off the mountain. The local assembly invited the community to come for food, drink, prayer, and encouragement. We spent much time in prayer that day, in addition to helping dig people out as we gave comfort and encouragement. Lunch that day came and went without any of the ministry team eating. We were just out trying to help.

We came back to the house in the early afternoon, tired, burdened for the situation and crying. It was an experience I'll never forget. Here we were, by God's grace, conducting these meetings and something like this happened. I was reminded that I had told God in Alaska that I would be willing to serve Him by life or by death, and I had narrowly escaped death. So many of the local believers had not escaped death, but of course they were with the Lord. The problem was with the thousands who had died who did not know the Lord Jesus as their personal Savior. Experiencing this catastrophe caused me to see afresh the urgency of winning the lost to Christ.

Staying to Help

Once everyone discovered that the Papacy Bridge was out, the concern was how to get down the mountains. With injuries, supplies, and safety becoming a growing concern, we knew there would have to be an evacuation. There were other people in the area, of course, who were from the lower part of India, and they were worried, too. What exit route was possible for us? We were encouraged when we learned that the Indian government was sending helicopters to Kalimpong to airlift people out. Brother Bakht Singh and the leaders thought about it and prayed about it, and sure enough the helicopters came the following day. There was a military helipad that normally was for bringing military supplies. Since this was an emergency, the government was not only engaging military aircraft, but was making the helipad accessible to civilians.

The day the helicopters came, we watched excitedly as two of them came up the valley. The pilots came out and greeted the people who were stranded, letting them know that they were happy to come to help get the people out. OM team members and those in Brother Bakht Singh's group helped people carry their luggage to the helipad and load up their suitcases. We filled the helicopter with all the bags we had brought with us, and I jumped out, to be with the other believers.

Some of the people watching me probably thought that since I was stranded and undoubtedly wanted to get out, surely I would be leaving on the helicopter. They wore looks of surprise when I jumped out of the helicopter. They asked me, "What are you doing? Are you staying? You are not going to take advantage of this opportunity to get out?"

I made it clear that I was with the local people: we were in this together, by life or by death. And of course they were touched by that. It wasn't like I was angry that I had come to this nation and this disaster had occurred. Like everyone else in the situation I was concerned. But I wasn't taking out my anxiety on the local people, blaming them for what happened and expressing some of the foolishness that some foreigners have been known to express. No, I was just happy for another day given by Jesus Christ to live for His glory and to do whatever He had in mind for me to do.

The Slow, Hard Journey to Calcutta

Information came to us about another exit, a back road from Kalimpong all the way down to the mainland of India. It was actually a secret military road that had been constructed in case of an invasion from China. It was a steep road and fortunately it was not affected by the earthquake and mudslides so it was useable. There were several in our group apart from those of us from Bakht Singh's compound who had come to the Kalimpong meetings, and they were eager to get back to the lower elevations of India.

Two days after their request, Brother Bakht Singh and the other believers received permission from the government to use the emergency back road. We were encouraged to get up early in the morning and begin walking toward the road, and then walking down the road to another section that was more accessible by buses. Many of the roads up to that point had been washed out. As we walked, we saw that the government had tractors staged all along the roads, parked for emergencies. We learned that there were often mudslides in the mountains, and the government had tractors set up to clear a path. As we began our journey, slowly but surely, down the mountainside, we saw that the tractors had pushed away most of the mud that had slid over the road at that point, and we just walked directly ahead.

After several hours of making our way down the mountain, we reached a location where we were able to get public transport. At that point there were many transportation agencies lined up to help people coming out of the mountains. We boarded a bus for the rest of the way out of the mountains. As we looked back on and spoke about that experience, our hearts were full of praise. We were thankful for the Christians in Kalimpong, for their continued faith, for their determination to live for God's glory and witness to the people in their area. We were determined to encourage their hearts and help them in any way possible as they carried on the Gospel ministry for our Lord and Savior, Jesus Christ.

Arriving in Calcutta, Returning to Hebron

We made our way to Calcutta, with its teeming millions, where we could get connections to all parts of India. Reservations were made for Brother Bakht Singh and those of us from Hebron returning to Hyderabad. We were going back with excitement because we knew that the believers had been praying for us at Hyderabad. We knew that the trucks were there, as was our literature; we also knew that others in OM were making plans for us to reassume our evangelism as soon as we hit the ground in Hyderabad.

Indeed, once we got back to Hyderabad, we initiated our same activities for outreach. There were groups of believers in many cities who were in fellowship with Brother Bakht Singh and they would encourage us to come. They would make a place for us to put our sleeping bags and prepare food for us. We went from cities like Calcutta to cities like Delhi to cities like Ahmadabad, to cities like Jabalpur, to cities like Vellore to cities like Nippur.

This traveling was a vast source of education. As we traveled, we carried literature in the different languages of the people. There are sixteen major languages in India, with hundreds of dialects in each of those languages, and all this in a country one-third the size of the United States. By God's grace, we had literature in most of the major languages. God provided the funds, and as a result, the church in India grew.

Some of this literature was being produced by Operation Mobilization, and some of it we obtained from the Bible Society. Fortunately, we were able to buy and distribute Bibles that the Bible Society had stored up for years. Our conviction was that God's Word should be distributed, not stored. People gave some money to make that possible, of course, but one disadvantage in India was that people did not have much money. God miraculously stretched the donations.

Onward, Christian Soldiers!

When I think of our activity at Hebron, and throughout Europe and the Middle East, I think of Erwin Rommel, the German general known as the Desert Fox. Rommel was considered one of the most skilled commanders of desert warfare ever. It is said that in the North Africa campaigns of WWII, if the Allies knocked out the German tanks, they were all rolling again in the morning. Rommel simply did not allow for any excuses. The movement was forward.

It was simply amazing to experience how the Lord gave Brother George Verwer and the leaders of OM the wisdom to carry out this mobilization of the church. The goal of Operation Mobilization was to move Christian soldiers, to move literature, and to reach the lost masses. There was no time to sit around waiting, praying that something would happen. It was a matter of believing God to move an army, believing God to move a group, and believing God to move forces to reach lost people at the outermost ends of the world. It was intense— very intense—and we were astounded at what God did.

For the first time Bakht Singh's group had meetings in many of the small towns that we went to, because they didn't have the mobility that OM afforded them. So if there were five or six people in those new villages that really wanted to know more about the Word of God, then Brother Bakht Singh would send specially chosen, mature brothers and sisters to teach them and help them to grow in the Lord. That's how, after a period of time, more than 300 assemblies under the administration of Brother Bakht Singh came to be. It was the fastest growing evangelical Christian group in all of India, and Brother Bakht Singh was already up in age at that time, about 69.

Convocations at Hebron, Madras, and Elsewhere

Every year Brother Bakht Singh would have what is called a "holy convocation" which is a large annual meeting or spiritual conference, in Hyderabad. People would come from many cities all over India to the convocation meetings. It was amazing to see how they were accommodated at Hebron. Places were arranged for thousands of attendees to sleep, refresh themselves, and eat. Much prayer was made before, during, and after the convocations, and the Lord used Bakht Singh and some of the senior elders to share from the Word of God morning, noon, and night. Many went away revitalized and encouraged in their Christian walk. At times, Brother Bakht Singh would hold these convocations in southeast India in the city of Madras, and on the western coast in the city of Ahmadabad.

From Ahmadabad we would reach other surrounding cities like Surat and Pune (formerly Poona), on the west coast. These cities led down to the city of Mumbai (formerly called Bombay). Between these cities lived millions and millions of people in rural areas to which we traveled by truck, sometimes accompanied by Brother Bakht Singh. That was a real shot in the arm for all of us. It proved that he, too, was a Christian soldier. Christians made him comfortable in the many places where he went, but his background, of course, was always one of adaptation to any situation in terms of reaching the people with the Gospel.

The Curious Ask about an African American Missionary in India

While in Madras, I had a chance to speak at several of the assemblies. Some of the local people came to me and expressed how happy they were to see an African American missionary in India. They asked how it would be possible to get more African Americans to come to India to minister the Gospel, especially since they had never seen one in India before. Many of their countrymen had complexions as dark as mine, and yet the missionaries they had seen were Caucasians. The local people loved them, they knew that they preached the Gospel, but they had this big question: Are there Christian African Americans in the U.S.?

I said, "Yes, there absolutely are African American Christians." I explained that there were a lot of complex social reasons behind the fact that such Christians do not go overseas as missionaries. I pointed out that these included the legacy of racism in our country: in the past, many white Bible schools and seminaries did not admit African Americans, and many white mission agencies refused to send African Americans to the field—even if they had the required credentials. Also, because of the nature of many black churches, congregations were not challenged to have a vision for overseas missions, at least not in places such as India.

I tried to round out the picture a bit more. There were one or two other African Americans who were from some universities or secular groups in India, but as far as missionary activity, there were practically no other Black missionaries working consistently. Some African Americans would come from time to time, but their movement and ministry was limited and restricted to small areas. Therefore, many of the

Christians in India never got a chance to see and dialogue in fellowship with African Americans like the Lord afforded me as part of the Operation Mobilization team.

Compelled to Reflect on the Next Phase

At times I thought that maybe the Lord would have me stay in India for the rest of my life, especially since I had the opportunity, the special privilege actually, to get an extended visa. I loved the country and I loved the people. I was quite comfortable among them and I was thankful for the opportunity to be nurtured by such a man as Bakht Singh. In various places where we ministered I was cordially invited for meals and to spend time with families. Some of these families had beautiful, educated young women around my age any of whom would have made a suitable wife for me.

No one ever asked me outright if I was considering staying in India, settling down and getting married, but I did pick up vibrations from some families, and even from Brother Bakht Singh that this was desirable and would have made him and others happy. I was sensitive to the unstated suggestions that I take an Indian wife, but I thought that it would not be God's plan. While I was waiting for God to answer my prayer for a wife, there were, of course, temptations.

The World Answers with Temptations

I think of the beautiful young woman who was offered to me when I was hitchhiking from Turkey to Lebanon. Then later while in India, one evening I was invited to dinner at a Christian professor's home, Professor Enoch, and on my way there I got somewhat lost. As I passed a house, I heard someone whispering, "Pssst, pssst, pssst." Among the shadows of the dark night, I saw the shapely silhouette of a beautiful woman standing in the door of the house. She was obviously a prostitute. For a few seconds, my feet seemed unable to move. It was as though they were nailed to the ground while thoughts went through my head. The devil showed up again, saying, "Here you are, all alone. All you have to do is take a few minutes, and it will be all over. No one will ever know. You've never known a woman before and here is your chance."

After a few seconds I cried out, "Lord, help me." God gave me the grace, and it was only God's grace, to tell the devil to back off. I took off running.

India's Enduring Impact

The four years that I spent in India had a profound influence on my life and I love it still. To this day, India is still very much on my heart. I talk to members of the church sometimes by phone, email, and letter and by God's grace I have maintained contact with the church in India.

Quite a few of the believers who were in the assemblies in India have come to the United States over the years and many of them have flourishing businesses and are very successful. They send hundreds of thousands of dollars back to India to help the church. I also maintain contact and fellowship with them, and when my wife and I worship with them and they prepare Indian food for us, it brings back so many wonderful memories.

After the convocation and earthquake in Kalimpong in 1968, and the return to Hebron, George Verwer contacted me and indicated that perhaps during the coming fall I should prayerfully consider either going back to the United States or coming back to Europe to try to ascertain how the Lord would be leading from there.

Is This the Time to Seek a Wife?

During the time I was away from the United States, I thought about the young woman whom I had met in Chicago through her parents at a prayer meeting. She appeared to be interested in me and I was certainly interested in her. At that time she was a high school teacher and an excellent musician. She played the organ and xylophones at her church and she loved the Lord. While I was in India, she had come to Europe to take part in one of Operation Mobilization's summer crusades. I knew that she was in Europe, so when George Verwer wrote and suggested that it would be wise to prayerfully consider coming back to Europe to ascertain how the Lord might be leading after leaving India, I began making plans to do so.

Or Should I Stay: Discovering the Lord's Answer

It was extremely difficult for me to even think about going back to Europe. My heart had been so bound with the Indian people that after four years, I was considered one of their own. India was my home. There was a plant in Hyderabad that built jet airplane engines and the thought came to my mind that with my Air Force experience, I could get a job at that facility and provide for a family. I could have an Indian wife, George Verwer would have a permanent contact in India, and I would live happily ever after. Although this was actually some of my thought processing, I never got the feeling of peace from the Lord that this was His plan or His desire for me.

Even though it was heartbreaking to think about leaving India, I reminded myself that if it was the Lord's plan, He would certainly lead me back to India. I also knew that God does not make mistakes. That has been my testimony my entire Christian life. As I have submitted to God's will, He has never led me wrongly and He always leads into His perfect will, whether we understand it or not.

I did share with Brother Bakht Singh that George Verwer had challenged me to consider returning to Europe to ascertain God's further directions. He did not say it but clearly he was disappointed. Still, he said the same thing that the Lord had reminded me of. Bakht Singh said, "We're going to be praying for you, and the Lord can bring you back. The Lord makes no mistakes. In the hundreds of assemblies where you have gone, and the holy convocations where you have gone, the Lord's people have had an opportunity to meet you all over India; they know of your life and ministry and they will be praying for you."

One of the most beautiful things that happened at my departure from Hyderabad was that Brother Bakht Singh gave me a white wool shawl that his mother had given to him. I almost wept at this man of God extending such a loving gesture toward me, giving me a shawl which his mother had given to keep him warm and protect him from the chill.

One of my main thoughts was how to get back to Europe from Hyderabad. One of Operation Mobilization's trucks was coming from southern India heading north, and I knew I was going to hitch a ride back to Delhi from Hyderabad. Then I would prayerfully consider how to get back to Europe.

God Always Knows Best: Talk to Him!

Prayer was a very important part of what we did in Operation Mobilization. Each day we spent time in prayer. Every day. No matter what our responsibilities were. Our brother George Verwer pleaded with us to take time before the Lord, to pray individually and together, to pray for the people in the countries of the world—whether you were being led to go there or not—pray for them so that they might be reached with the Gospel of Jesus Christ.

CHAPTER EIGHTEEN

Reunions and a New Mission

A Hard Departure

In 1969, I left Hyderabad and Brother Bakht Singh's compound at Hebron. I got a ride in one of Operation Mobilization's trucks headed for Delhi where I would prayerfully consider the best way to get back to Europe. I was sure I did not want to take a flight back because it would have cost too much. Even if anyone offered to pay for me to fly back, I would have, as lovingly as I knew how, let them know I disagreed with them. My thought, about which I wanted to pray for guidance, was to hitchhike back. I knew this would be another tremendous experience.

Once I arrived in Delhi at the OM base, I had refreshments and fellowship with the brothers there, and then after a day or two of prayer I was ready to start back toward Europe. The strategy was to take a train from Delhi to Lahore and then take a bus. The brothers made sure I got to the train station, prayed with me and sent me off. I knew it was going to be a challenge. I had my sleeping bag under my arm, a little pouch with some snacks in it, and a scarf in case I needed it at night. I wore a thick wool shirt; it was autumn and I was going toward the mountains, so the temperatures were moderately cool. I was on my way back to Europe.

Surprising Encounters with Hindus and Muslims

On the train from Delhi going up toward Lahore, I passed out some Gospel tracts in Hindi to Muslims and Hindus. I felt pretty safe, that no one would attack me or try to beat me up. After passing out a few tracts and returning to my seat, two men sat down with me and looked at the tract.

After a few minutes of looking at me, they said, "We are Muslims. Our parents are Muslims. Our great-grandparents were Muslims. As far as we can go back in our history, our families have always been Muslims."

I was a little excited as to what else they would tell me.

They kept talking. "We don't really believe that Islam is the answer. We don't really believe that Mr. Mohammed is the answer."

By this time I was really excited. To my surprise, they said, "We really believe that Jesus Christ is the Savior of the world. But"—and I experienced that as being a very loud "but"—"we will not take it from the hands of a white man."

Whoa! I thought: *Where shall I go from here?*

The Window is Wide Open for People of Color

As I was thinking about their words and studying their faces, I realized the tremendous opportunity people of color have to reach out with the Gospel in certain areas. At this time, there were very few people of color on the mission field. I could understand the people back home and the people around me, in terms of the influences of history, but I knew that the issue of the moment was the Gospel.

I tried to refocus the two men on the tract. One of the verses in the tract was John 3:16, and with the Lord's help, I tried to help them to realize that God so loved the world—the whole world, Muslims, Hindus, Buddhists, Animists, Catholics, Presbyterians, the entire world—that He gave His only begotten Son, that whosoever believeth in Him should not perish but have everlasting life! (See John 3:16.)

Since I did not exchange contact information with the two men, and therefore have not kept in touch with them, it's difficult to say how much our conversation remained with them over the years. Still, the dialogue and fellowship remained within my heart. It was a wonderful moment and a powerful example of God's presence with me during my journey back to Europe.

Visiting Colleagues and Friends in Lahore and Kabul

The train arrived in Lahore. From Lahore, I took a bus over the border of India to Islamabad and through the Khyber Pass going toward Kabul, Afghanistan. I had friends in Kabul, DC and PC, an OM couple who pioneered the work in Afghanistan. I knew them before they were married. I spent time in ministry in Bombay (now Mumbai), India with Sister C. Brother P was a student at Wheaton College and was with one of the early OM teams in India. They had gotten married and were now living in Kabul where the Lord had given them a burden to reach the people of Afghanistan with the Gospel. I stopped off at their home for a few days, to be refreshed and have a time of fellowship before hitchhiking back to Europe.

It was in Kabul that I came across a bus owner who had driven all the way from England. He had brought a group of students that he had charged a nominal fee to go to Afghanistan. Some of them got off his bus in Turkey, Iran, and a few other countries, but apparently he had made a profit to go as far as Afghanistan and he was looking for riders going back.

I was a bit hesitant to join the small group of riders that paid for seats back to England. I engaged him in conversation to see what would come up and he was eager to accommodate me. Since I had very little money I indicated there was an element of poverty to consider. He kept quoting prices for me, and one price he quoted fell within my capability. I let him know what I'd be willing to pay and he accepted it. For a few seconds I hesitated, knowing that it would be cheaper to hitchhike and I could learn a lot on the way if I chose that option, but my better thought was that I should take the bus.

I would be going through unknown territory, alone other than with Jesus Christ. Chances were that He provided this bus for me. So, I took the bus.

A Bus Ride: Kabul to Tehran and Istanbul

We traveled through the remaining portion of Afghanistan, a mountainous, semi-desert area. It almost felt like an excursion, seeing the local people and stopping at various roadside restaurants. At several of these restaurants the bus would stop and everyone on board would buy some food. I had a few cents left, so I got some, too. The food was excellent: nice hot beans and rice, soup, yogurt, chicken, pork, and lamb, all at a reasonable price. You couldn't ask for anything better than that. Afterwards the bus driver would say, "We're on our way."

So, we re-boarded the bus and before long, we were going through Iran. The next stop we came to was Tehran. We passed through Tehran, and then we came to Istanbul, Turkey. At this point, the bus driver told me, "With the money that you gave me, this is far as I can take you."

I had reached the edge of Istanbul, a little distance from the border. It was time to use another form of travel.

Hitchhiking in Turkey, Yugoslavia, and Italy

So, I hitchhiked a short distance from that point, going toward the border. I got a ride in a truck, which took me into the city of Istanbul and I wanted to go farther to the border, hitchhiking my way back to Europe.

I reached the city of Edirne, located at the border of Turkey and Bulgaria. Along with others, I lined up to be processed through customs. At this point two men came to me and asked if I needed a ride.

I said, "Yes, how much would you charge?"

They said, "Well, come on, get in, we'll see."

Getting in and seeing what they were going to charge me later wasn't a wise thing to do, but I did it. As we went through Bulgaria, we came to a service station and they paid for the gas. I didn't say or indicate by gesture that I would contribute anything to pay for the gas. My dollars were very short and they didn't say anything. But when we got to the Yugoslavian border, they were indicating that well, this is the end of your ride; we can't take you any further. Our problem was poor communication: I didn't know how to communicate clearly in their language and they seemed to have the same inadequacy. I didn't know how to explain to them that I had a very few dollars and wanted to negotiate.

So, I accepted the challenge of continuing to hitchhike. The weather was good and I thought that it was not very far from the Yugoslavian border with Italy, which would put me back in the heart of Europe. The only thing slightly challenging about this was the approach of night. I stepped off the road to a little side street because I knew that if the secret police apprehended me, they might arrest me. I had my passport but I knew they would be suspicious of a single man like me hitchhiking through Yugoslavia. I'd had a snack along the highway, so I wasn't very hungry. It was dark, and after finding a somewhat suitable nook I rolled out my sleeping bag, got in it, and slept. I was tired from hitchhiking, and I slept and slept and slept.

In the morning I got up early, got back on the highway to hitchhike and lo and behold, the last two men who had given me a ride in their car came by. They saw me hitchhiking, and they were smiling and seemed quite glad; it was like they'd found the lost wanderer, the lost sheep. They reached out toward me and were beckoning, come on, come on, get in! I got the impression they felt guilty about our last encounter when they'd pretty much dropped me off without any further ado.

With God, There Is Always Provision

It was so wonderful how the Lord was providing for me to get rides all the way from India. My bus ride from Kabul was so comfortable and scenic. I was blessed to be able to take a modern bus for such a small price. What I was experiencing, of course, was how the Lord takes care of His children.

Earlier when the men asked me to get out of their car and I got out, they did not say it harshly. It was more like "Well, this is the end of the road. Nice knowing you, 'bye." I'd accepted that and here I was early in the morning, about to continue hitchhiking, and the same persons came by, eager and excited to take me as far, it seemed, as I wanted to go.

A Reunion in Trieste

But I really only wanted to go as far as Trieste, Italy and this is where they dropped me off. In the city of Trieste I again visited a dear brother, Dave Bormann, with whom I had been on an OM team. He was one of the early members of Operation Mobilization. He and his wife Lidia lived in Trieste. Lidia was a Spanish young lady whom Dave had met on OM in Spain and they had gotten married. I had spent time with them in the fall of 1964 when I had an opportunity to do some undercover missionary work in Yugoslavia. Their home in Trieste, Italy is near the border of Yugoslavia. So I spent a few days with Brother and Sister Bormann in Trieste. Dave had an excellent command of the Italian language. We had a good time of fellowship.

During my time with Dave and Lidia Bormann, he shared how the Lord had helped them start a church in Trieste. They were beginning to disciple and to teach individuals how to grow in the Lord.

Another Reunion, in Spain

I was with Dave and Lidia for a few days and then I continued my journey back to Europe. I had contacted OM and gotten permission to stop off in Spain, where an African American sister that I was interested in, I'll call her Deborah, was living at the time. We had been corresponding for a while and she had made her way over to take part in the summer crusade in 1969 on an Operation Mobilization team.

Naturally I wanted to go to Spain and see Deborah. I was thinking she might become my wife, and I looked forward to spending some time with her. So, I made contact with the team in Spain and they gave me a place to stay. Deborah and I met in the mornings for our devotions together. We prayed together, read the Bible together, and talked about different things.

Meanwhile, Operation Mobilization had chartered an airplane to take students back to the United States from Europe. By this time, there were large numbers of students coming over in the summers, and this particular summer a very large group had come, so it was much more equitable to charter an airplane to transport students.

A Hopeful Idea

When I got back to England and met with George Verwer, he suggested that I take the plane back to America with the aim of having meetings in local churches to burden them to pray for the ministry of Operation Mobilization. At the same time, I could challenge other young African Americans about the possibility of coming with Operation Mobilization to Europe for times of ministry.

Well, I had about a week or two to pray about his suggestion before it was time for the charter flight's departure. I thought it was a good idea and considered other facets he and I hadn't talked about. Deborah entered my thoughts, not only in terms of my interest in her and the fact that if I went back I'd be able to spend more time with her because she was due to return also. In America, I thought maybe we could arrange some meetings in black churches where she could give her testimony as an African American female and I could give mine as an African American male.

To my mind, this was an unprecedented opportunity to be an effective witness in black churches. We could stir up an interest in global missions since we were two African Americans just returning from the foreign mission field. We could facilitate many joining Operation Mobilization. I also thought that perhaps in the future, were we to become husband and wife, she and I could work with OM as a team in some other part of the world.

So, I let Brother Verwer know that I was in agreement—I felt it would be wise to return to America for a time. At this point, I had been away from the United States for approximately eight years. I'd never planned to stay away from the United States that long. I only planned to go for a summer crusade, but the Lord led me. The Lord allowed me to experience certain spiritual lessons of dedication and commitment, and placed opportunities before me; I had embraced them and almost eight years had passed. Volumes of information, knowledge, and experiences were stored in my mind. I had made many friends, traveled to many different countries, and it didn't seem like it was eight years but it had been. And now I was preparing to return to my homeland, the United States of America. I was excited!

A New Mission

I truly thought that as I went to African American churches and challenged young people that they would be eager, literally running, to take advantage of the opportunity to enter the mission field. I thought that many would prayerfully consider joining Operation Mobilization and taking up a ministry in some part of the world to make Christ known to those who knew not Him as their personal Savior. At one point I actually thought it would only take about three months to mobilize a large group of African American young people to move out for missions.

I was so wrong. It was 1969; it took many more years to even begin a trickle. But I did not know this at the time.

CHAPTER NINETEEN

The Sojourn Home: God Beckons

Launching Hope for the Future

Almost as soon as the charter plane arrived in America, the issue arose of where I would be staying. Of course, many people would think I should have straightened out this detail before I got back, but remember—the Lord led me along a different path. I had hitchhiked through Europe; lived by faith for eight years on that continent and in India; so naturally, I was prepared to do the same at this point. It didn't really bother me not to know exactly where I would be sleeping.

Deborah's mother and father met her at the airport. She was taking them to her apartment, and she and her parents encouraged me to stay a few days in the apartment with them. It would allow me a chance to get to know her better, of course. Her parents would be there as chaperones to make sure everything was on the up and up. This was a plan I wanted to be part of.

First, though, I had ministry business to tend to. I went to the Operation Mobilization headquarters in Wyckoff, New Jersey. The staff told me that if I wanted some money to support myself until I could get established in New York this could be arranged. I realized it would be a challenge to survive in New York. However, I knew I had a place to stay for a few days. I also knew that once the visit with Deborah was over, while I was challenging young people for the mission field, I would be living by faith. The Lord would lead me, surely, and show me how to make some money to support myself.

So I shared my thoughts on the matter with my brothers and sisters in Wyckoff, and thanked them very much for wanting to financially support my stay and ministry in New York. Graciously, I turned down their offer. They assured me that they would be praying for me. Evening was approaching; I left the office in Wyckoff and headed for Deborah's apartment.

Grounded?

That evening I had a good encounter with Deborah and her parents. At this point we weren't kissing and hugging and all of that, but I thought they greeted me warmly and it seemed that we were growing closer. I stayed the night in her apartment, and the next morning she left to take care of some business. She was a schoolteacher and even though school was still out for the summer, I guessed she needed to prepare for the coming fall.

When she returned to her apartment, Deborah told me that her time in the ministry of Operation Mobilization was really challenging for her. She said she was greatly encouraged by my own life and testimony. She went on to assure me that she would continue to pray for me as I pursued the Lord's will in my life, but there was no possibility of a personal relationship with her. She said this graciously, but firmly. She added that after what she had seen in Europe and what she felt in her heart after meeting me and spending time with me she was convinced, before the Lord, that it was not the Lord's will for us to pursue a relationship. We did not need to spend any more time together.

Even though I was trying to take it on the chin, I was really torn up inside. I didn't know what to say. Her mom and dad were still there during this announcement. Perhaps their presence affected me in my silence. I recall that I did sit down on the couch and I tried to be cool. They offered me lunch that day and I ate with them.

Deborah said, "Where will you stay?"

I said, "I'm not sure. I'm sure the Lord will provide some place."

She said, "Well, I know of a YMCA that's not far from here."

When she said that, I must admit that I felt a glimmer of hope. I thought that maybe she wasn't as sure as she'd sounded; maybe she really wanted a temporary break in our relationship and she wanted me to stay close by in case her feelings changed. Thoughts swirled through my mind.

She gave me the telephone number of the YMCA. I called from her apartment, and they had a room for me. I could easily afford the rent because the YMCA only charged $5 a day at that time. So, in as manly a way as I knew how, I tried to accept the situation. I would be moving my things out and going to the YMCA, only about 10 minutes from where she was living.

Before I left, I tried to get her to agree to the possibility that I might call her every now and then, or in some way maintain a connection with her. But she made it very clear that it wouldn't be wise. She indicated that she really wouldn't like to hurt my feelings, but as far as a personal relationship, it was over.

I bowed out on that note. I told her that I would be praying for her and asking the Lord to continue to use her and guide her as she served Him. I embraced her mom and dad. I thanked them for their prayers, and assured them that I would be praying for them and talking to them from time to time. I was out the door, going toward the YMCA.

Upside Down and Inside Out

My heart, my emotions, my thoughts were really in turmoil. I scrolled back in my mind to when I first met Deborah and her parents in Chicago; I'd written many letters encouraging her to prayerfully consider coming and giving her life and talents to Operation Mobilization. She had chosen the country of Spain and had written that she felt comfortable there. It seemed that she felt good about being in Spain even though we were worlds apart because I was in India. The testimony of the OM team members was that she was a lovely girl, as I knew, that she had established a very effective ministry witnessing to people and was quickly becoming fluent in Spanish. I'd been so happy when I finally arrived in Spain and we had a chance to spend some time together, talking and having devotions together.

On the one hand, after Deborah said that our relationship was over, I felt a strong desire to try to get her to change her mind. On the other hand, I was trying to convince myself that it was over; it was a Dear John situation and that was that.

Receiving Solace

Since I did not know what to do, I decided to consult several close brothers. I had made it a habit never to make very important decisions without getting wise counsel from these brothers in New York and across the country. I had such a difficult time wrapping my head around the fact that Deborah was not the one whom God had in mind for me. When I shared this turmoil with my spiritual mentors, they said, in so many words, "God has something better."

But, I told myself, "How could there be something better? This is a beautiful young lady, a schoolteacher who loves the Lord, and who attends midweek prayer meetings. To top it all off, she is gifted musically and plays the piano for the church on Sundays. How could there be something better?"

Really, I didn't want to hear my mentors' response. In my heart I wanted them to tell me what I wanted to hear. I did not realize it then, but I wanted my way as opposed to God's way. God was in control. He is always in control. It just took me some time before I could bring myself to accept that fact.

I visited another godly friend, Dr. Suzto, a Chinese brother and I explained what happened. He said, "Well, Brother, we'll pray. God knows your heart. He has a special life partner for you somewhere, and we can trust Him."

I heard what he said, and I thanked him for his advice and supportive prayer, but the stress and turmoil did not subside.

Heartache Hurts

After a few days at the YMCA, I felt ill. It seemed like I was having heart trouble so I thought I should go to a doctor and check it out. After all, I'd been away in India for a long time and I hadn't had a physical examination since the initial exam that Operation Mobilization requires of all of its entering students. Maybe in coming back from India, with the stress and strain of hitchhiking and the irregular meals and irregular sleep, a physical examination would be in order.

Fortunately there was a hospital not too far from the YMCA, just up the hill. After the physician checked my heart and other vital signs and completed the rest of his exam, he asked me, "Do you have a girlfriend?"

I paused. He caught me off guard. Why did he ask me such a question? As far as I could see, he should be telling me about my physical condition, but I decided to answer his question. I told him that I had one, but she broke it off.

He said, "What happened?"

I told him the story, and he then said, "Well, I'd like to report to you that there's nothing wrong with your heart." He told me that what I thought was heart trouble was probably the emotional turmoil of the breakup.

Once it was clear to me that I did not have heart trouble, I realized that I simply had to rely on the Lord to get me through this. I needed to trust that God would help me accept the breakup as fact, and allow the Lord to give me the grace and peace that only He could provide on a day-by-day basis.

Get to Work

I left the hospital, went back to the YMCA, and began thinking about a job. I had little money; I had to do something to create a cash flow. The YMCA where I was staying was in New York City's borough of Queens, near a busy shopping area not far from a major street, Jamaica Avenue.

At that time Jamaica Avenue was one of New York's largest shopping areas. Tourists who came to New York City, including those from other boroughs and Long Island, could board special buses and come to Jamaica Avenue to shop. It occurred to me to go to Jamaica Avenue and look for a job washing dishes, sweeping floors, or something of that nature. So I went to a few restaurants, and several of the managers simply said,

"Well, we have the dish washers and workers that we need." It was afternoon; some indicated that if I wanted work, I should search early in the morning.

This made sense and by God's grace, at one restaurant I was told, "Yes, we would love to hire you, can you come to work tonight?"

I said "Yes!" and was on the night shift of this particular restaurant. A large number of people ate there, many of them drug dealers and prostitutes working the street. The place was packed all night and they did a lot of business. There were a lot of dishes to wash but I was happy to do it. I was making $8 an hour, which wasn't bad at that time. I was glad to have that job on Jamaica Avenue, washing dishes, or as some called it, "busting suds" at a local restaurant. Even though I was grateful for the job I viewed it as temporary. I wanted the night shift mainly so I could look for another job during the day.

A number of job offers appeared in the newspaper, which I sought out during my off hours from work. One or two of these opportunities were chauffeur jobs. At first, I thought, no way am I going to get a job as a chauffeur. But then I thought, I can drive, it won't be strenuous, and it won't be a job that will have me tied down so I can visit churches and challenge young people to join the mission ministry. Also, I thought that from time to time, I might travel to other cities.

As it turned out, I did get a job as a chauffeur driving for a legal and real estate corporation based in Manhattan. The job was very simple. In the morning I picked up one of the firm's partners from his home and took him to the office. I was then free until four in the afternoon when it was time to drive him home. After I dropped the partner off, I parked the car at the limousine company and went back to the YMCA. On several occasions my passenger asked me to help out in the kitchen and do light cleaning in his home, but he saw that I was not happy with the housecleaning duties. I continued to look for another job.

One day I met another limousine driver who told me that they were hiring at the airport. As I was on the bus going to the airport to check out this job lead, I met an airline captain. He told me that after submitting a job application with the airlines it would be good to stop by the employment office every week or so to check the progress on my application. The secret was for them to see your face and the consistency and frequency of you coming to check on the job. This would really impress them that you wanted the job. He knew of several cases where individuals were hired in a matter of a few weeks because they followed this procedure.

CHAPTER TWENTY

Persevering by God's Grace

Air Time

At first I worked with Allied Cleaning Service which had a contract with National Airlines. Then, for about four months National Airlines hired me as a ground technician. As on previous occasions during my time as a dish washer, I sensed that this was but a temporary position. Trans World Airlines was next door to National Airlines. I submitted an application to the employment office at TWA and stopped in once a week to see if they had processed my application.

This proved to be a good strategy: in 1969 TWA hired me. I ended up working for TWA for 18 years and it was such a blessing because I had flight privileges to many different cities and countries.

Rewards

I could fly around to various cities and challenge young African Americans to participate in foreign short-term missions. Since TWA flew to many countries, I also had the opportunity to fly overseas and visit Christians in other lands. In addition, I could attend convocations and conferences on standby status and not have to pay air fare.

Consequences

While there were rewards to the job at TWA, I also experienced some of the results of the sacrifices I had made—gladly—because I had been in service to the Lord overseas. When I arrived back in the United States after being away for almost eight years, I experienced culture shock. So many things were different from the way I remembered them. The television programs and the popular music were unfamiliar. More importantly, I had missed the entire Civil Rights Movement with Dr. Martin Luther King and the fight against Jim Crow laws and segregation. To this day, someone will ask me about a song or an event that happened in the sixties and I am clueless.

It is as though there is a big blank page in my life regarding America and what happened here during those eight years. I remember seeing metal pop tabs from soda cans, strewn on the street and wondering what they were. When I left for Europe, glass bottles had claw-like caps and were opened with bottle openers. I felt as though I was coming up for air and moving in slow motion after having been involved in intense evangelism for so long.

Still, there is a deeply personal and positive consequence to describe, too. While engaged in evangelism, I was involved in dialogue with thousands of students from different parts of the world, from different cultures, who spoke different languages;

we shared the Gospel and saw God work mightily. As the only African American in such an environment, it was, to say the least, quite an experience. I saw the power of the Gospel actively moving in people's lives all over the world, among many tribes and nations, and it was a challenge to my heart. I felt humbled that Jesus, the Creator of the universe, entrusted me with this burden and commissioned me to take His message and go forth across the lands. I had planned to go for just one summer, but my journey ended up lasting eight years to more than twenty-eight different countries. I will never be able to fully tell the story of what I experienced as I, with the Lord's help, made an effort to obey His call on my life.

And then there were personal costs. After being dropped like a hot potato by a young lady whom I felt was the one the Lord had chosen to be my partner, I initially went into a spin. Many young people whom I'd met and numerous others of my age range already had their soul mates. They'd met one another while part of OM or just got together and got married as human beings tend to do in the course of ordinary life. I wondered when the Lord would direct my path toward my life's partner. But after wrestling with my emotions I acknowledged that as I had reminded myself in other situations, God does not make any mistakes concerning His servants.

Fellowship and Prayer

I turned to the Word of God and prayer. I took time to be alone with Him, reading His Word and enjoying fellowship with Him. I reviewed His claim on my life and the fact that I had been bought by His blood. It was a day-by-day battle because I was having a spiritual conflict with the devil, but going to the Word of God every day was strengthening. It cleared my vision and brought peace to my own heart. I realized that my relationship with Deborah was really a very short-lived experience in my overall walk with God. He allowed me to experience the pain that He might teach me deeper and greater lessons concerning His sovereignty.

Coming Down to Earth: African Americans as Missionaries

My efforts to recruit African Americans to the mission field did not go as I expected. Before I returned to the States, I had thought the recruitment would be easy. In my mind, it was already a done deal. I truly believed that within a few months after I returned and shared the vision, hundreds of young people would be marching off to take part in missions as they obeyed the Great Commission. I was not prepared for what I encountered: the lack of vision and education about missions, especially global missions, in the black church.

I did visit African American churches to present the opportunity for young people or anyone who would be exercised to join forces in reaching a lost world. I was surprised at the number of times that the pastor or youth leader rebuked me and reminded me we have to evangelize here in America first before we can worry about overseas. While perhaps some of the reaction was due in part to African Americans' intense focus on what was happening to them within their own country, it was still dismaying to hear it. Certainly, the Bible does not say that we should worry about ourselves before we evangelize among other people. The Bible says that God expects us to do ministry *simultaneously* at home and abroad:

> ...and ye shall be witnesses unto me *both* in Jerusalem, and in all Judaea, and in Samaria, and unto the uttermost part of the earth (Acts 1:8, emphasis added).

The Lord showed me that it was going to take much longer than I thought to stir up African American churches for missions. But I know that He is faithful, and I have seen fruit over the years.

The Fruit of a Widespread Tree

Today, over fifty years later, Operation Mobilization has over 6,000 workers from over 100 nations serving in 110 countries.

Over the years, OM has launched four ocean-going Gospel ships. Way over 150 missions agencies to varying degrees trace their birth back to Operation Mobilization and many books about missions have been written by former OMers.

The book *Spiritual Revolution: The Story of OM* by Ian Randall (2008) was written to celebrate and tell the story of fifty years of Operation Mobilization. It begins with George Verwer's conversion and OM's early outreach in Mexico and continues through God's faithfulness as OM has grown to include thousands of workers serving in hundreds of countries. In the book, Ian Randall emphasizes the spirituality that underlies the organization, and the fact that OM was a pioneer in short-term missions.

In his book of 1989, *A Revolution of Love*, George Verwer says that Christianity is a "revolution of love," and he is convinced that nothing is more important in all the world. He says that since God is love, and since He has told us to love one another, we cannot be effective if we do not obey. We are reminded in Galatians 5:22-26 (KJV) that the fruit of the Spirit is love:

> [22]But the fruit of the Spirit is love, joy, peace, longsuffering, gentleness, goodness, faith, [23]Meekness, temperance: against such there is no law. [24]And they that are Christ's have crucified the flesh with the affections and lusts. [25]If we live

in the Spirit, let us also walk in the Sprit. [26]Let us not be desirous of vain glory, provoking one another, envying one another.

In his book, George Verwer points out that since Christianity is a revolution of love, God's people must not only have "right" or "orthodox" doctrine, but they must exhibit love and humility and brokenness. This involves loving those we are trying to win and relating to other Christians with a meek and gentle spirit which esteems them better than ourselves.

Rooted in a Missionary's Love

I often experienced this kind of love in Operation Mobilization and from George Verwer himself. This love is based on the fact that God is love and He demonstrated His love by sending Jesus to give His life for us on the Cross.

There are many who testify to the reality of the love George Verwer showed to those in Operation Mobilization and to the fact that George lives what he preaches in *A Revolution of Love.* One is Virgil Amos, a former OMer who in the 1980s founded Ambassadors Fellowship, a missions agency for ethnic minorities. Virgil is a good friend of mine who was the second African American to join Operation Mobilization. He also attended Moody Bible Institute. When I was leaving Moody, he was just beginning his studies there. Virgil joined OM in the sixties and led the work in Iran. I saw Brother Virgil and his family in Bombay (now Mumbai), India and in Iran while he was with Operation Mobilization.

In January 2000, while attending the fortieth wedding anniversary of George and Drena Verwer in England, Virgil Amos was asked if he thought the celebration was worth the miles of travel. Virgil responded, "A thousand times worthwhile!" Virgil went on to say, "Back then missions didn't accept black folks, so OM was my opportunity to get involved. George paved the way to making OM multicultural. He has modeled 'loving others better than yourself,' and broken down barriers. George puts into practice what other people just talk about. That's what makes him a radical. His vision, his zeal, has been a powerful influence in my life." (OM News Release, January 31, 2000 by Debbie Meroff) Virgil said that he came to the celebration because George invited him, and he added that he would have come if it had been in India.

Many of the young people who have come on Operation Mobilization for a short-term mission experience have gone back to their own countries, and after further schooling in colleges and seminaries, have not only started their own missions, but have actively promoted missions in their churches. The Spirit of God used OM to give them the initial jolt toward missions. Reaching lost people is on the heart of God and this is why His Spirit gives His people the love and compassion for lost people necessary to reach them.

I am thankful and deeply humbled that when I became a "new man in Christ" while in Alaska, I was then privileged to be allowed to take part in reaching some of those on God's heart. God used me to go into all the world and preach the Gospel; the missionary journeys of this African American prove God's faithfulness.

EPILOGUE

The job at Trans World Airlines turned out to be a tremendous blessing. I was able to travel almost free on TWA flights and at a deep discount on other airlines. This made it possible for me to fly to various cities and share about short-term missions, and to go to conferences and network with other mission-minded believers. I nearly always travelled with lots of Christian literature and often set up book tables at missionary conferences. I did whatever I could to promote, support, and encourage African American involvement in foreign missions.

Not long after I returned to the States, I visited my good friend Virgil Amos in Iran to encourage his heart. He was a field leader in Iran with OM at the time and later started the mission Ambassadors Fellowship based in Colorado Springs, Colorado. Besides Iran, I also travelled to Sierra Leone, Liberia, Ghana, Nigeria, and Uganda. As a result of visits to several churches in New York City, two African American young men, one from a church in Queens, and one from a church in Brooklyn went on a short-term summer crusade with OM. As I mentioned, I quickly learned that it would take much longer than I initially thought to raise up an army of African American young people ready to go to the mission field.

Just as He always does, God gradually began to make His will clear to me as I settled into life back in the United States.

One person who was a great help in this regard was Rev. George Perry. George was a pastor at a church in the Bronx in New York City and we became great friends. He was instrumental in helping me to adjust to re-entry into life in the States. This warm, caring man took a personal interest in me. We spent hours together, the two of us or with his wife and children, just doing ordinary things, having a hamburger, riding in a car, all the while talking and sharing as he was advising and counseling me. In time I became his assistant pastor and he encouraged my involvement in the church's outreach ministry and the prison ministry.

As I had done many years before while attending Moody Bible Institute, I got really involved with a prison ministry. I became a volunteer chaplain with the clergy volunteer program at several inmate centers in New York City. At one point, I was the coordinator of fifteen volunteer chaplains. I also worked as a liaison between state prisoners and their families, including some families in the church who had sons in prison. I was an associate pastor with Rev. George Perry for seven years, from 1970 through 1977.

Not long after I returned home to the States, I felt God leading me to finish my bachelor's degree, but I resisted at first. I thought, with all the experience I've acquired on the mission field, why did I need a degree? But God was clearly leading in that direction and He used George Perry to encourage me to re-enroll in school and obtain my degree. I began by taking some courses at Queens College of the City University of New York and I finished at Nyack College in Nyack, New York, receiving a Bachelor of Science from Nyack in 1974. It was not easy working fulltime at TWA and continuing with my prison ministry efforts while attending school, especially once I began going to Nyack since it was almost an hour away from the city. But time and time again, God proved Himself faithful. He had called me to go back to school, and as He said in His Word in I Thessalonians 5:24:

Faithful is he that calleth you, who also will do it.

While I was ministering for seven years with George Perry at the Full Gospel Christian Church (formerly Bethany Alliance Church) in the Bronx, I was ordained by the Christian and Missionary Alliance denomination in 1975. Later I was an associate minister from 1977 through 1979 at Ebenezer Baptist Church under Rev. Timothy Mitchell in Flushing, Queens and I was ordained by the Eastern Baptist Association in 1977. As always, in keeping with what I believed was what God had called me to do, I was involved in the outreach ministries of the churches more so than within the four walls.

September 20, 1975 was a momentous day. On that day I was joined in holy matrimony to my miracle wife, Cynthia. It was amazing how God put us together. We met in the home of an elderly sister, Carrie Cokes in Chicago. Sister Cokes was 87 at the time. I'd stopped by to visit her because she had faithfully prayed for me and sent me monetary gifts when I was overseas with Operation Mobilization. I was living in New York and I went to Chicago to attend a Christian conference there in July, 1975. Sister Cokes mentioned that Cynthia was staying with her temporarily until she could move into her own apartment. When Cynthia came home from work that day, it turned out that we were going to the same Christian conference, so we went together.

It was unbelievable how God worked in both our hearts that very night to bring us together. We believe that He had already worked it out; He only had to bring us together. After the conference, and before we went to sleep, the Spirit of God impressed upon both of us that we should be together. We did not hear voices, but as we prayed separately, we both had a strong sense from God that He was putting us together.

The next day I proposed—I came right out and asked her to be my wife. Cynthia said later that she was not as surprised as she might have been because of the experience she had had the night before. She told me that she would pray about it. Three days later she said "yes." She said that while she was thinking and praying about the proposal, she had complete peace that this was God's will. Another miracle: Not only did both of us have complete peace about our sudden engagement, when we shared it with church elders, family, and friends (some of whom were prayer warriors), no one objected. They also had peace about it. We met and were married in less than three months.

As I write this, I celebrate thirty-six years of marriage to Cynthia. We are quick to say that we do not recommend this for everyone. God did a special thing for us. So many people had prayed for a wife for me over the years that we believe God had already worked our union out; we just had to meet. I cannot put into words how thankful I am that God has given me a godly wife, one who loves Him, His Word, and prayer.

Cynthia was saved while a junior at the University of Illinois at Chicago. There was a Christian young man in two of her English classes who always used to give her Gospel tracts and talk about a "personal" relationship with the Lord. He also had some of his Christian friends praying for her for about a year when he invited her to hear an evangelist from Harlem named Tom Skinner. Tom had been a former leader of a violent street gang called the Harlem Lords when he heard the Gospel on the radio and came to Christ. Cynthia says this was the first time she heard the Gospel presented clearly. She responded and was wonderfully saved. Ironically, she began going to Westlawn Gospel Chapel, the African American church that I was involved with while at Moody Bible Institute before I went overseas. When they discovered that Cynthia had accepted a quick marriage proposal, it was fortunate that I had kept in touch and the elders knew me!

After God put my wife and me together, it was full steam ahead. A few weeks after we were married in Chicago at Westlawn Gospel Chapel, we returned to my apartment in New York and I began a course in clinical pastoral education. I took two semesters of this, traveling from Queens to Manhattan four days a week, Monday through Thursday. These courses focused on hospital chaplaincy, which I was very interested in as a result of the years I had volunteered as a chaplain in the jails. I learned a lot from these courses; hospitals and jails are full of people who desperately need to hear about the love of God and their need of a Savior.

In 1981, and as a result of an earlier suggestion of a landlord, my wife and I started a small business. For fourteen years we had a waste oil collection business, collecting waste crankcase oil from service stations, auto repair shops, and transmission stations and taking it to a recycling station. We also had contracts with a major utility, Con Edison, and with Pan American World Airways, Eastern Airlines, and Sky Chefs. For a time we also delivered home heating oil. We named the heating oil business Capstone Fuel Oil. We got the name "Capstone" from Psalm 118:22 (NIV, 1984):

> The stone the builders rejected has become the capstone;

I drove the tanker trucks and my wife did the paperwork and covered the phones. The business was meant to provide extra income for the ministry, and it did just that for quite a few years. We even named one of the tanker trucks "The Widow's Pot" after the story in II Kings 4:1-7 where a widow's lone pot of oil was multiplied miraculously and used to fill many, many pots. Likewise, God blessed our small business, kept the trucks full of oil, and helped us, many times in miraculous ways. Eventually the value of recycled oil went way down, and the nature of our contracts with the utility became less profitable, while the cost of doing business, such as rent, permits, and insurance was rising. So we closed the business after fourteen years.

The same landlord who had given me the vision for starting a business, a Jewish man named Mr. Mazus, also suggested that I should invest in real estate. When he first mentioned this, I was single and in no position to invest in anything. As a matter of fact, I could barely pay my rent. I had the same reaction as when he suggested that I start a small business. At first I thought, "Why is this man always mentioning these impossible pipe dreams to me? I do not have any money. I cannot start a business and I cannot invest in real estate." But I believe that God used him to plant a seed in my mind both about a business and about real estate. Over the years I thought about both things and God helped me to do both. As with the suggestion about starting a business, the advice about real estate turned out to be valuable. Over time my wife and I bought several houses, as well as vacant land and made profits, some of which were used to spread the Gospel.

The years 1975 through my retirement from Trans World Airlines in 1988 were extremely busy. In addition to working fulltime at TWA, I was also involved in ministry, working with the waste oil business, and going to college. And yet there was more that the Lord wanted me to do. The argument I gave the Lord about returning to school to get my bachelor's was mild compared to the one I gave Him when I felt the Lord leading me to go to seminary.

"Seminary?!! Why seminary?" I asked the Lord. *"I have enough schooling. I went back to school and finished my bachelor's degree. And now You want me to go to seminary. Why, Lord? I have been all over the world preaching the Gospel. Besides, I'm too busy. I have too much to do. And anyway, some instructors at seminaries are not biblically sound."*

As in the past, when I argued with the Lord about something He wanted me to do, I lost the argument. I obeyed and submitted to His will. I ended up attending two seminaries and received a Masters of Professional Studies from one and a Masters of Divinity from the other. I know for a fact that when God says to do something, it is important to obey, even if you do not understand it at all.

At one point I was working fulltime and involved with the business, the ministry, and family life as well as going to school. All of this would have been impossible without my miracle wife Cynthia. She worked alongside me and helped in every way and in every area. She prayed with me and for me and helped to keep all of the balls in the air. While I was in seminary, it was helpful that Cynthia had a master's degree in English; I had a live-in proofreader for all of my papers.

In 1983, God blessed us in a special way. Our family expanded when our son Daniel came into our home at three and a half months by way of adoption. Three years later, our daughter Lisa was added to our family at four and a half months, also by way of adoption. As I look at them now as adults, Daniel, age 29, and Lisa, age 26, I agree with those that say children often teach us more than we teach them. They are both blessings from the Lord.

My wife and I took full advantage of the flight privileges which came with my job with TWA. We travelled a lot during the eight years before the children and later we traveled as a family with them. The first place I took Cynthia was India. We could barely afford it at the time, but after we had been married a year, I wanted so badly for her to see the country where I had spent four continuous years under the tutelage of the godly man Bakht Singh and the Christian assemblies in India. We stayed for almost two weeks at Hebron, the missionary compound with Bakht Singh and the indigenous missionaries under his leadership. It was so wonderful to be back and see everyone again and introduce my wife to the believers. The women showed Cynthia how to put on a sari, the dress of Indian women, and she wore one each day. We had a chance to eat at the table with Bakht Singh and to travel a bit to several nearby villages and attend some meetings. Like me, Cynthia loved the food and her heart was quickly knit with the warm, loving people.

After India, my family and I visited other countries. The list was quite large: Egypt, Portugal, Greece, Italy, England, Israel, Zambia (just Hoise and Daniel); Senegal (the whole family went to encourage African Americans in this way of doing missions); Spain (Cynthia and the children visited Virgil Amos' daughter and her husband in the field with his mission); and Canada. We also visited many islands, some several times, including Bermuda, Jamaica, Barbados, Bahamas, Hawaii, Puerto Rico, and many states in the United States. Much of this travel was in conjunction with missionary and biblical interests. Since I was saved in Alaska, the burden to see others come to Christ has always been with me, so whenever possible, no matter where we went I tried to engage others in a conversation about the Lord. Often we passed out tracts and Gospel booklets as a family.

In spite of my unbelievably busy schedule, I was privileged to be able to take some short-term mission trips. Three were with my good friend and former OMer Fouzi Ayoub. Fouzi had married his English sweetheart Wendy, and they were living in Wolverhampton, England. He founded a mission to Arabs called The Arabic Evangelical Centre in Wolverhampton. I went with Fouzi to Sicily twice, in 1990 and 1991, and to Morocco once, in 1992. Each trip lasted about ten days and we did a lot of literature distribution and encouraging Christians in those countries. Morocco was especially difficult because it was an Islamist country and special precautions had to be taken to hide the literature. Fouzi was able to get a van and have the inside panels outfitted so that literature could be hidden behind the panels.

After I retired from TWA in 1988, I continued working part-time at Kennedy Airport with several companies until 1999. After 1999, I was able to focus more on various aspects of the ministry.

Another series of mission trips occurred when I went to Timbuktu in Mali, West Africa three times in 2000, 2001, and 2006. A Malian pastor friend of Brother Fouzi introduced me to another Malian pastor, Pastor Nouh Ag Infa Yatarra who was in the United States working on a master's degree at a seminary in Philadelphia. When Pastor Nouh returned home to Timbuktu, he invited me to visit. South Africa was the destination of a short-term mission trip with Carver Bible College of Atlanta in 2000, and I also went to Ecuador in 2003. I consider myself especially blessed to have been able to take these short-term mission trips in the midst of my busy schedule.

Over the years as I went to many church- or parachurch-sponsored mission conferences, particularly those with a vision for encouraging African Americans to go to the mission field, I have been able to meet and network with many who have a real heart for the Great Commission given in Matthew 28. This effort is an important part of what I devote my time and energy to more recently. Currently, I am involved with promoting the vision for short-term missions at four churches in Atlanta where my wife and I have lived since 2009 (we lived for thirty-four years in Queens, New York City). Even though I had an unrealistic vision when I first returned from Europe, that it would take only a few months to raise up a huge army of young African Americans ready to go to the mission field, I also realized that God had a plan. He always does. As He says in Jeremiah 29:11-12 (NIV):

> [11] For I know the plans I have for you," declares the LORD, "plans to prosper you and not to harm you, plans to give you hope and a future. [12] Then you will call upon me and come and pray to me, and I will listen to you.

God's time is not my time. I have learned to relax and be confident of His sovereignty. I have tried to exercise the same faith when I returned from overseas that I exercised while overseas on the mission field. Whether it has had to do with employment, education, marriage and family, business, or ministry, I know that the Lord has a plan for my life and He will help me every step of the way. He has done just that. And He continues to do it.

ABOUT THE AUTHOR

Hoise Birks likes to refer to himself as a servant of God. At any given point in his life, he has been a jet engine specialist, a global missionary, a prison chaplain, an entrepreneur, a church planter, an international book and literature distributor, and a pastor. Hoise gives God all of the glory for such a rich life. He and his wife Cynthia have two grown children, Daniel and Lisa.

Copies of A New Man *may be ordered at: info@HoiseBirks.com and at HB Publishing, P.O. Box 2171, Stockbridge, GA 30281.*

The Old Man

Growing Up in Cincinnati

*That ye put off concerning the former conversation
the old man, which is corrupt according to the deceitful lusts;
And be renewed in the spirit of your mind;
And that ye put on the new man, which after God
is created in righteousness and true holiness.
Ephesians 4:22-24*

*Six years old
in grandfather's
backyard*

High School – 11th Grade

First Year College- Miami University, Oxford, Ohio

A man of the world - just before Air Force, 1956

Air Force

Hoise Birks Becomes a New Man

*Therefore if any man be in Christ,
he is a new creature, old things are passed away:
behold, all things are become new.
II Corinthians 5:17*

*Airman 1st Class - honored as most outstanding Airman
on Ladd Air Force Base - 1956*

Jet Engine Specialist at Ladd AFB

Overnight Survival in Alaska, 1955

*Overnight Survival - the temperature
is minus 25 degrees*

On top of ice in Alaska

MOODY BIBLE INSTITUTE

Birks, Hoise

1960 Yearbook picture – Moody Bible Institute

*Hoise with first group of Moody students heading for Mexico,
Christmas break, 1958
George Verwer, founder of Operation Mobilization,
is second from right at the top*

Impossible? God uses OM to open Christian bookstores:

Mexico

Spain

Turkey

EUROPE

London, England - 1962
Stayed with George Verwer and his family, took part in meetings
introducing Operation Mobilization

TEENS & TWENTIES

Dave and...

Scores of young people will meet in Paris to plan b

IT'S 'OPERATION MOB

ON 1st July this year, scores of young people
of many nationalities will meet in Paris.
In their minds and hearts will be
thoughts and plans of revolution!
Their's will be a revolution motivated by love.
Their arms and ammunition will be Gospel
tracts and portions of Scripture. But make no
mistake, this revolution will be real. These
pieces of paper are potent. And the young
people who will unite to distribute 25 million of
them during the months of July and August,
will expect to see dynamic results.

The man behind this spiritual revolution to
take daring, decisive action in reaching Europe's
untold millions for Jesus Christ, is 23-year-old
George Verwer. We have already told some of
his story—how attempts to get the Gospel behind
the Iron Curtain have resulted in his expulsion
from two Communist countries. But experience
gained as a result of this, convinces George that
the task is not impossible.

Bearing this in mind, as a future development
of his work, he is now turning his attention to
free Europe, and this project is known as *Operation
Mobilisation*. Thousands of pieces of literature
across
many
in this
e are

George Verwer (left) discusses preliminary
plans for " Operation Mobilisation" with
co-workers Tim Withy and Jose Birch

finalising preparations across Europe. In Spain,
a dedicated young man who belongs to the
Brethren has given up his job as an insurance
agent to devote all his time to this task. Another
young man, born of German parents in Poland,
is now in Austria and Germany preparing the
way. He speaks German and English fluently.
With previous experience of a similar crusade in
Mexico, a young man of Chinese descent, born
of Buddhist parents, is laying the groundwork in
France. He speaks fluent English, French and
Spanish. Two young ladies are included in the
team of leaders ; one is Spanish and the other
comes from East Germany.

Will the young people participating in
Operation Mobilisation be expected to speak
another language ?

"No," said George Verwer when we put this

*Portion of an article from a Christian
newspaper in London, 1962, showing
George Verwer, Tim Withy, and Hoise Birks
discussing plans for an Operation Mobilization campaign;
Hoise and George were the first two recruiters in the U.K.*

Missions in France: girls' team and driver, Hoise - 1962

International Sextet - singing to the Glory of God in France:
two Dutch, two English, one Greek, and one African American

Three-member Operation Mobilization
team, Zagreb, Yugoslavia, 1964

Dr. Branko and his wife,
Christian contacts in Yugoslavia,
a closed Soviet bloc country;
they hosted us when we did
undercover ministry

Hoise with John Carling
and a Yugoslavian Christian leader
in Zagreb, 1964

With a youth leader active
in Zagreb's underground church

With Dr. Branko and
Operation Mobilization
team member
John Carling in Zagreb

In the market in
Zagreb where
John Carling and I
met an African student

With an African student leader from Ghana at
University of Zagreb, 1964

With a group
of communist
students from
Ghana, at
University of
Zagreb

IRAQ

The Desolation of Babylon

Therefore the wild beasts of the desert
with the wild beasts of the islands shall dwell...therein:
and it shall be no more inhabited for ever;
neither shall it be dwelt in
from generation to generation.
Jeremiah 50:39

With Fouzi Ayoub and John Carling at gate to Ancient City
of Babylon, Iraq - 1964

With Fouzi and John at one of the ancient ruins of Babylon
". . . I will raise up against Babylon, and against them
that dwell in the midst of them that rise up against me, a destroying wind."
Jeremiah 51:1

*Fouzi, Hoise and John walking down the main street
in the Ancient City of Babylon – April 1964*

Original designs on the walls of the Ancient City of Babylon, Iraq

Ruins in Babylon
"Because of the wrath of the LORD it shall not be inhabited,
but it shall be wholly desolate...." Jeremiah 50:13

Ruins in Babylon
"To make their land desolate, and a perpetual hissing;
every one that passeth thereby shall be astonished,
and wag his head." Jeremiah 18:16

Ruins in Babylon
*"I will also make it a possession for the bittern, and pools of water:
and I will sweep it with the besom of destruction,
saith the Lord of hosts." Isaiah 14:23*

INDIA

*One of the OM trucks driven across the continent
from London to India – 1964*

Bakht Singh of India – leader of an Indigenous Christian Movement
Operation Mobilization teams worked with Christian Assemblies
established by Bakht Singh

Bakht Singh praying at an open-air meeting in India

Hoise preaching with an interpretation into the Indian language of Telugu from the back of an OM truck – 1966

*Hoise Birks as a student at Allahabad Bible Seminary
with other seminary students - 1966*

*Open-air teams from Bakht Singh's compound Hebron in
Hyderabad, India - 1967*

*Leading an open-air outreach in Kalimpong, India
- high in the Himalayan Mountains, 1968*

Hoise being honored with a "Global Jacket" by George Verwer, founder of Operation Mobilization - August, 2011

George shares about their relationship from day one with OM.